## DEBBIE BROWN'S

# enchanting
# magical cakes

will be the back of the wings).

**Safety tip:** Sewing black on black can be tricky, so work in good light.

**3** Place the two light-grey ear shapes on one bat body. Sew them in position with a triangle of three stitches in light-grey sewing thread. With black thread, sew two black seed beads on for eyes (three or four stitches per bead) and backstitch a curved smile. For vampire fangs, make a few small stitches with white sewing thread.

**4** Fold the length of narrow black ribbon in half to form a loop and, with 1cm overlapping the felt, sew the ends to the top of the second bat body using dark-grey thread.

**5** Sandwich the wings between the two bat body shapes (ensure the sides of the wings where you finished the stitching face backward). Line the bodies up and pin all three layers. Sew together by stitching around the edge with dark-grey thread and small running stitches. Turn the bat over and back again as you sew, finishing on the back.

# Halloween Bats

# Woo-hoo!

No tricks in these family Halloween makes – they're all a treat!

These fab felt bats are even more spooky as 'vampire' bats, simply add fangs with white thread. Wool felt is best for fairly stiff wings, or thicker craft felt, or cut extra thin felt.

## YOU WILL NEED (FOR EACH BAT)

- 15 x 18cm of black felt
- 9 x 12cm of dark-grey felt
- Black stranded embroidery thread
- Small pieces of light-

- grey felt
- Two black seed beads, size 8/0
- 15cm-wide black ribbon
- Scissors, pins, needles
- Matching sewing threads

**1** Use the templates *(overleaf)* to cut out two black wing shapes, two dark-grey body shapes, and two light-grey ears.

**2** Pin two wing pieces together. Cut a length of black thread and set aside half the strands (so for six-stranded thread, use three). Using the thread and a large needle, sew the wings together with running stitch, turning the wings over and back again as you sew so the line is neat and straight on both sides. Sew the four dotted lines across the wings first, sewing along each line and then back again, filling in the gaps to create a continuous stitch. Sew around the edge of the wings, finishing neatly on one side (this

# Debbie Brown's enchanting magical cakes

MURDOCH BOOKS

# Contents

4

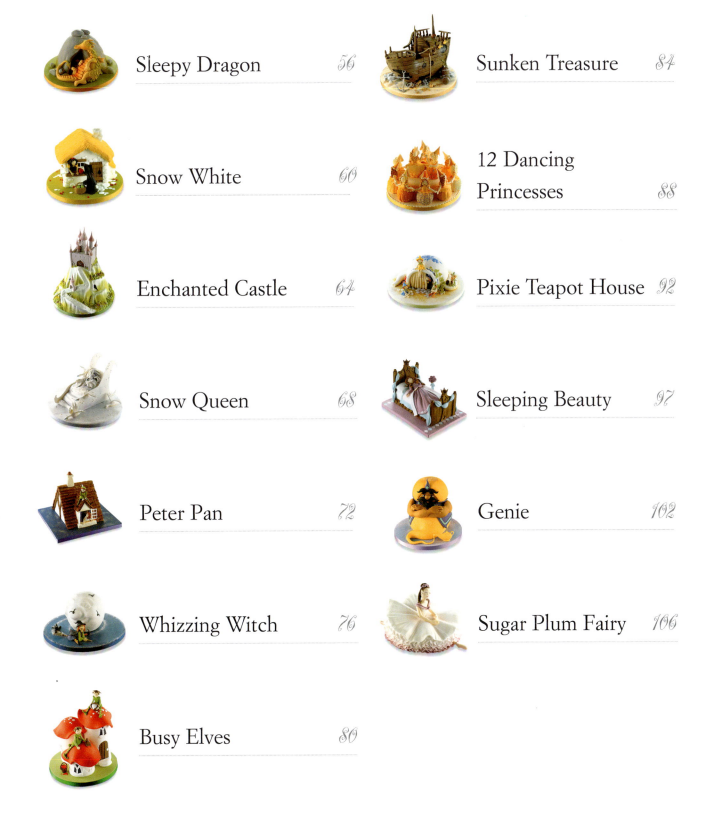

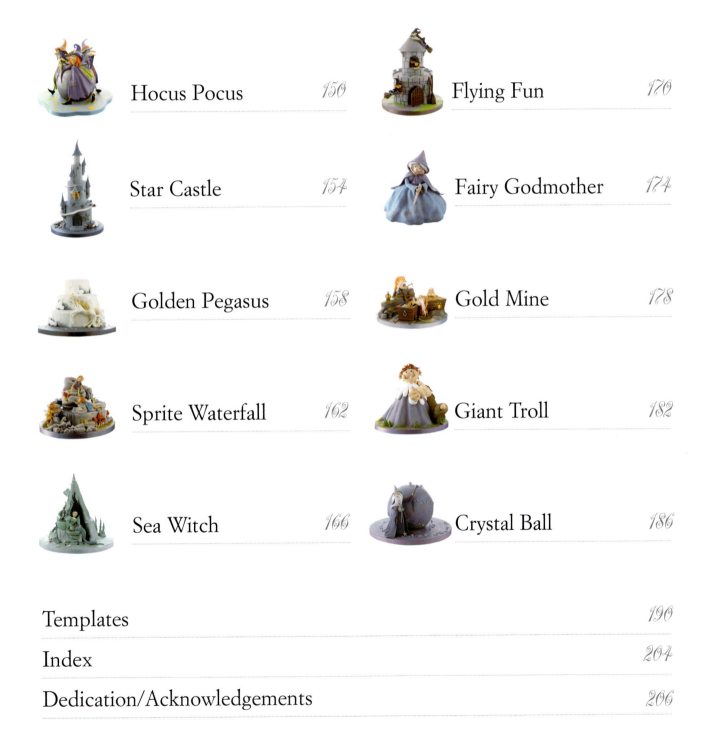

# Introduction

*Enchanting Magical Cakes* is a pretty subject to base cake designs on. It was quite easy to think of ideas because of the broad range of enchanting tales and folklore that are ever popular with children.

At certain moments, when thinking deeply about designs, I must admit that childhood tastes came flooding back. I'm afraid that up until the age of eight I thought everything beautiful should be coloured pink! Pink dresses, pink ribbons, pink bedroom. Blue was for boys. Green only for grass and trees. Thank goodness colour tastes change when you grow up.

I must admit that I did bear this in mind when designing some of these cakes as girls' tastes haven't changed that much. When making Cinderella, the most enchanting figure of fairy tales, I considered colouring her dress blue, which in my grown-up head I thought would look rather nice. But the child in me said 'pink!' A compromise was reached and I gave her a white dress, dusted it with a little pink dusting powder (petal dust/blossom tint) and added lots of extra sparkle.

Some of the cakes in this book are quite involved, with lots of detail that appeal to children and adults alike. I have made them this way so that there are lots of ideas and you can take the elements from them that you want, or leave out parts if you are short of time.

Many of the cakes will still look pretty with less detail in them. The Bewitching Mermaids cake (see pages 22–5) and Pixie Teapot House (see pages 92–6) would look complete with only half the modelling projects. Or a single, pretty fairy on top of a cake would look just as enchanting as three or four, and can be lifted off and given to the birthday girl, as a special treat when the cake is cut.

Because of the enchanting subject of all these cakes, many can be mixed around to give different looks. The Busy Elves (see page 80–3) would not look out of place sprucing up the Pixie Teapot House (see pages 92–6) instead. The Enchanted Tree (see pages 51–5) could be home to the Fruit Fairies (see pages 38–41), especially as it is meant to be a crab apple tree, and the Whizzing Witch (see pages 76–9) could be flying around the Enchanted Castle (see pages 64–7) for a change.

I hope you use this book as inspiration for your own creative ideas too. If you make cakes as a hobby or business, or even just for the occasional birthday, you have a creative streak that should not be neglected. Don't be afraid to try things out. The basics of cake modelling are covered in most projects in this book. Have a go yourself and I guarantee that you will be pleasantly surprised.

Happy cake decorating!

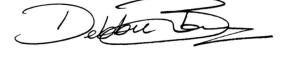

# Recipes and Materials

## MADEIRA SPONGE CAKE

*Madeira is ideal for shaping without crumbling.*

The secret of successful cake decorating is to use a firm, moist cake that can be cut and shaped without crumbling. Madeira cake is a good choice and can be flavoured for variety. To make a madeira cake, follow the steps below. For the ingredients and bakeware required, see pages 18–21.

1 Preheat the oven to 160–170°C/ 325°F/Gas 3, then grease and line the bakeware.

2 Sift the self-raising and the plain/ all-purpose flour together in a bowl. Then, put the soft margarine and caster/ superfine sugar in a large bowl and beat until the mixture is pale and fluffy.

3 Add the eggs to the mixture, one at a time with a spoonful of the flour, beating well after each addition. Add any flavouring required (see right).

4 Using a large spoon, fold the remaining flour into the mixture. Spoon the mixture into the bakeware, then make a dip in the top of the mixture with the back of the spoon.

5 Bake in the centre of the oven until a skewer inserted in the middle comes out clean (see pages 18–21 for baking times).

6 Leave the cake to stand for about 5 minutes, then turn out on to a wire rack and leave to cool. When cold, store in an airtight container until ready to use.

## Madeira cake flavourings

- **Vanilla** Add 5ml (1tsp) of vanilla essence/extract to every 6-egg mixture.

- **Lemon** Add the grated rind and/or the juice of 1 lemon to every 6-egg mixture.

- **Almond** Add 5ml (1tsp) of almond essence and 30–45ml (2–3tbsp) of ground almonds to every 6-egg mixture.

- **Chocolate** Add 30–45ml (2–3tbsp) of unsweetened cocoa powder mixed with 15ml (1tbsp) of milk to every 6-egg mixture.

- **Chocolate swirl cake**
A delicious and unusual alternative to the chocolate cake is to fold in 155g (5oz) of dark melted cooking chocolate into each 6-egg madeira mixture, until a swirling effect is achieved. For a marbled effect, gently stir in the chocolate. Spoon the mixture into the required bakeware and follow cooking instructions. For an even more luxurious chocolate swirl cake, fold in 75g (2½oz) each of melted white and dark cooking chocolate into each 6-egg madeira mixture.

*Chocolate swirl cake.*

## SUGARPASTE

*Sugarpaste is an easy, smooth cake covering.*

I recommend using ready-made sugarpaste (rolled fondant), which is of high quality and is available from cake decorating suppliers and supermarkets. The sugarpaste used in this book is firm but pliable – it smoothes well and keeps its shape when drying. Try different sugarpastes to find your own preference or use the recipe below.

*Makes 625g (1¼lb)*
- *1 egg white made up from dried egg albumen*
- *30ml (2tbsp) liquid glucose*
- *625g (1¼lb/5 cups) icing (confectioner's) sugar*
- *A little white vegetable fat (shortening) if required*

1 Put the egg white and liquid glucose into a bowl, using a warm spoon for the liquid glucose.

2 Sift the icing (confectioner's) sugar into the bowl, adding a little at a time and stirring until the mixture thickens.

3 Turn out onto a work surface dusted with icing sugar and knead the paste until it is soft, smooth and pliable. If the paste is a dry and cracked, fold in a little vegetable fat (shortening) and knead again.

4 Put into a polythene bag, or double wrap the paste in cling film (plastic wrap), and store in an airtight container.

## BUTTERCREAM

*Buttercream gives a smooth surface for sugarpaste.*

As well as making a delicious filling between layers of cake, a thin coat of buttercream spread all over the cake fills any small gaps and also provides a smooth surface on which to apply the sugarpaste. Buttercream can also be flavoured (see below).

*Makes about 500g (1lb/2 cups)*
• *125g (4oz/½ cup) butter, softened or soft margarine*
• *15ml (1tbsp) milk*
• *375g (12oz/3 cups) icing (confectioner's) sugar*

1 Put the butter or soft margarine into a mixing bowl. Add the milk and/or any flavouring required (see box below).
2 Sift the icing (confectioner's) sugar into a bowl, a little at a time, and beat well after each addition, until all the sugar has been incorporated and the buttercream has a light, creamy texture.
3 Store the buttercream in an airtight container until required.

### Buttercream flavourings

• **Vanilla** Add 5ml (1tsp) vanilla essence (extract).
• **Lemon** Replace the milk with 15ml (1tbsp) fresh lemon juice.
• **Chocolate** Mix the milk and 30ml (2tbsp) unsweetened cocoa powder to a paste and add to the mixture.
• **Coffee** Mix together the milk and 15ml (1tbsp) instant coffee powder to a paste and add to the buttercream mixture.

## MODELLING PASTE

*Modelling paste is pliable to use and dries hard.*

Modelling paste is a sugarpaste (rolled fondant) with a gum additive. When the gum is incorporated, it makes the paste firm but pliable so it is easier to work with. Items modelled from modelling paste will dry harder and will also keep their shape.

A natural gum called gum tragacanth, which is widely used in the food industry, is usually used to make modelling paste. There is a man-made alternative called carboxy methyl cellulose (CMC), which is cheaper than gum tragacanth and also goes further.

However, if you do not want to make your own modelling paste before embarking on the projects in this book, there are some ready-made modelling pastes available that give good results. Even more useful, they can be obtained pre-coloured. All items are available from cake decorating suppliers.

*Makes about 500g (1lb)*
• *10ml (2tsp) gum tragacanth*
• *500g (1lb) sugarpaste (rolled fondant)*

1 Put the gum tragacanth on a work surface and knead it into the sugarpaste (rolled fondant).
2 Double wrap the modelling paste in polythene or cling film (plastic wrap) and store in an airtight container for at least an hour before use.

## ROYAL ICING

*Royal icing is used to pipe fine details and hair.*

Royal icing is used to pipe fine details, as well as hair and for sticking items together. Ready-made royal icing can be obtained in powder form (follow the instructions on the packet). If you prefer to make your own, use the recipe below.

*Makes about 280g (9oz)*
• *1 egg white made up from dried egg albumen*
• *250–280g (8–9oz/2 cups) icing (confectioner's) sugar*

1 Put the egg white into a bowl. Beat in the icing (confectioner's) sugar a little at a time, until the icing is firm and glossy and forms peaks when the spoon is pulled out.
2 Cover the bowl with a damp cloth for a few minutes before use.

### Food colouring

Food colouring can be obtained in a rainbow of colours from cake decorating suppliers and many supermarkets. When deep or brightly coloured sugarpaste is required, I recommend using paste food colourings as they are more concentrated and will not drastically change the texture of the paste. Food colouring in liquid form is also available but only use these for pastel shades as they will make the paste sticky and difficult to use. Food colouring in powder form is good for dusting your cake to achieve subtle shades. (See page 16 for more on how to colour sugarpaste.)

## PASTILLAGE

*Pastillage dries very hard.*

When pastillage icing is rolled out and left to dry, it dries so hard it snaps when broken. It will not bend or lose its shape when dry, although extremely damp conditions will affect it.

When using pastillage, you have to work quite quickly as it forms a crust soon after being exposed to the air. It is therefore unsuitable for modelling unless you mix it 50:50 with sugarpaste.

Pastillage can be obtained in high-quality powder form from cake decorating suppliers, but this recipe is very simple and just as good.

*Makes about 375g (12oz)*
• *1 egg white made up from dried egg albumen*
• *345g (11oz/2³⁄₄ cups) icing (confectioner's) sugar*
• *10ml (2tsp) gum tragacanth*

1 Put the egg white in a bowl and add 280g (9oz) of icing (confectioner's) sugar a little at a time, mixing well.
2 Sprinkle the gum tragacanth over the top and put the mixture aside for about 10 minutes.
3 Turn the mixture out onto a surface and knead in the remaining icing sugar.
4 Double wrap in polythene or cling film (plastic wrap) and store in an airtight container until required.

## PETAL PASTE

*Petal paste produces delicate flowers.*

Petal (or flower) paste produces very fine results and, as its name suggests, is ideal for making flowers and leaves, such as those on the Fairy King and Queen cake (see pages 30–3). It can be bought ready-made from cake decorating suppliers (either direct or by mail order) or you can make your own as follows:

*Makes about 500g (1lb)*
• *25ml (5tsp) cold water*
• *10ml (2tsp) powdered gelatine*
• *500g (1lb/4 cups) icing (confectioner's) sugar*
• *15ml (3tsp) gum tragacanth*
• *10ml (2tsp) liquid glucose*
• *15ml (3tsp) white vegetable fat (shortening)*
• *1 egg white made up from dried egg albumen*

1 Mix the water and gelatine in a small heatproof bowl and leave to stand for 30 minutes. Sift the icing (confectioner's) sugar and gum tragacanth into the bowl of an electric mixer and fit the bowl to the machine.
2 Place the bowl with the gelatine mixture over a saucepan of hot water. Stir until all the ingredients have melted.
3 Add the dissolved gelatine mixture to the icing sugar, along with the egg white. Fit the beater to the machine and turn it on at its lowest speed. Beat until mixed, then increase the speed to maximum and continue beating until the paste is white and stringy.

## SUGAR STICKS

*Sugar sticks keep figures' heads secure.*

Sugar supports for models can be made from left over modelling paste or preferably pastillage or petal paste. Roll or cut thin sticks of paste and leave to dry. Insert the sugar stick into the modelled body, then gently push on the head, using sugar glue to secure. Alternatively, use pieces of raw, dried spaghetti.

## SUGAR GLUE

Sugar glue is required to stick pieces of sugarpaste (rolled fondant) together. Egg white made up from powdered egg albumen is a good glue, as is royal icing (see page 12), or sugarpaste and water mixed together to make a thick brushing paste.

Alternatively, a glue made from gum arabic is popular, which, along with commercial sugar glues, are available from cake decorating suppliers. Mix 5ml (1tsp) gum arabic powder with a few drops of water to make a paste. Store in an airtight container in the refrigerator.

To stick sugarpaste pieces together, slightly dampen the paste with sugar glue using a fine paintbrush. If you apply too much, the piece may slide out of place. Gently press in position, holding for a few moments. Small pieces of foam sponge can be used for support until dry.

### Storing the decorated cake

Store in a cardboard cake box in a warm, dry room. NEVER leave in the refrigerator where the dampness will make the cake spoil. You should decorate the cake within one week of baking.

# Equipment

*A blossom plunger cutter.*

*A circle cutter.*

**Blossom plunger cutter** is used for cutting simple flower shapes.

**Bone tool** is used to indent paste, when making ears, eye sockets, shaping curves.

**Cake smoother** is used to create a smooth surface on sugarpaste (rolled fondant). The type with a handle is the most useful. Smooth it over the paste in a circular motion to level out an uneven surface.

**Calyx cutter** is used to make flower calyxes, hats or hair.

**Cocktail sticks** (toothpicks) are ideal for indenting small details and handy for applying food colouring to sugarpaste.

**Crimping tool** (serrated) is a simple way to add texture and pattern to sugarpaste. The crimping tool pinches up sugarpaste between the pinchers at the end of the tool. Lines are pinched horizontally, letting the serrated teeth scratch vertical lines. Practise on a spare piece of paste.

**Circle cutter** is used to cut out or indent various circular shapes.

**Foam sheet** is useful for drying modelled items or figures because the air can circulate underneath.

**Foam sponge** is for supporting decorative pieces while they are drying.

**Garrett frill cutter** is used for cutting out frills that can be arranged as the layers of a dress or simply for achieving a decorative finish.

**Grater** (small) is used to texture paste to produce effects including sand and grass.

**Kitchen paper** is useful for blotting and removing excess paint from a brush.

**Leaf cutter** is used to cut leaf shapes and also fairy costumes.

**Leaf veiner** is used to mark the veins in the leaf shapes.

**Petal cutter** is used to cut petal shapes for dragon scales and fairy costumes.

**Paintbrushes** are essential for painting and dusting the cakes, and marking details using the handle.

**Piping bags** and a variety of tubes (tips) are used for piping royal icing to make hair for the figures.

**Plastic dowelling** can be used to support internally cakes that are built up.

**Rolling pins** (large and small) are essential for rolling out paste. White polypropylene pins are recommended.

**Scissors** are needed for cutting out templates and some modelling.

**Sharp knife** is essential for making clean, accurate cuts in cakes and various pastes.

**Square cutter** is used to cut out square shapes, such as windows and doors.

**Star cutter** is used to make various decorative shapes.

**Star tube** (tip) creates a grass-like effect when pressed repeatedly into sugarpaste.

**Sugar shaker** is for holding icing (confectioner's) sugar.

*A crimping tool*

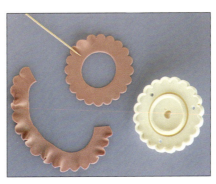
*A Garrett frill cutter.*

# Basic Techniques

## CUTTING & SHAPING CAKES

### Cake sculpting

To sculpt cake into different shapes, use a sharp, serrated knife. Cut a little at a time, shaving off small pieces until you have the required shape. If you shave off more than you need, pieces of cake can be stuck back on with a little buttercream but take care not to do this too much because it may cause the sugarpaste (rolled fondant) to slip when applied.

*Use a sharp knife to sculpt cakes.*

### Balance

When building up a high cake, make sure each layer is completely straight and that the cake is perfectly balanced. If part of the cake is left only slightly uneven it will look much worse when covered with sugarpaste and may cause the cake to lean.

## USING SUGARPASTE

### Colouring the paste

Add food colouring to the sugarpaste (rolled fondant) a little at a time with a cocktail stick (toothpick). Knead it into the sugarpaste, adding more until you have the required shade. Wear plastic gloves as the food colouring can stain your hands. Alternatively, pre-coloured packs of sugarpaste are now obtainable from cake decorating suppliers and supermarkets.

*Use a cocktail stick to apply colour to the paste.*

### Preparing sugarpaste

Knead thoroughly until warm and pliable before rolling out onto a work surface covered with a sprinkling of icing (confectioner's) sugar. Keep moving the paste around so that it does not stick and roll it to a thickness of 3–4mm (⅛in), unless otherwise stated.

To lift a large piece of rolled-out sugarpaste, lay a large rolling pin on the centre and flip the paste over it. Lift it, position, then roll the paste into place. Use a sharp, plain-edged knife to cut the paste. To avoid the paste 'pulling', cut cleanly downwards. Keep wiping the blade to remove excess, or a layer of paste will build up and make cuts untidy.

When the sugarpaste is dry, polish the surface with your hands to remove excess icing sugar and to give it a sheen.

## Covering the cake board

Roll out the sugarpaste, lift and cover the board. Use a cake smoother to give a smooth surface. If the paste has not stuck to the board, lift the sugarpaste around the edge and moisten with a damp paintbrush. Trim any excess downwards with a sharp knife. You may wish to remove the sugarpaste from the area of the board on which the cake will sit. Because the cake is moist, the sugarpaste beneath has a tendency to become sticky. Leave boards to dry for at least 12 hours.

*Use sugarpaste to cover the cake board.*

### Covering the cake

Spread a layer of buttercream over the surface of the cake to help the sugarpaste stick. Roll out sugarpaste and cover the cake completely, smoothing around the shape and trimming any excess. If required, rub the surface with a cake smoother to produce a smooth surface.

*Gently lower the sugarpaste onto the cake.*

# MODELLING PEOPLE

*The modelled pieces of a figure.*

The head, hair and clothes will vary, depending on the design, but the general principles of body, arms and legs remain the same. The best material to use for making people is modelling paste, as it will hold the shapes you model. The head can be a round or teardrop shape. To make the arms and hands, roll the paste into a sausage, rounding off the end to make each hand. Press the hand to make it slightly flat, then cut a thumb on one side. Make three cuts along the top to form fingers. Gently twist each finger to lengthen it, then press in the palm to round off. Pinch in halfway to indent the elbow and pinch out at the back. To make legs and feet, roll out two long sausage-shaped pieces of modelling paste and pinch at the ankles to round the feet. Pinch each foot to lengthen and indent underneath each to make the foot arch. Halfway from the ankle to the top of the leg, push in at the back and pinch out at the front to mark the knee.

# PAINTING ON SUGAR

## Colour strengths

You can dilute food colouring pastes with cool boiled water. The amount of water dictates the strength of the colour. For a really pale, watercolour effect, dilute the colouring until very pale and transparent. For a stronger colour, only add a few drops of water until the food colouring paste is liquid enough to paint with.

## Applying colour

When painting on sugar, the brush must be kept only slightly damp to avoid paint running or even the sugar melting. Blot excess liquid from the paintbrush using a

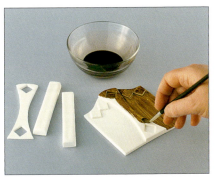

*Apply colour with diluted food colouring.*

dry cloth or some absorbent kitchen paper. If you are nervous about painting, practise on a sheet of plain paper first. Remember, any painted mistakes on dried paste can be removed with a damp cloth.

## Mixing colours

To make a different shade of one colour, you can add a minute amount of another colour – for example, if you have a basic green and want a bright grass green, add some yellow. Likewise, if you are using basic green and want a dark, muddy green,

*Coloured dusting powder provides subtle shades.*

add a touch of brown. Experimenting is part of the fun, but if you are nervous about mixing your own colours, use different shades of the same colour from the vast range of pastes available.

## Stippling

Stippling food colouring onto paste is a simple, effective and controllable method of adding colour. Preferably use a medium-sized firm bristle paintbrush and only collect a little diluted food colouring onto the tip. Blot excess liquid off the brush with a cloth or absorbent kitchen paper, then repeatedly dot over the surface of the paste, keeping the paintbrush vertical.

*Use a stippling action to achieve this paint effect.*

# FINISHING TOUCHES

When your decorated cake is complete, brush off any excess icing (confectioner's) sugar. Apply the finishing touches by dusting it with powder (petal dust/blossom tint) or glitter to set it off and give it a sparkle. Dusting powder adds colour, lustre powder will give your cake a bright sheen and sparkle powder will make it glisten. Using confectioner's varnish will create a shine.

*Edible glitter gives a sparkle.*

# Cake Quantities

| Cake | Page | Bakeware | Eggs | Self-raising flour | Plain/all-purpose flour | Butter/soft margarine | Caster/superfine sugar | Baking time |
|---|---|---|---|---|---|---|---|---|
| Bewitching Mermaids | 22 | 25cm (10in) square tin | 6 | 375g (12oz/ 3 cups) | 185g (6oz/ 1½ cups) | 375g (12oz/ 1½ cups) | 375g (12oz/ 1½ cups) | 1–1¼ hours |
| Persian Palace | 26 | 25cm (10in) square tin | 6 | 375g (12oz/ 3 cups) | 185g (6oz/ 1½ cups) | 375g (12oz/ 1½ cups) | 375g (12oz/ 1½ cups) | 1–1¼ hours |
| Fairy King and Queen | 30 | 20cm (8in) square tin | 5 | 315g (10oz/ 2½ cups) | 155g (5oz/ 1¼ cups) | 315g (10oz/ 1¼ cups) | 315g (10oz/ 1¼ cups) | 1–1½ hours |
| Magical Wizard | 34 | 25cm (10in) square tin | 6 | 375g (12oz/ 3 cups) | 185g (6oz/ 1½ cups) | 375g (12oz/ 1½ cups) | 375g (12oz/ 1½ cups) | 1–1¼ hours |
| Fruit Fairies | 38 | Two 1l (2 pints/4 cups) ovenproof bowls | 5 | 315g (10oz/ 2½ cups) | 155g (5oz/ 1¼ cups) | 315g (10oz/ 1¼ cups) | 315g (10oz/ 1¼ cups) | 1¼–1½ hours |
| Knight in Armour | 42 | 18cm (7in), 15cm (6in) and 12cm (5in) round tins (evenly fill each tin) | 8 | 500g (1lb/ 4 cups) | 250g (8oz/ 2 cups) | 500g (1lb/ 2 cups) | 500g (1lb/ 2 cups) | 1–1¼ hours for large cake<br><br>45 mins–1 hour for other cakes |
| Cinderella | 46 | Two 18cm (7in) square tins (evenly fill each tin) | 8 | 500g (1lb/ 4 cups) | 250g (8oz/ 2 cups) | 500g (1lb/ 2 cups) | 500g (1lb/ 2 cups) | 45 mins–1 hour |
| Enchanted Tree | 51 | 25cm (10in) square tin | 6 | 375g (12oz/ 3 cups) | 185g (6oz/ 1½ cups) | 375g (12oz/ 1½ cups) | 375g (12oz/ 1½ cups) | 1–1¼ hours |
| Enchanted Tree Sleepy Dragon | 45 56 | 1l (2 pints/ 4 cups) ovenproof bowl and 20cm (8in) round tin (half fill bowl with third of mixture, then put rest of mixture into tin) | 6 | 375g (12oz/ 3 cups) | 185g (6oz/ 1½ cups) | 375g (12oz/ 1½ cups) | 375g (12oz/ 1½ cups) | 1¼–1½ hours for bowl-shaped cake<br><br>45mins–1 hour for round cake |
| Snow White | 60 | 25cm (10in) square tin | 5 | 315g (10oz/ 2½ cups) | 155g(5oz/ 1¼ cups) | 315g (10oz/ 1¼ cups) | 315g (10oz/ 1¼ cups) | 45 mins–1 hour |

All baking tins used are 8cm (3in) depth.
All ovenproof bowls used are Pyrex.

| Cake | Page | Bakeware | Eggs | Self-raising flour | Plain/all-purpose flour | Butter/soft margarine | Caster/superfine sugar | Baking time |
|---|---|---|---|---|---|---|---|---|
| Enchanted Castle | 64 | 20cm (8in) round tin, 15cm (6in) round tin and 18cm (7in) square tin (evenly fill each tin) | 8 | 500g (1lb/ 4 cups) | 250g (8oz/ 2 cups) | 500g (1lb/ 2 cups) | 500g (1lb/ 2 cups) | 45 mins–1 hour for each cake |
| Snow Queen | 68 | 20cm (8in) square tin | 5 | 315g (10oz/ 2½ cups) | 155g (5oz/ 1¼ cups) | 315g (10oz/ 1¼ cups) | 315g (10oz/ 1¼ cups) | 1–1½ hours |
| Peter Pan | 72 | 20cm (8in) and 15cm (6in) square tins (evenly fill each tin) | 6 | 375g (12oz/ 3 cups) | 185g (6oz/ 1½ cups) | 375g (12oz/ 1½ cups) | 375g (12oz/ 1½ cups) | 45 mins–1 hour for each cake |
| Whizzing Witch | 76 | Two 1l (2 pints/4 cups) ovenproof bowls | 5 | 315g (10oz/ 2½ cups) | 155g (5oz/ 1¼ cups) | 315g (10oz/ 1¼ cups) | 315g (10oz/ 1¼ cups) | 1¼–1½ hours |
| Busy Elves | 80 | 25cm (10in) square tin | 6 | 375g (12oz/ 3 cups) | 185g (6oz/ 1½ cups) | 375g (12oz/ 1½ cups) | 375g (12oz/ 1½ cups) | 1–1¼ hours |
| Sunken Treasure | 84 | 25cm (10in) square tin | 6 | 375g (12oz/ 3 cups) | 185g (6oz/ 1½ cups) | 375g (12oz/ 1½ cups) | 375g (12oz/ 1½ cups) | 1–1¼ hours |
| 12 Dancing Princesses | 88 | Fill 12-hole cup cake tin, then put remaining mixture into 15cm (6in) round tin | 5 | 315g (10oz/ 2½ cups) | 155g (5oz/ 1¼ cups) | 315g (10oz/ 1¼ cups) | 315g (10oz/ 1¼ cups) | 20–30 mins for cup cakes<br><br>45 mins–1 hour for round cake |
| Pixie Teapot House | 92 | 2l (4 pint/ 10 cup) ovenproof bowl | 5 | 315g (10oz/ 2½ cups) | 155g (5oz/ 1¼ cups) | 315g (10oz/ 1¼ cups) | 315g (10oz/ 1¼ cups) | 1¼–1½ hours |
| Sleeping Beauty | 97 | 30cm (12in) square tin | 6 | 375g (12oz/ 3 cups) | 185g (6oz/ 1½ cups) | 375g (12oz/ 1½ cups) | 375g (12oz/ 1½ cups) | 45 mins–1 hour |
| Genie | 102 | 1l (2 pints/ 4 cups) and 625ml (1¼ pint/3 cup) ovenproof bowls (evenly fill each bowl) | 5 | 315g (10oz/ 2½ cups) | 155g (5oz/ 1¼ cups) | 315g (10oz/ 1¼ cups) | 315g (10oz/ 1¼ cups) | 1¼–1½ hours for large cake<br><br>45 mins–1 hour for small cake |
| Sugar Plum Fairy | 106 | 20cm (8in) round tin | 5 | 315g (10oz/ 2½ cups) | 155g (5oz/ 1¼ cups) | 315g (10oz/ 1¼ cups) | 315g (10oz/ 1¼ cups) | 1–1½ hours |

| Cake | Page | Bakeware | Eggs | Self-raising flour | Plain/all-purpose flour | Butter/soft margarine | Caster/superfine sugar | Baking time |
|------|------|----------|------|--------------------|-----------------------|----------------------|----------------------|-------------|
| Emerald City | 118 | 3 x 15cm (6in) round tins | 6 | 375g (12oz/ 3 cups) | 185g (6oz/ 1½ cups) | 375g (12oz/ 1½ cups) | 375g (12oz/ 1½ cups) | 1 hour |
| Pirate Dreams | 138 | 20cm (8in) square tin | 4 | 250g (8oz/ 2 cups) | 125g (4oz/ 1 cup) | 250g (8oz/ 1 cup) | 250g (8oz/ 1 cup) | 1 hour |
| Gold Mine | 178 | 20cm (8in) square tin | 5 | 315 (10oz/ 2½ cups) | 155g (5oz/ 1¼ cups) | 315g (10oz/ 1¼ cups) | 315g (10oz/ 1¼ cups) | 1¼–1½ hours |
| Hocus Pocus | 150 | 2 x 1 litre (2 pint/5 cup) ovenproof bowls | 5 | 315 (10oz/ 2½ cups) | 155g (5oz/ 1¼ cups) | 315g (10oz/ 1¼ cups) | 315g (10oz/ 1¼ cups) | 1¼ hours |
| Crystal Ball | 186 | | | | | | | |
| Flying Fun | 170 | 2 x 15cm (6in) round tins 18cm (7in) round tin (evenly fill each tin) | 6 | 375g (12oz/ 3 cups) | 185g (6oz/ 1½ cups) | 375g (12oz/ 1½ cups) | 375g (12oz /1½ cups) | 1 hour each |
| Wizard's Helpers | 142 | 10cm (4in) round tin 15cm (6in) round tin 20cm (8in) square tin (put half of mixture in 20cm (8in) tin, then fill remaining tins) | 7 | 440g (14oz/ 3½ cups) | 220g (7oz/ 1¾ cups) | 440g (14oz/ 1¾ cups) | 440g (14oz/ 1¾ cups) | 50 mins–1 hour largest tin 1–1¼ hours other tins |
| Baby Dragon | 147 | 3 x 625ml (1¼ pint/3 cup) oveproof bowls (fill two bowls evenly and third bowl with 60ml (4tbsp) of mixture) | 4 | 250g (8oz/ 2 cups) | 125g (4oz/ 1 cup) | 250g (8oz/ 1 cup) | 250g (8oz/ 1 cup) | 1 hour each 30 mins smaller bowl |

| Cake | Page | Bakeware | Eggs | Self-raising flour | Plain/all-purpose flour | Butter/soft margarine | Caster/superfine sugar | Baking time |
|---|---|---|---|---|---|---|---|---|
| Sea Witch | 166 | 10cm (4in) round tin 12cm (5in) round tin 18cm (7in) round tin (evenly fill each tin) | 6 | 375g (12oz/ 3 cups) | 185g (6oz/ 1½ cups) | 375g (12oz/ 1½ cups) | 375g (12oz/ 1½ cups) | 1–1¼ hours each |
| Golden Pegasus | 158 | 10cm (4in) round tin 15cm (6in) round tin 20cm (8in) round tin (evenly fill each tin) | 6 | 375g (12oz/ 3 cups) | 185g (6oz/ 1½ cups) | 375g (12oz/ 1½ cups) | 375g (12oz/ 1½ cups) | 1 hour each<br><br>40 mins smallest tin |
| Rock Monster | 114 | | | | | | | |
| Ramshackle Village | 122 | 25cm (10in) square tin | 7 | 440g (14oz/ 3½ cups) | 220g (7oz/ 1¾ cups) | 440g (14oz/ 1¾ cups) | 440g (14oz/ 1¾ cups) | 1¼ hours |
| Star Castle | 154 | | | | | | | |
| Wizard Owl | 130 | 25cm (10in) square tin | 6 | 375g (12oz/ 3 cups) | 185g (6oz/ 1½ cups) | 375g (12oz/ 1½ cups) | 375g (12oz/ 1½ cups) | 1 hour |
| Labyrinth | 134 | | | | | | | |
| Sprite Waterfall | 162 | 10cm (4in) round tin 20cm (8in) round tin (evenly fill each tin) | 4 | 250g (8oz/ 2 cups) | 125g (4oz/ 1 cup) | 250g (8oz/ 1 cup) | 250g (8oz/ 1 cup) | 1 hour larger tin<br><br>40 mins smaller tin |
| King Neptune | 126 | | | | | | | |
| Giant Troll | 182 | 18cm (7in) round tin 20cm (8in) round tin (evenly fill each tin) | 6 | 375g (12oz/ 3 cups) | 185g (6oz/ 1½ cups) | 375g (12oz/ 1½ cups) | 375g (12oz/ 1½ cups) | 1 hour larger tin<br><br>50 mins smaller tin |
| Dragon Castle | 110 | | | | | | | |
| Fairy Godmother | 174 | 2 litre (4 pint/ 10 cup) ovenproof bowl | 5 | 315g (10oz/ 2½ cups) | 155g (5oz/ 1¼ cups) | 315g (10oz/ 1¼ cups) | 315g (10oz/ 1¼ cups) | 1¼–1½ hours |

# Bewitching Mermaids

*Deep, dark oceans hold many secrets, none more captivating than tales of beautiful mermaids. This is how I imagine they would be, playing happily with the sea creatures.*

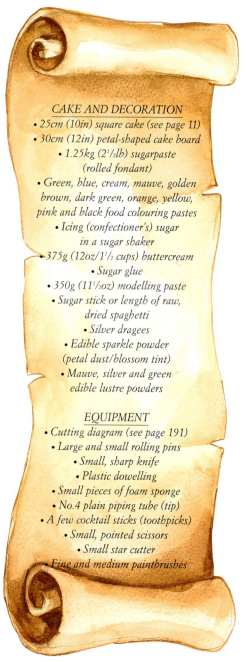

## CAKES AND BOARD

1 Colour 1.17kg (2lb 5½oz) of sugarpaste (rolled fondant) mid-green. Roll out 500g (1lb) and cover the cake board completely. To create a rippled effect, press the rolling pin into the surface and gently roll. Trim any excess away from around the edges. Model some flattened pebbles of different sizes using some of the trimmings and stick these around the cake board edge. Put the cake board aside to dry.

2 Cut the cake as shown in the cutting diagram on page 191. Cut the corners from each cake, then trim to round off. Stack them on top of one another in height order to ensure that they sit evenly and are balanced.

*Stack the cakes up to check that they sit evenly.*

Then take them apart again to cover with sugarpaste. Spread the surface of each cake with a layer of buttercream. Roll out 280g (9oz) of mid-green sugarpaste and cover the large cake completely, smoothing around the shape

*Cover each cake with sugarpaste.*

and tucking the sugarpaste underneath. Position on the centre of the cake board.

3 Colour 45g (1½oz) of sugarpaste pale blue. In order to vary the shade of the cake from green at the base to blue at the top, knead a small amount of blue food colouring paste into the remaining mid-green each time one of the cakes is covered. Stack the cakes up again, turning each slightly and making sure that each one is well balanced. Once you have done this, secure them in place using sugar glue. Carefully push the plastic dowelling down through the top of the cake to provide extra support for your ocean scene.

## THE MERMAID'S BODY

4 Next, model the mermaids that are swimming around the cake. Colour 140g (4½oz) of modelling paste cream. To make a mermaid's body, roll 30g (1oz) into a tapering sausage, twisting the tail to a point. One-third of the way from the rounded end, press in all the way around to shape the waistline and round off the chest, then smooth up a neck at the top.

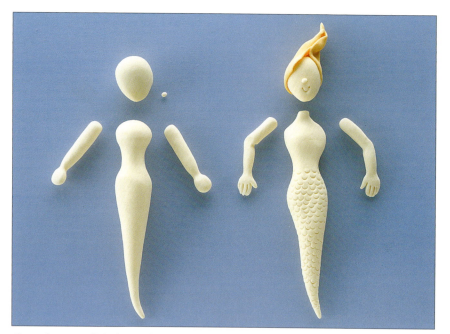

*Create the mermaid's body out of modelling paste and add arms, head and hair when in position.*

## THE MERMAID'S HAIR

Split 30g (1oz) of modelling paste into three pieces. Colour one golden brown, one mid-golden brown and the last piece dark golden brown. Thinly roll out 7g (¼oz) of each and fold around the mermaid's head, twisting up at the end to form the base for the hair. You will add the rest of her hair in step 12.

*Add her fins, tail and shell-shaped top.*

Lay the mermaid down and smooth her stomach flat. Press gently at the top to help flatten her back. The mermaid is shown on the work surface for clarity but it is best to place her on the cake at this stage, using pieces of foam to support the pose while she is drying. Indent the scales on her tail by repeatedly pressing the no. 4 plain piping tube (tip) in at an angle over the surface.

### THE MERMAID'S FACE

Roll 7g (¼oz) of cream modelling paste into a teardrop-shaped head. For the top mermaid, use a sugar stick or length of raw spaghetti to support the head by pushing gently into her neck, moistening the base with sugar glue, then pressing on the head. Stick a small ball in the centre to make a nose. Indent a smile with a no.4 plain piping tube pressed in at an angle and dimple each corner with the tip of a cocktail stick (toothpick).

### THE MERMAID'S FINS

Colour 30g (1oz) of modelling paste pale mauve. Using 7g (¼oz) split in half, shape the two fins, marking in lines with a cocktail stick. Model two small teardrop shapes, flatten slightly, then mark lines with a cocktail stick to produce the shell-shaped top. Flatten two very small oval shapes of pale mauve paste and stick in place for the shoulder straps.

### THE MERMAID'S ARMS

To make the arms, split just under 7g (¼oz) of the cream modelling paste in half. Roll a sausage shape, rounding it off at one end. Press the rounded end slightly flat, then cut the thumb on one side. Cut the fingers across the top, keeping them straight. Gently twist each finger to lengthen. Halfway up the arm, press in to form the elbow, then pinch out at the back. Make two more mermaids following these steps.

*Small details add the finishing touches to your cake.*

### THE SEAWEED

Colour 22g (¾oz) of modelling paste dark green. Roll long, thin tapering sausage shapes and stick them into place twisting up over the cake. Colour 30g (1oz) of modelling paste orange and 15g (½oz) dark mauve. Put aside half of the orange paste, then using the step photograph as a guide,

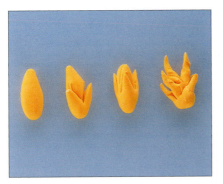

*Twist the seaweed into spiral shapes.*

*Indent smiles on the faces of all the sea creatures with a no.4 plain piping tube.*

make the different-sized pieces of seaweed, twisting the orange paste into spirals and smoothing the mauve seaweed into points.

make the fish, form teardrop shapes with the remaining yellow paste, marking smiles as before. Decorate each fish with tiny thin stripes of orange modelling paste and miniature teardrop shapes for fins.

### THE OCTOPUS AND FISH

To make the octopus, first colour 60g (2oz) of modelling paste yellow. Using the photograph below as a guide, shape 45g (1½oz) of it into an oval, indenting around the centre. Cut eight legs, twisting each until long and thin, and curl up each end. Dampen your fingers slightly if the legs become dry before you have finished. Indent a smile as you did in step 5 with the mermaids. To

### THE STARFISH

Colour 15g (½oz) of modelling paste pale pink. To make a starfish, thickly roll out and cut a star. Pinch at each point, twisting up at the ends, then pinch a small ridge along the top. Make more starfish, varying the colours by kneading in a small amount of orange modelling paste. Place them around the base of the cake.

*Add the rest of the mermaid's hair.*

### FINISHING TOUCHES

With the remaining white paste, make shells and the eyes for the octopus. Stick the silver dragees over the cake. To finish the mermaid's hair, roll out some golden brown paste. Cut thin strips, twisting each into a spiral and stick in place. When the cake is dry, paint little dots for eyes with the fine paintbrush, using black food colouring paste diluted with a drop of water.

Dust the cake with sparkle powder (petal dust/blossom tint). Then dust the cake randomly with mauve lustre powder, the mermaids' tails with mauve and silver powder and the edge of the board with green powder.

*Model the octopus in yellow modelling paste.*

*Place the starfish and seaweed around the cake.*

# Persian Palace

*I could have added a genie, flying carpet and fantasy birds to this design but had to stop somewhere. If you are short on time, dust cream-coloured turrets with gold lustre powder for an exotic look.*

## CAKE AND DECORATION
- 25cm (10in) square cake (see page 11)
- 30cm (12in), 25cm (10in) and 20cm (8in) square cake boards
- 1.25kg (2½lb) sugarpaste (rolled fondant)
- 440g (14oz/1¾ cups) buttercream
- Cream, mauve, yellow, green, orange, blue, pink, turquoise, brown and black food colouring pastes
- Icing (confectioner's) sugar in a sugar shaker
- Sugar glue
- 1.185kg (2lb 6oz) modelling paste
- Three sugar sticks or lengths of raw, dried spaghetti
- Gold edible lustre powder (petal dust/blossom tint)

## EQUIPMENT
- Non-toxic glue stick
- Large and small rolling pins
- Small, sharp knife
- Cutting diagram and templates (see page 193)
- Length of thread
- 1cm (½in) square cutter
- Miniature square cutter
- Smocking (lined) rolling pin
- No.4 plain piping tube (tip)
- Fine paintbrush
- Small pieces of foam sponge
- A few cocktail sticks (toothpicks)

### CAKES AND BOARD

1 Stick the cake boards together using glue stick. Colour the 1.25kg (2½lb) of sugarpaste (rolled fondant) cream. Roll out 500g (1lb) and cover the boards, smoothing the edges to shape the steps. Trim excess and allow to dry.

2 Cut the cake as shown in the cutting diagram on page 193. Sandwich the three square cakes together using buttercream, then position centrally on the board. Trim the edges from the four strip cakes to make cylinder

*Stack the cakes up to make the palace shape.*

shapes and position them at each corner of the cake. Sandwich the small square on top of the larger square to shape the tower. Spread a layer of buttercream over each cake to help the sugarpaste stick. Put the tower cake aside until later.

3 Split 625g (1¼lb) of cream sugarpaste in half. Using one half, roll out and cut oblongs to fit the cake sides, leaving the turrets uncovered. To cut the right amount of sugarpaste,

*Cover the cakes with cream sugarpaste.*

measure each side using a length of thread. Cut the thread to size and use as a cutting guide. Roll out the other half and cut pieces to cover the turrets, measuring as before and secure against the sugarpaste cake sides with sugar glue.

### THE TOWER

4 Using 60g (2oz) of cream sugarpaste, roll out and cut a square to cover the top of the cake, trimming off each corner. Leave the

*Make a square tower to go on top of the cake.*

tops of each turret uncovered. Roll out the remaining cream sugarpaste and cut a strip to fit around the tower, measuring as before. Stick the join with sugar glue, then smooth with your fingers to close. Position centrally on top of the cake.

### THE PALACE WALLS

5 Colour 375g (12oz) of modelling paste cream. To add detail to the palace walls, thinly roll out 75g (2½oz) and cut out strips that will form the palace base – cover the sides first and then each turret. Roll out 100g (3½oz), then roll the smocking (lined) rolling pin over the surface to indent even lines. Cut in between the lines to form different sized strips to decorate the palace walls – secure with sugar glue. Using the templates (see page 193), cut out a doorway in the front, a window at the front of the tower and a window on each turret. Colour 155g (5oz) of modelling paste dark mauve. Thinly roll out 22g (¾oz) and cut pieces to fill each space.

### THE TOWER ROOF

6 To make the tower roof, roll the remaining cream modelling paste into a ball. Bring up a point by turning and pinching gently around the top. Turn upside down, then cut out the centre to hollow it out and reduce the weight. (If the roof is too heavy, it may cause the cake covering to wrinkle slightly.) Colour just under 15g (½oz) of sugarpaste blue. Thinly roll it out and cut six strips, each tapering to points, and stick evenly around the tower roof. Colour 170g (5½oz) of modelling paste yellow. Thinly roll out a pea-sized amount and cut very thin, tapering strips out of it and stick into place either side of the blue strip. Shape the detail on the top of the roof with the remaining blue and yellow paste and secure in place. Position the roof on the tower, making sure it is well balanced, then stick with sugar glue.

7 Using the remaining cream modelling paste, roll it into a thick sausage. Cut two mini towers, each measuring 4cm

*Make green chequered strips for the turret roof.*

(1½in) in height to go either side of the tower on the cake top. Mark a long window slit in each using a knife, then stick them in place with sugar glue.

### THE TURRET ROOFS

8 Colour 100g (3½oz) of modelling paste pink, 100g (3½oz) turquoise and 60g (2oz) orange. Use 100g (3½oz) of modelling paste for the turret roofs and 45g (1½oz) for the mini towers. Make the turret roofs in yellow, turquoise, dark mauve and pink, hollowing out as before. Make the mini towers yellow and orange.

9 Colour 45g (1½oz) modelling paste green. To make the green and yellow stripy-and-chequered effect roof, roll out 15g (½oz) of green,

then press with the lined rolling pin lengthways and across to indent tiny squares. Cut into strips, then cut the ends of each into points. Stick on the roof, spacing evenly, then make yellow chequered strips as before and carefully slot in to fill the spaces. Make the chequered turquoise strips for the yellow turret roof in the same way. For the zig-zag turret, use orange modelling paste very thinly rolled out and cut squares in two even lines to create zig-zag shapes using the square cutters. For the turquoise roof, model tiny teardrop shapes of dark mauve – graduate them in size as you work towards the top, with the smallest right at the tip. When the roofs are complete, stick them in place with sugar glue.

### PALACE DETAILS

10 Use the left-over coloured paste to decorate the walls. Cut pink circles from very thinly rolled out modelling paste, and then cut them again into halves and quarters. Thinly roll out and cut dark mauve squares of paste and cut these into triangles. Roll out yellow and cut miniature yellow circles using the tip of the no.4 piping tube (tip). To make the finials, use different paste trimmings to decorate the top of the turret and tower roofs with flattened circles and pointed teardrops. The palace is now complete and you are ready to model the characters.

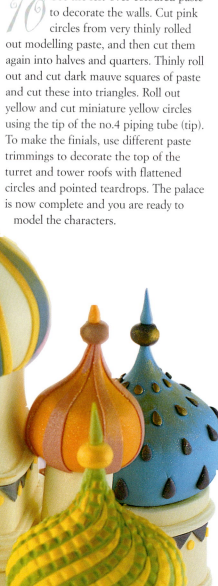

## THE ELEPHANT

*11* To make the elephant's body, first colour 125g (4oz) of modelling paste grey. Roll 90g (3oz) into a rounded sausage. Cut a cross into the base to separate the legs. Pinch around each to lengthen the legs, then press down on the work surface to flatten each foot. Push a sugar stick down into the neck, leaving 2–3cm (³/₄–1¹/₄in) protruding and secure with a little sugar glue.

*12* To make the head, roll 22g (³/₄oz) of paste into a ball, then pinch gently to bring out the trunk. Pressing carefully, mark lines on the trunk with a cocktail stick (toothpick). Then, using the end of a paintbrush, indent two holes for the tusks and at the end of the trunk. Cut a curve under the trunk to make his smile, then smooth his mouth open with the damp paintbrush. Hold the head carefully and push down onto the sugar stick, securing with sugar glue. If necessary, use a piece of foam to support it while it is drying. With the remaining grey, model two ears and a curly tail. With a little white, model the two tusks, two oval-shaped eyes and flattened half circles for the feet. Thinly roll out dark mauve trimmings and cut a hat and seat for the elephant. Trim these with tiny rolled sausages of yellow and mark with a cocktail stick to create a rope effect. Model tiny tassels for the ends.

## MODELLING THE FIGURES

*13* To make the prince and princess, first split just under 7g (¹/₄oz) of dark mauve modelling paste into four equally sized pieces to make their shoes. Roll each into long, tapering teardrops and curl up the ends to make pointed toes. Flatten a little at the heel by pressing gently. For the trousers, model a large teardrop using 15g (¹/₂oz) of turquoise trimmings and cut to separate the legs. Smooth to remove the ridges. Make green trousers for the prince in the same way. Start assembling the prince and princess on the cake, sticking each of the pieces together with sugar glue as they are completed.

## THE PRINCESS

*14* Colour 7g (¹/₄oz) of modelling paste pale brown. Split into four pieces, making one slightly larger than the others. Put this piece aside for the prince. With one piece, shape the body of the princess, gently pinching up a neck. Roll out pink trimmings and cut a cumberband and model a tiny flattened circle for the centre of her crown. With a tiny amount of turquoise trimmings, shape her top with two flattened circles as the straps. Model her crown, sticking on the pink circle and put aside. Roll another piece of brown into an oval shaped head, marking her smile with the no.4 plain piping tube pushed in at an angle. Dimple the smile by pushing the tip of a cocktail stick into the corners. Using a sugar stick to help secure it, stick her head in place.

*Modelled pieces for the princess.*

*15* With the third piece of brown, model her nose, then split in half and roll sausages with rounded ends for her arms. Flatten the ends, cut the hands (see page 17) and stick in place. If necessary, use foam pieces for support while she is drying. Colour the rest of the paste black. Shape two tiny dots for the eyes of the elephant. Roll the remaining black into long teardrop shapes for her hair, then stick on her crown.

## THE PRINCE

*16* For the prince, split 7g (¹/₄oz) of yellow into three pieces. Shape a small oval with one piece for his top, indenting the chest. Thinly roll out mauve trimmings, then cut a cumberband as before and two triangles for the waistcoat. Model teardrop-shaped sleeves with the other two pieces, pushing the end of the paintbrush to make hollows for the hands.

*17* Using the last, larger piece of brown, shape a neck and press the base in the top for his chest, then make a head, nose and hands. Shape two flat green teardrops for his turban and a yellow teardrop to go in the middle. When dry, paint black dots for eyes on both figures with the paintbrush. Finally, apply gold edible lustre powder (petal dust/blossom tint) to the whole cake.

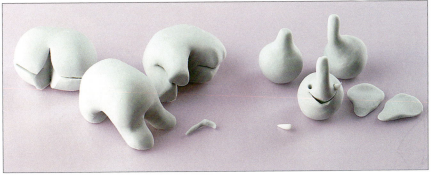

*Using grey sugarpaste, first model the elephant's body and then add the head.*

# Fairy King and Queen

*I decided to crown these fairies with roses after watching rose petals falling. I wanted the king and queen to look as though they were being carried away on a breeze, floating majestically over their fairy kingdom.*

## CAKE AND DECORATION
- 20cm (8in) square cake (see page 11)
- 35cm (14in) oval cake board
- 280g (9oz) petal paste (gumpaste)
- 1.13kg (2lb 4oz) sugarpaste (rolled fondant)
- 315g (10oz/1¼ cups) buttercream
- Icing (confectioner's) sugar in a sugar shaker
- 60g (2oz) royal icing
- 230g (7½oz) modelling paste
- Cream, egg yellow and black food colouring pastes
- Sugar glue
- Two sugar sticks or lengths of raw, dried spaghetti
- Pink, yellow and blue edible dusting powder (petal dust/blossom tint)
- Edible sparkle powder

## EQUIPMENT
- Large and small rolling pins
- Small, sharp knife
- Templates (see page 191)
- Plastic dowelling
- Large and small rose petal cutters
- Rose petal veiner
- Fine and medium paintbrushes
- Miniature circle cutter
- A few cocktail sticks (toothpicks)
- Paper piping bags
- Small pieces of foam sponge

### PETALS

1 Make the petal-shaped arms and backs of the thrones first, to leave plenty of drying time. To make the throne arms, thinly roll out 15g (½oz) of petal paste and cut a large petal with the template (see page 191). Roll the edges with the small rolling pin to thin and frill. Using the plastic dowelling, roll up the petal from the narrow petal base so that the arm rest will sit just above the side of the throne. Make three more petal-shaped arms and leave to dry. Make two more petals for the back of each throne. Roll

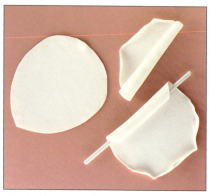
*Use the plastic dowelling to curl the edges.*

up half of each petal, using the dowelling as support as shown in the photograph above. Put them aside to dry.

2 Using 60g (2oz) of petal paste, thinly roll out a little at a time and cut out petals with the large and small rose petal cutter. Press into the petal veiner to shape. Make 40 large petals and 20 small petals – leave to dry. Using 22g (¾oz), thinly roll out and cut four large fairy wings using the template (see page 191), curling the edges round as before.

*Cut out rose petals and leave to dry.*

### CAKE AND BOARD

3 Roll out 500g (1lb) of sugarpaste (rolled fondant) and cover the board. Press the large rolling pin over the surface to indent and create a rippled effect. Trim excess, then put aside to dry.

4 Cut the crust from the cake and slice the top flat. Cut the cake into four equal squares by cutting in half, then half again. Using buttercream, sandwich them together to make two

*Cover the cakes with white sugarpaste.*

square cakes, then spread a layer of buttercream over the surface to help the sugarpaste stick. Roll out 315g (10oz) of white sugarpaste and cover one of the cakes completely. Smooth around the shape stretching out any pleats and trim excess from around base. Cover the second cake in the same way and put aside. When the petal sides are dry, press them in position using royal icing to secure. Make two more large petals as before and stick in position draped over the front of each throne.

*Stick the throne arms in place when dry.*

### THE FAIRY QUEEN

5 Colour 100g (3½oz) of modelling paste cream. Split 30g (1oz) exactly in half. To make a leg, roll one piece into a sausage, rounding off one end for the foot. Pinch out the foot pulling gently to lengthen. Indent around the ankle to round off the heel. Mark toes by pressing in along the edge with the tip of a knife. Press on the tip of the large toe with the end of a paintbrush to indent the toe nail. Halfway from the ankle to the top of the leg, pinch up the

*Make the queen's skirt with layers of petals.*

knee and press in at the back to indent. Smooth the shin, keeping the back of the leg rounded for the calf. Stick in place on the throne using sugar glue to secure. Make the other leg in the same way.

6 Roll 15g (½oz) of cream modelling paste into a rounded teardrop and stick on top of the throne up against each leg. To make the petal skirt, thinly roll out 30g (1oz) of petal paste and cut petals, one at a time, using the template (see page 191). Curl the edges as before, then stick one at a time, overlapping around her body. Trim side and back petals so that they tuck under.

7 To make her bodice, roll 22g (¾oz) of white modelling paste into a teardrop. Press down into the rounded end to indent her chest. Smooth the waistline, then cut the base straight. Stick in position using sugar glue, taking care that it is well balanced and the waistline sits completely straight. Split a 7g (¼oz) piece of cream modelling paste in half and roll into a ball. Pinch up halfway to shape her neck. Stick the rounded end into the top of her bodice, smoothing it flat. Supporting her neck, gently push one of the sugar sticks or a length of raw, dried spaghetti down into it, leaving a little protruding to help support the head.

8 Roll 15g (½oz) of cream modelling paste into an oval shape for her head. Push down onto the sugar stick and smooth at the chin point to narrow. Stick a tiny ball of cream paste onto the centre of her face to make her nose. Press the miniature circle cutter in at an angle to mark her smile. To dimple the corners of the smile, gently press in the tip of a cocktail stick (toothpick) and lift slightly. Stick on two minute flattened ovals of white modelling paste to make her eyes.

9 To make her arms, split just over 7g (¼oz) of cream modelling paste exactly in half. Roll one half into a sausage rounding off one end for the hand. Press the rounded end flat. Cut a thumb, slightly to one side. Make three straight cuts along the top for her fingers. Gently smooth each finger pulling gently

to lengthen. Press in the palm to indent and shape the hand. Indent around the wrist area to round off the hand. Make an indent halfway between her wrist and shoulder for her elbow, pinching out at the back. Make the other arm and stick both in position, resting the appropriate hand on the throne arm.

10 Roll out some petal paste trimmings and cut two petal-shaped sleeves using the large rose petal cutter. Indent in the veiner as before then cut the base of each petal straight. Stick in place over the top of each shoulder. Stick one of the small petals made earlier onto the front of her bodice. Thinly roll out and cut a strip for her belt and stick in place crossing over at the back.

11 To pipe her hair, first colour 30g (1oz) of royal icing pale yellow using a touch of egg yellow food colouring paste. Put into a piping bag and cut a small hole in the tip. Pipe long, wavy strands of hair down and over her

*Pipe the queen's hair with royal icing.*

shoulders, with shorter strands around her face. Stick small petals into the piped hair to make her crown.

12 Dust all the petal centres with pink edible dusting powder (petal dust/blossom tint) and all the bases with a little yellow. Push two

*Attach the wings into her bodice carefully.*

*Use two petals to make the king's waistcoat.*

pinching out at the back. Stick them in place together with the hands that were made earlier. Arrange small petals around his neck, securing with sugar glue. Stick a small, flattened ball of white paste on top for a collar. With the remaining cream modelling paste, make a head and nose as before. Pipe the hair using the remaining pale yellow royal icing, sticking small petals around his head for his crown. Stick two large petals into his back for the base of his wings and cut two small openings as before for the large petal wings.

large rose petals into the back of the queen's bodice to make the base of her wings. With the tip of the knife, push into the back of her bodice twice, just above these two petals to create small openings for the long petal wings to slot in, but do not stick these into position yet. Position the queen's throne on the cake board, leaving a space for the king's throne.

### THE FAIRY KING

*13* Split 7g (¹/₄oz) of the cream modelling paste into three pieces. Model two pieces into oval shapes and make two feet as for the queen. To make the king's legs, split 45g (1¹/₂oz) of white modelling paste exactly in half. Roll two sausages, tapering in each at one end for the ankles. Pinch each halfway up to shape the knee, indenting at the back to shape. Stick them in position on the feet, securing with sugar glue. Split the third piece of cream modelling paste in half and make two hands out of flattened teardrop shapes as for the queen. Then put aside until later.

*14* Press 7g (¹/₄oz) of white modelling paste around the top of the king's legs to create a base for his petal tunic. Thinly roll out 7g (¹/₄oz) of petal paste and cut

six more petals using the large petal cutter. Indent the veins as before, then stick four in position around the top of his legs. To make his body, roll 30g (1oz) of white modelling paste into an oval shape and stick in place making sure it is well balanced and completely straight. Hold in position, then carefully push a sugar stick or length of raw, dried spaghetti down through the body, leaving a little protruding at the top to help support the head. Indent down the centre of the body with a knife, and mark buttons using the tip of a cocktail stick. Carefully position the throne on the cake board.

*15* Stick the remaining two petals in place either side of his body to make his waistcoat. Split just over 7g (¹/₄oz) of the white modelling paste in half and roll two sausages for his sleeves. Indent the centre of each to mark the elbow,

### FINISHING TOUCHES

*16* Using dabs of royal icing on the end of each, carefully slot each petal wing in place using foam pieces to support them while they dry. Make sure that none of the wings protrude further than the back of the thrones or the back pieces will not sit flush. Stick the back pieces in position, again using royal icing and foam pieces for support.

*17* Dust the cake board with blue dusting powder. Mix a little blue dusting powder with water and paint a small circle on each eye. Lightly dust around the cake with pink and yellow dusting powder. Add a little pink to the king and queen's cheeks to give a slight blush. Using the remaining royal icing, stick all the rose petals in position, building up more at one end of the board, and scatter some randomly on each throne. Dilute black food colouring paste with a few drops of water. Using a fine paintbrush and a little black colour, paint the pupils, eyelashes and eyebrows. Dust the whole cake with sparkle powder.

# Magical Wizard

*This is my idea of a kindly old wizard, keeping himself busy by taking spells from his magical book and mixing potions as rewards for those doing good-hearted deeds.*

### CAKE AND DECORATION
- 25cm (10in) square cake (see page 11)
- 30cm (12in) hexagonal cake board
- 1.315kg (2lb 10oz) sugarpaste (rolled fondant)
- Blue, mauve, black, green, cream, brown, chestnut, yellow and red food colouring pastes
- Icing (confectioner's) sugar in a sugar shaker
- 470g (15oz/2 scant cups) buttercream
- 655g (1lb 5oz) modelling paste
- Sugar glue
- Edible silver
- Edible sparkle dusting powder (petal dust/blossom tint)

### EQUIPMENT
- Large and small rolling pins
- Small, sharp knife
- 2cm (3/4in), 5cm (2in) circle cutters
- Plastic dowelling
- Template (see page 193)
- Piece of foam sponge
- Fine paintbrush
- A few cocktail sticks (toothpicks)
- Small star cutter
- Bone tool

### CAKE AND BOARD

1. Colour 375g (12oz) of sugarpaste (rolled fondant) blue and 440g (14oz) mauve. For a marbled effect, knead the blue and 90g (3oz) of mauve together until the paste is streaky in colour. Roll it out and cover the cake board completely, trimming any excess from around the edge, then put aside to dry. Trim the crust from the cake and slice the top flat where it has risen. Cut out a 16cm (6½in) square from a corner of the cake and then cut this piece in half. Put one on top of the other to make the table.

2. From the remaining cake, cut out four strips measuring 13cm (5in), 10cm (4in), 9cm (3½in) and 6cm (2½in) in length. Stack these centrally, one on top of the other, graduating in size. Trim from the top, sloping down to shape the back of the wizard. Trim either side from the top, taking off the corners. Sandwich all the layers together with buttercream, then spread a layer of buttercream over both cakes to help the sugarpaste stick.

*Cake shapes for the wizard and table.*

### THE TABLE

3. Colour 440g (14oz) of sugarpaste pale grey using a touch of black food colouring paste. Roll this out and cover the table cake, smoothing around the shape and trimming excess from the base. Mark horizontal ridges around the table for a rock effect. Roll the trimmings into four legs and stick these at each corner with sugar glue. Colour 60g (2oz) of sugarpaste dark green. Thinly roll out and cut a square measuring 15cm (6in) for the tablecloth, and position over the top of the cake.

*Lay the tablecloth on top of the table cake.*

### THE WIZARD

4. Colour 200g (6½oz) of modelling paste mauve. Thinly roll out 15g (½oz) and cut strips to edge the tablecloth. Make a feature of the joins at each corner by marking another line to make a diamond shape. Roll out 100g (3½oz) of mauve sugarpaste and cover the front of the wizard. Position the wizard up against the back of the table, sticking him in place with sugar glue. Split 90g (3oz) of mauve modelling paste

*Attach the sleeves in place with sugar glue.*

in half for the sleeves. To make a sleeve, roll the paste into a long teardrop shape and pinch into the wide end to open it up. Indent halfway and pinch out at the back to mark the elbow. Make the second sleeve and stick it in position using sugar glue.

5 Thinly roll out 7g (¼oz) of the mauve sugarpaste and cut out a circle using the 5cm (2in) circle cutter. Stick this in position on top of the wizard to make his collar. Push the dowelling down through his body, leaving 4cm (1½in) protruding from the top to help hold the head in place. Colour 90g (3oz) of modelling paste cream. Using 75g (2½oz) of this, roll into a ball, then from the centre pinch out a hooked nose. Carefully push this down onto the dowelling and secure at the base with sugar glue.

*Use plastic dowelling to fix his head to his body.*

6 Model the wizard's hat using 75g (2½oz) of mauve modelling paste, pinching a rim that fits over the top of his head and around the back and sides. Don't pinch this too thin. Twist up a point at the top of the hat, then bend it over. Stick it in position on his head, ensuring that the back is balanced. Roll out the remaining mauve sugarpaste and cut the cloak using the template (see page 193). Re-work the buttercream in case it has started to set. Moisten down his side and tops of arms with sugar glue. Wrap the cloak over his back and turn the top over to form a collar.

7 Colour 22g (¾oz) of modelling paste blue. Using 15g (½oz) of blue and a small ball of mauve modelling paste, knead them together until you get a streaky effect, then roll into a ball to make the globe he will hold. Stick it onto the wizard's front, just above the top of his sleeves, and support with a piece of foam until secure. Model the top part of the wizard's beard using 22g (¾oz) of white modelling paste. Indent lines using the side of a paint-brush, then stick it in place with the point tucked in behind his sleeve. With just under 7g (¼oz), model the tip of his beard, marking lines as before, and stick just under the base of his sleeve letting it trail over his cloak.

8 Using 7g (¼oz) of white modelling paste, model two long tapering teardrop shapes for his moustache, two small flattened balls for eyes, two tiny white teardrop shapes for eyebrows and two small teardrops for his hair, sticking them just under the hat rim. Using another 7g (¼oz), stick on different-sized flattened pieces around his head for more hair. Split another 7g (¼oz) in half and model two long tapering teardrops for hair and stick at his temple on either side, letting them fall down over his cloak. With a minute amount of green trimmings, stick flattened circles on each eye for irises.

9 To make hands, split just over 7g (¼oz) of cream modelling paste in half. Model a teardrop shape and press a little flat. Cut a thumb on one side, then make three cuts along the top edge to create separate fingers. Pinch and

*Trail his hair and moustache over his cloak.*

twist each finger to lengthen them. Mark fingernails using the end of a paintbrush. Twist gently at the base to create a wrist and stick into the sleeve and against the globe using sugar glue. Make another hand in the same way. If necessary, use the piece of foam for support while drying.

10 Colour 45g (1½oz) of modelling paste mid-brown. To make the staff, roll just over 7g (¼oz) into a long uneven sausage with a rounded end measuring 14cm (5½in) in length. Make the top more angular than the bottom by pinching it flat, then put it aside to dry on a flat surface.

11 To make the open spell book, roll out 15g (½oz) of mid-brown modelling paste and cut an oblong shape measuring 9 x 5cm (3½ x 2in). Mark the binding by indenting with the back of a knife. For the pages, thickly roll out 75g (2½oz) of white modelling paste and press down in the centre with a knife to mark the centre. Use the flat of the knife to open up and create the dip in the page. Smooth the pages either side so that they slope down, then cut them slightly smaller than the cover. Make small cuts with a knife on three sides of the book to mark page lines. Stick the book on the centre of the table.

12 To make the book pile, thickly roll out 75g (2½oz) of white modelling paste and cut four

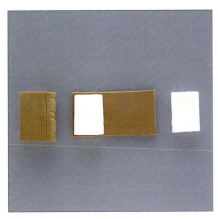

*The modelled pieces of the book.*

oblong shapes, one large, two medium and one small. Mark page lines around three sides of each one as before. Colour 15g (½oz) of modelling paste chestnut brown and roll out and cut a cover to fit the larger oblong. Wrap the covering around the book pages. Indent the binding, and stick onto the front of the cake board with the book binding facing outwards. Roll out 15g (½oz) of mid-brown paste and cover the two medium oblong shapes as before, and stick centrally on top of the large book, with the pages facing outwards. Colour 15g (½oz) of modelling paste dark brown. Make the small book using half, sticking it on top of the book pile with the binding facing outwards.

*13* Colour 7g (¼oz) of modelling paste green. Roll into a ball, then pinch around the top to create the neck of a bottle. Indent an opening in the top using the end of a paintbrush. Model a small sack with the remaining dark brown modelling paste, pinching a wide opening. Using a pea-sized amount of cream, roll into a thin sausage and mark lines at an angle using a cocktail stick (toothpick) to create a rope effect. Wrap this around the top of the sack. Thinly roll out 7g (¼oz) of white modelling paste. Cut out 11 stars using the star cutter and stick into the green bottle building them up quite high. Cut out six circles using the smaller circle cutter, and cut into each again to make the half moon shapes and stick these into the sack.

## THE MICE

*14* Colour 7g (¼oz) of modelling paste pale brown for the mice. Model a small teardrop shape for each body and, using the end of a paintbrush, indent two small holes for the legs to slot in. Stick in place on the cake. To make legs, bend a tiny sausage halfway and gently pinch out a heel. Indent twice to mark toes. Pinch the top of the leg to a point and slot in position using sugar glue to secure.

*15* For the mouse on the spell book, model two tiny flattened teardrop-shaped paws, and indent twice into the top as before. Roll tiny sausage-shaped arms for the mouse sleeping on the pile of books, rounding off the end of each and marking as before. Model tiny teardrop-shaped heads. For the sleeping mouse, indent an open mouth just under the point using a cocktail stick. Roll minute tapering sausages for the tails. For the ears and nose, use white modelling paste. Indent into tiny teardrop shapes using the small end of a bone tool for the ears.

## THE CANDLES

*16* To make the candles, first model the candle holder for the dripping candle using the remaining mid-brown modelling paste. Model a ball for the base and press in the centre to indent. Model a small flattened circle to go on top, then a thin handle.

*The pieces of the candle and holder.*

Shape the candle using white paste, with two minute teardrop-shaped drips. For the second candle, model two flattened circles of cream modelling paste for the candle holder. Model the candle as before and colour a small piece of modelling paste yellow. Put aside a minute amount for later, then model two teardrop shapes for flames. Mix a little red and yellow food colouring pastes together with a drop of water and paint the centre of each flame. Stick the candles in place on the table using sugar glue.

## THE BOTTLES

*17* To make the mauve bottle on the table, knead a tiny piece of white modelling paste into a small piece of mauve until it is streaky. Model a bottle as in step 13 and press into the top to indent it using the end of a paintbrush. Colour some trimmings red. Knead together the red and the minute piece of yellow that you put aside earlier until the paste is streaky. Roll a ball for the base of the bottle, then a smaller ball for the neck. Push into the top with the end of a paintbrush as before. Make a blue and mauve streaky bottle as before. With the remaining dark brown, model three tiny teardrop shapes for corks and stick into the top of each bottle, with their points downwards.

## FINISHING TOUCHES

*18* To make the scrolls, thinly roll out the remaining white modelling paste and cut out two 5cm (2in) squares. Make small cuts around the edges, then roll them up and stick them onto the cake board at the side of the table. Dilute a little black food colouring paste with a drop of water and paint the eyes and the spells on the book. Paint silver stars and moon shapes over the wizard and the edge of the tablecloth, and paint the cut-out moons and stars in the sack and bottle. Paint a tiny silver highlight on each of the wizard's eyes. Dust the whole cake with edible sparkle powder (petal dust/blossom tint). Stick the staff against the side of the table.

# Fruit Fairies

*All flowers and leaves can have their very own fairies, so why not fruit? I decided to make them plump, just like the ripest fruit, and full of fun playing happily together in their apple-shaped house.*

## CAKE AND BOARD

1 Colour 315g (10oz) of sugarpaste (rolled fondant) bright green. Roll out and cover the cake board completely, trimming any excess from around the edge and put aside to dry.

2 Trim the crust from each cake and slice the tops flat. Sandwich them together with buttercream to make a ball shape, then spread a layer of buttercream over the surface of the cake.

## THE APPLE HOUSE

3 Colour 875g (1¾lb) of sugarpaste pale green. Roll out and cover the cake completely, stretch out any pleats and smooth the paste downwards around the shape. Trim excess from around the base and position the cake on the centre of the cake board. Smooth the surface with a cake smoother.

*Trim the excess sugarpaste away from the base.*

4 Using the large circle cutter, cut a curve for the top of the doorway by pressing the circle cutter in at an angle. Cut either side and at the base for

*Use a small circle cutter to make the windows.*

a doorway, removing the sugarpaste. Cut two windows either side using the smaller circle cutter.

## THE BANANA ROOF

5 Colour 155g (5oz) of sugarpaste using egg yellow food colouring paste with a touch of brown. Thinly roll out 15g (½oz) and cut two small circles to fill the windows. Roll the remaining yellow into a tapering sausage and, using the photograph below as a

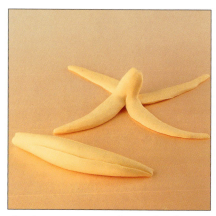

*Cut the sugarpaste into a banana-skin shape.*

guide, make the banana skin. Open up the four cuts and position on the top of the house securing with sugar glue.

### THE DOOR AND WINDOWS

6 Colour 7g (¼oz) of modelling paste brown. Roll out and cut a door slightly smaller than the width of the doorway. Mark lines with a knife for the wood grain. Using trimmings, roll little sausages of brown paste to make the stalk window frames and ledges. Colour 45g (1½oz) of modelling paste orange. Using 7g (¼oz), model little flattened pieces for the curtains, sticking them into the window corners with sugar glue. With the pale green trimmings, model the top of the windows and door by shaping a sausage indented in the centre, press flat, then curve around.

*Use brown paste for window frames and ledges.*

### FAIRY WINGS

7 Colour 15g (½oz) of modelling paste bright green. Thinly roll out half and cut 10 leaves using the leaf cutter. Indent and shape using the leaf veiner, then put aside to dry.

### THE FRUIT

8 Colour 60g (2oz) of modelling paste dark red. Using 15g (½oz), split into four pieces and make the cherries, indenting the top of each with the end of a paintbrush. Make the cherry stalks with brown paste and stick in place with the cherries. If necessary, use foam pieces for support while they dry.

9 Dilute some red dusting powder (petal dust/blossom tint) with icing (confectioner's) sugar, then dust the cake base with the medium paintbrush.

To make the blueberries, colour 45g (1½oz) of modelling paste dark mauve using black and mauve food colouring paste. Using 22g (¾oz), roll 15 small balls and mark the top of each by pressing in gently with the end of a paintbrush. Use a cocktail stick (toothpick) to tear around the edge of the indent, then stick in place on the cake board, with one on the door for the door handle.

### TANGERINE FAIRY

10 Roll the remaining orange paste (from step 6) into a ball and 'texture' by pressing the tip of a cocktail stick repeatedly over the surface. Indent with the large end of a bone tool to create a hole for the arms and legs. Colour 75g (2½oz) of modelling paste cream. Using 7g (¼oz), roll an oval-shaped nose and an oval-shaped head. Indent a smile by pressing the miniature circle cutter in at an angle and dimple the corners by pressing in the tip of a cocktail stick and lifting it gently. Stick the head onto the body, then attach the nose.

11 Divide 5g (just under ¼oz) of cream modelling paste into four pieces; two slightly larger than the others. Make the legs with the two larger pieces by rolling sausages and rounding off each end. Pinch the rounded ends to shape each foot and indent around the ankle to narrow and shape each heel. Using the two smaller pieces, make the arms in the same way, but press the rounded end flat. Cut a thumb, slightly to one side, then make three cuts along the top to separate the fingers. Twist each

*Position the arms of the tangerine fairy so that she looks as though she is waving.*

*The pieces of the blackberry fairy.*

to remove any ridges, then press on the palm to round off the hand. Using sugar glue, stick in place as each is made.

*Apply two coats of confectioner's varnish to make the fruit fairies shine.*

### THE OTHER FAIRIES

*12* Colour 22g (³⁄₄oz) of modelling paste apricot and 30g (1oz) bright red. The strawberry fairy is a rounded teardrop shape, indented with the end of a paintbrush to texture the surface. Colour the royal icing cream – pipe tiny pips with the no.0 plain piping tube (tip). The blackberry and raspberry fairies are oval shapes, then small flattened balls are stuck over the surface. The apricot fairy is ball-shaped. Support their poses with small foam pieces until dry.

*13* Roll out the remaining bright green modelling paste. Cut six hats using the calyx cutter then stick each in place with sugar glue. Model tiny stalks with the

*Use a calyx cutter to make the fairies' hats.*

trimmings. Stick two leaves onto the back of each fairy for their wings. With the remaining dark red modelling paste, roll into tiny berries, indenting into the top of each with the tip of a cocktail stick, and scatter over the cake board.

*14* Dilute a little black food colouring paste with a few drops of water and paint eyes using the fine paintbrush. Dilute a little brown and streak the banana skin, concentrating the colour on the top and bottom. To give all the fruit fairies a shine, except for the apricot fairy, paint on two thin layers of confectioner's varnish, leaving the first layer to dry before applying the next.

*Position the apricot fairy on top of the blueberries at the door.*

# Knight in Armour

*It is always easier to design enchanted cakes for girls than boys, so I decided to include this jousting tent, complete with knight in armour, to capture the magical mystery of medieval times.*

### CAKE AND DECORATION
- 18cm (7in), 15cm (6in) and 12cm (5in) round cakes (see page 11)
- 25cm (10in) round cake board
- 440g (14oz/1¾ cups) buttercream
- 1kg (2lb) sugarpaste (rolled fondant)
- Black, blue, red, yellow and green food colouring pastes
- Icing (confectioner's) sugar in a sugar shaker
- Sugar glue
- 75g (2½oz) modelling paste
- Edible silver food colouring

### EQUIPMENT
- Small, sharp knife
- Large and small rolling pins
- No.8 star piping tube (tip) or dinner fork
- 2cm (¾in) square cutter
- Templates (see page 191)
- Sheet of foam sponge
- Medium paintbrush

## CAKES AND BOARD

Trim the crust from each cake and slice the tops so that they are flat. Trim the top edge from the smallest cake, cutting it at an angle down to just above the base to create the sloping roof. Stack the cakes one on top of the other, graduating them in size. Trim away the edges from the roof so that it slopes out and down to the base, removing any jagged pieces. Sandwich the layers together with buttercream, position

*Trim the cakes to make a tent shape.*

the cake slightly towards the back of the cake board then spread buttercream over the surface to help the sugarpaste stick.

Colour 15g (½oz) of sugarpaste (rolled fondant) dark grey, using black food colouring paste. Thinly roll out a strip and use it to cover the front of the cake to make the tent opening. Colour 200g (6½oz) of the sugarpaste green. Roll out a little at a time and position it around the cake board. Press the star piping tube (tip) or dinner fork into the green sugarpaste repeatedly to create a grass effect around the edges.

*Use a star piping tube or fork to create the grass.*

## THE TENT

Roll out 500g (1lb) of white sugarpaste and cut it into an oblong shape (12 x 48cm/5 x 19in). Dust with icing (confectioner's) sugar, roll it up at both ends, and then lift and wrap it around the cake until the two ends meet at the dark grey strip at the front, leaving the roof uncovered. Trim any excess, leaving a small gap for the tent opening. Pinch around the base to create a slightly wavy edge.

*Roll the white sugarpaste around the cake.*

*Cut a decorative trim for the top of the tent.*

4 To cover the roof of the tent, roll out 200g (6½oz) of white sugarpaste and place it on the top of the cake, trimming any excess away from around the edge. Gently indent the surface of the roof in order to achieve a fabric effect. Then moisten around the roof base with sugar glue. Roll out 75g (2½oz) of sugarpaste and cut a long strip measuring 2.5 x 48cm (1 x 19in). Cut a row of squares evenly along this strip using the square cutter as shown above. Stick the strip in position, hiding the roof join and trim off any excess.

**THE BANNERS AND FLAGS**

5 To make the banner and flag poles, roll long, thin sausage shapes using 7g (¼oz) of white modelling paste. Indent the banner pole slightly so that the two parts stick together neatly. Press on small flattened balls at the ends and on the top of the flag pole. Stick the banner pole together with sugar glue and place on the foam sheet with the flag pole to dry.

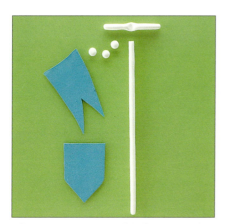

*The various components of the banner.*

6 Colour 22g (¾oz) of modelling paste blue. Thinly roll out 7g (¼oz) and cut a strip to go around the base of the tent. Thinly roll out the remaining blue and cut three shields, the banner and the flag using the templates (see page 191). Stick one shield and the banner flag onto the banner pole and wrap the flag around the flag pole, leaving it to dry completely on the foam sheet. Stick the remaining two shields on either side of the tent.

*The knight's banner.*

7 Colour 7g (¼oz) of the modelling paste red. Thinly roll it out and cut strips to decorate the flags and shields. Model tiny flattened balls to go on the banner flag. With the remaining red, thinly roll out and cut out the knight's cloak. Pinch gently to encourage pleats.

8 Colour 7g (¼oz) of modelling paste yellow. Thinly roll out and cut strips and tiny squares to decorate the flag, shields and tent. Put aside a pea-sized amount for later, then roll the remaining piece into a ball and press on the top of the tent. Push down into the centre with a paintbrush to make a hole for the flag pole to sit in.

*Cut out the flag with the template on page 191.*

*Stick the shields to either side of the tent.*

*Use grey modelling paste to make the knight's armour and add the red cloak that was made in step 7.*

### THE KNIGHT

9 Colour 30g (1oz) of modelling paste grey. To make the knight, first model the chest using 7g (¼oz), shaping a flattened oval. Press in the base to narrow the waist, then indent a line down the centre with a knife. With 7g (¼oz), roll two sausage-shaped legs and roll again in the centre of each to indent the knee. Model two teardrop-shaped feet and two flattened ovals for the knee caps. Thinly roll and cut out the skirt, indenting the top with a knife. Stick it in place wrapping it around the body.

10 Split 7g (¼oz) of the grey modelling paste into three pieces. With the first piece, split it again to make two sausage-shaped arms, rounding off each end. Roll in the centre of each arm to indent an elbow. Press each rounded end flat and cut a thumb into each of them. Stick the body onto the cloak, then stick the arms in place, bending up one arm so that it is ready to hold the banner pole. With the second piece, roll out and cut four squares – two for the shoulders and two for the skirt. With the third piece, make three flattened circles – two for the neck and one for the chest, and make two flattened ovals for each elbow.

11 With the remaining grey, model a ball-shaped helmet, marking indentations with the tip of a knife. Shape the mouth guard, pinching gently in the centre to create a ridge, and cut a long triangle to go on the top of his helmet. Following manufacturer's instructions, apply the silver colouring to the armour. With blue trimmings, cut out two squares for the armour. Thinly roll out the remaining yellow and cut a strip for the cloak and two tiny squares for the armour. Leave the knight to dry, preferably overnight.

12 Stick the knight in position in front of the tent using sugar glue. Remove the banner pole from the foam sheet and rest it against the tent with the knight holding it.
To create the finishing touch, stick the flag pole into the indented ball that is situated on the top of the tent.

*Stick the finished knight in position, with the banner resting against his hand.*

45

# Cinderella

*Cinderella, dressed in her beautiful ball gown, rushing down the steps and leaving her glass slipper behind, has to be the most memorable scene from this enchanting fairy tale.*

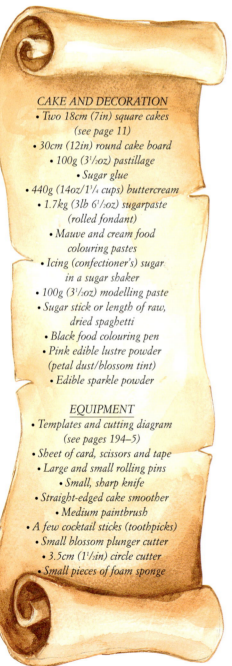

### CAKE AND DECORATION
- Two 18cm (7in) square cakes (see page 11)
- 30cm (12in) round cake board
- 100g (3½oz) pastillage
- Sugar glue
- 440g (14oz/1¾ cups) buttercream
- 1.7kg (3lb 6½oz) sugarpaste (rolled fondant)
- Mauve and cream food colouring pastes
- Icing (confectioner's) sugar in a sugar shaker
- 100g (3½oz) modelling paste
- Sugar stick or length of raw, dried spaghetti
- Black food colouring pen
- Pink edible lustre powder (petal dust/blossom tint)
- Edible sparkle powder

### EQUIPMENT
- Templates and cutting diagram (see pages 194–5)
- Sheet of card, scissors and tape
- Large and small rolling pins
- Small, sharp knife
- Straight-edged cake smoother
- Medium paintbrush
- A few cocktail sticks (toothpicks)
- Small blossom plunger cutter
- 3.5cm (1½in) circle cutter
- Small pieces of foam sponge

### THE ROOF

1 Cut out two roof templates using card (see page 195). Tape the join together on one template to make a support for the pastillage roof to sit over while it is drying. Thinly roll out the pastillage and cut out the roof shape using the second template. Using sugar glue, stick the join together on the pastillage roof and position over the top of the taped template and leave to dry. Roll out the pastillage trimmings and cut the clock with the circle cutter, again putting aside to dry.

### CAKES AND BOARD

2 Roll out 375g (12oz) of white sugarpaste (rolled fondant) and cover the cake board completely, trimming any excess away from around the edges. Put it aside until it is dry. Trim the crust from each cake and slice the tops flat where they have risen in the oven. Cut one of the cakes into four equally-sized squares and stack them up, one on top of the other. Trim off the corners so that you are left with a tall cylindrical shape, which will form the tower, as shown below.

*Use the template on page 195 for the roof.*

3 Cut the second cake diagonally into two pieces (see cutting diagram on page 194). Turn the smaller piece of cake upside down and position it on top of the larger cake, lining it up at the back in order to create a sloping front. Trim the sides from the top, sloping out and down towards the base. Trim the steps out of the sloping front, cutting 1cm (½in) into the cake, then trimming vertically to meet the cut.

### THE TOWER

4 Sandwich the layers together with buttercream and then spread buttercream over the surface of the tower and steps to help the sugarpaste stick in place. Colour 1kg (2lb) of sugarpaste mid-mauve. Roll out 60g (2oz) and cut a circle to cover the top of the tower. Roll out 625g (1¼lb) and cut an oblong to fit around the tower. Position the cake down onto the mauve sugarpaste and roll the sugarpaste around it. Trim any excess sugarpaste away from the join, moisten with sugar glue and then smooth the join closed. Roll the tower over the

*Stack the cakes up to make the tower and stairs.*

*Roll an oblong strip of paste around the tower.*

work surface to create a smooth finish.
Lift the cake, holding it at the top and
bottom, and position on the cake board,
leaving room for the steps.

### THE STAIRCASE

Colour 235g (7½oz) of sugarpaste
pale mauve. Roll out 220g (7oz) and
cover the top of the stairs, trimming
any excess away from the sides and base.
Smooth around the shape with your
hands to bring out the cut steps. Press in
with a straight-edged cake smoother
along each step and riser to create edges
to the steps. Position the cake in the
middle of the cake board, lining up the
top step with the tower.

### TOWER AND STAIRCASE DETAILS

Trim out a curved doorway from
the tower at the top of the stairs.
Colour 15g (½oz) of sugarpaste
dark mauve. Roll it out thinly and cut
a piece to fill the doorway. Thickly roll
out 15g (½oz) of pale mauve and cut a
step for the doorway, sticking it in place
with sugar glue.

*Press the paste to make the edges of the steps.*

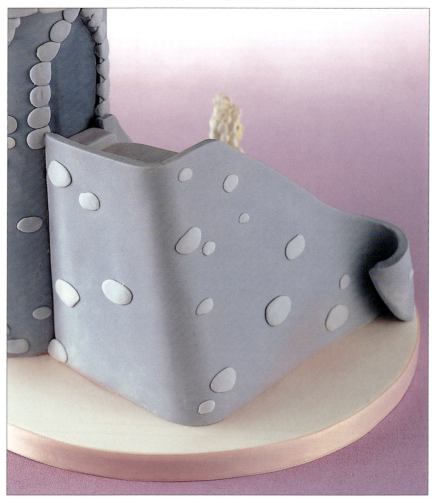

*Use the template on pages 194–5 to cut out the staircase side and back and secure with sugar glue.*

Roll out 100g (3½oz) of mid-
mauve sugarpaste and cut out the
tower side and banisters of the
staircase using the template on page 108.
Using sugar glue, stick the staircase side
in position. Curl the end of the staircase
round into a small spiral and stick it in
position holding it for a few moments
until it is secure. Using the remaining
mid-mauve sugarpaste, cover the other
side in the same way using the back and
side template on pages 194–5.

### CINDERELLA'S BODY AND DRESS

To make Cinderella's dress, first
shape a skirt support using 30g (1oz)
of white modelling paste, pinching it
up at the back so that it sits firmly on the
staircase without leaning – then stick in
position with sugar glue. Roll out 7g
(¼oz) of white modelling paste and cut
out one skirt piece using the template on
page 195. Press the side of a paintbrush
into the surface to create the pleats.

*Make the pieces of Cinderella's skirt and bodice.*

Gently press the end of the paintbrush
along the bottom edge to scallop the
hem. Then stick this onto the skirt base.
Make four more skirt pieces and stick
them in place around the skirt base, each
overlapping the last, until the whole skirt
base is covered. Press the tip of a cocktail
stick (toothpick) into the skirt to create a
lace pattern.

Shape the bodice using a small ball of white modelling paste. Press your finger into the top to create an indentation for Cinderella's chest. Colour 7g (¼oz) of modelling paste pale cream. Use a pea-sized amount to shape the chest, pinching up to shape her small neck. Stick this onto the top of the bodice with sugar glue and place the whole piece in position on top of the skirt. Moisten the sugar stick with a little sugar glue and push it down through the neck, bodice and skirt, leaving 1.5cm (½in) protruding from the top to help support the head. You may find that this process thickens her neck slightly – to put this right, simply moisten it with sugar glue to prevent the paste from cracking and smooth the neck gently upwards.

To finish the skirt, make two skirt side panels, the train and the top part of the skirt that wraps round and joins at the front – use the templates on page 195 and 15g (½oz) of white modelling paste. Make the side panels first, marking pleats and edging as before and stick in position curling around Cinderella's body. Make the train next, by curling it up behind her over the stairs. Mark pleats in the top part of the skirt and stick it into position, wrapping it around the back of her and pulling it up to join at the front. Mark the lace pattern as before, then edge the bodice. Make two sleeves next using two very small balls of modelling paste. Press into the base of each with the end of a paintbrush to create a small hole to help hold the arm in place. Pinch gently around the edge of this small hole to frill the edge slightly, then stick in position.

### CINDERELLA'S ARMS AND FEET

To make her arms, roll two very small, thin sausages of cream modelling paste and make a bend in the centre of each to shape elbows. Push the arms into the sleeves and secure with sugar glue. To make a glove, slightly flatten a tiny teardrop shape of white modelling paste and cut a thumb on one side. Make three cuts across the top for the fingers. Gently smooth each finger to lengthen, and twist gently at the wrist to shape. Make another glove. To hold them

each in place, model small flattened sausage shapes for cuffs. With a pea-sized amount of cream, shape a small foot, twisting up an ankle.

### CINDERELLA'S HEAD AND HAIR

To make Cinderella's head, first put aside a minute amount of cream modelling paste, then roll the remaining cream into an oval shape. Press with the side of your little finger into the eye area to shape the face, and gently stroke the chin to a softened point. Model a minute teardrop-shaped nose and stick in place on the centre of the face with the point uppermost. Smooth out the join either side and at the top of the nose between the eyes by gently rolling a cocktail stick over the surface. Moisten the sugar stick with sugar glue, then carefully push the head in position. Gently push the end of the paintbrush into the mouth area to open.

For Cinderella's hair, shape different-sized balls of modelling paste and stick over her head.

*Model Cinderella with cream and white paste.*

Make a larger ball for the top of her head, and edge with little blossom flowers made by cutting and shaping with the blossom plunger cutter. To make the feather, model a tiny, long, flattened teardrop and mark the centre line with a cocktail stick. Make small cuts using

*Trail Cinderella's skirt up the staircase behind her to make it look as though she is running.*

*Use different-sized balls of modelling paste for her hair.*

sized flattened pieces of paste over the roof, building up from around the base and finishing up with a teardrop shaped finial. Stick the roof on top of the tower. Shape flattened pieces of pale mauve paste – stick these over the staircase sides and tower, and edge the doorway. Make four teardrop shapes for the roof supports, bend each one round and stick in place.

### FINISHING TOUCHES

*15* To make the clock, draw the face striking 12 using the black food colouring pen. Draw Cinderella's eyes, pressing gently with the tip of the pen. Use a minute ball of pale mauve modelling paste for the centre of the clock, then stick the clock in position using foam pieces for support while it is drying. Using pale mauve trimmings that are left over, roll two long sausages using pea-sized amounts for each, rounding off each end. Stick each in place to edge the clock on opposite sides. As a finishing touch dust Cinderella and the whole cake with pink edible lustre powder (petal dust/blossom tint) and sparkle powder.

a knife and stick it in position curling it around her head. Make a tiny slipper using a pea-sized amount of white modelling paste.

*14* Using the mauve trimmings and 75g (2½oz) of white sugarpaste, knead white and mauve together, making various shades of mauve, ranging from almost white through to pale mauve. When the pastillage roof is dry, stick different

*Stick flattened pieces of paste on pastillage roof.*

*Draw the clock face with a black food colouring pen and edge with shaped mauve trimmings.*

# Enchanted Tree

*Sometimes when you create a face, it ends up looking like someone you know. When I finished creating the kind, cheerful face on this enchanted tree, it reminded me of my Uncle Charlie.*

## CAKE AND DECORATION
- 25cm (10in) square cake (see page 11)
- 30cm (12in) round cake board
- 440g (14oz/1¼ cups) buttercream
- 1.25kg (2½lb) sugarpaste (rolled fondant)
- Brown, black, green, blue, yellow, golden brown and pink food colouring pastes
- Icing (confectioner's) sugar in a sugar shaker
- Sugar glue
- 200g (6½oz) modelling paste
- Red, dark green, black and brown dusting powders (petal dust/ blossom tint)

## EQUIPMENT
- Large and small rolling pins
- Fine and medium paintbrushes
- Small, sharp knife
- Leaf cutter
- Leaf veiner
- No.8 star piping tube (tip)
- 1.5cm (½in) circle cutter
- A few cocktail sticks (toothpicks)
- Miniature circle cutter
- Sheet of kitchen paper

## CUTTING THE CAKE

1 Trim the crust from the square cake and slice the top flat where the cake has risen. Cut it into four equally-sized squares, by slicing the cake in half, and then cutting each strip in half again. Put one cake on top of the other. Trim off each corner, cutting downwards at an outwards angle so that the top is slightly narrower than the base. Trim a little more from around cake in order to round it off. Position the cake in the centre of the board, and arrange the cake trimmings around the base.

2 Sandwich the layers of cake together with buttercream and sandwich the trimmings around the base of the cake to make the shape of the roots of the tree. Spread a layer of buttercream over the surface of the cake to help the sugarpaste (rolled fondant) stick in position. Colour 1kg (2lb) of sugarpaste brown. Roll 22g (¾oz) of paste into a circle to cover the top of the cake and stick in place.

## THE TREE

3 Roll out 750g (1½lb) of brown sugarpaste into an oblong shape measuring 20 x 40cm (8 x 16in). Carefully roll up the length of paste from both ends so that it meets in the middle. Position against the cake, then carefully unroll the sugarpaste around the cake, making sure that the widest part of the base is covered. There will be some excess at the join, especially at the top where the cake is narrower. Carefully trim this away and smooth the join closed using a little sugar glue. Smooth upwards around the cake to create a lip at the top of the tree. Trim any excess from around the base and smooth the sugarpaste into recesses.

4 To texture the wood effect on the trunk, first press in with your hands and side of a paintbrush, marking indented lines from the base upwards all round the cake. Follow these with small cut lines using the back of a knife, then mark tiny horizontal lines randomly over the surface.

*Stack the pieces of cake into a tree shape.*

*Use a knife to create the wood effect.*

*The components of the face.*

*Smooth the facial features into the trunk.*

Using the step photograph as a guide and the brown sugarpaste trimmings, make the facial pieces next, texturing each as before. Stick in position with sugar glue, smoothing the ends into the surface of the tree to remove join lines. Add a tiny amount of brown food colouring to a pea-sized amount to get a slightly darker shade and make the pupils.

5 Split 75g (2½oz) of brown sugarpaste in half and make the two tree branches for the sides of the cake. Use the finished photograph as a guide of where to position them. Stick in place with sugar glue and smooth the join closed. When sticking the top branch in position, you will need to hold it for a few moments until it is secure and then texture it as before. Stick the lower

branch against the cake sides to create a ledge for the squirrel to sit on.

6 Colour 30g (1oz) of modelling paste black. Shape flattened pieces for the tree holes around the base of the cake and under the tree branch. Stick and smooth them so that they line up with the surface of the cake, then shape the mouth piece and slot it into the mouth. Smooth in place with a damp paintbrush.

7 Roll different-sized tapering sausage shapes for roots and stick them in place framing the 'holes' around the front of the cake using 45g (1½oz) of brown sugarpaste. Using 60g (2oz), shape wedges of brown sugarpaste and cut out steps using a knife. Cut the base and back straight, then smooth the steps in position against the cake. Press down on the top of each step to make a dip to create a well-worn look.

### THE NEST AND APPLES

8 To make the nest, first put aside a small ball of brown sugarpaste, then roll out the remaining brown and cut thin strips. Stick in position on top of the cake, building up a twig nest. Colour 15g (½oz) of modelling paste pale green. Split into three different-sized pieces and make the apples, indenting the base of each with the end of a

paintbrush. Stick them in position on the branches of the tree, holding them for a few moments until secure. Colour just under 7g (¼oz) of modelling paste bright green. Thinly roll out and cut eight leaves using the cutter. Indent the veins using the veiner and stick in place with sugar glue.

9 Colour the remaining sugarpaste bright green. Roll out strips, one at a time, and position them around the cake board, butting up against the cake sides. Texture with the star piping tube by pressing repeatedly into the surface.

### THE BIRDS

10 Colour just under 15g (½oz) of modelling paste blue and just under 7g (¼oz) yellow. To make the two birds, first split 7g (¼oz) of blue in half and model teardrop shapes. Pull each point to lengthen it, make three cuts in each, then smooth them upwards to make the tails. Put aside a pea-sized amount for later, then, with the remaining blue, model four wings, cutting the bottom edges with a knife to make the feathers and also make two oval-shaped heads. With a pea-sized amount of white modelling paste, press a flattened teardrop on the front of each bird to make their chests and flattened ovals for eyes. Knead a minute amount of blue into two pea-sized amounts of white until they are streaky and then

*Use thin strips of brown sugarpaste to make the bird's nest.*

shape them into eggs and place them in the nest. Model two triangular-shaped beaks using a minute amount of yellow modelling paste. Stick the birds in place, with one perched on the edge of the nest.

### THE HEDGEHOG FAMILY

*11* Colour 30g (1oz) of modelling paste brown. Split it into three different-sized pieces. To make the hedgehog family, model the paste into ball shapes, then press down on the work surface to create a flat base on each. Pinch gently to pull out the hedgehogs' muzzles. Press into the body repeatedly with the star tube to texture the prickles, leaving the face smooth. Indent the eye sockets with the end of a paintbrush. Make the eyes and snout using a pea-sized amount of black modelling paste, indenting each snout twice with the tip of a cocktail stick (toothpick).

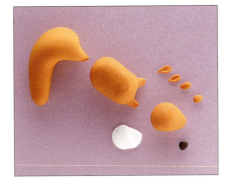

*The pieces of the squirrel.*

ears, indenting in the centre of each with a cocktail stick. With the remaining dark golden brown paste, shape the long teardrop-shaped tail, marking lines on it with a knife. Curl the top over and stick it in position with sugar glue. Flatten a small piece of white modelling paste and stick this onto the front of the squirrel for his tummy patch. Make his nose with a tiny amount of black modelling paste.

### THE BEES

*13* With the remaining black, yellow and blue modelling pastes, make all the little bees. Indent their smiles with the miniature circle cutter pressed in at an angle. Cut very thin stripes of black for their bodies and shape their wings with minute blue teardrop shapes. Stick in a cluster around the 'hole' under the branch, with one settling on the tree's nose.

*Stick the bees to the tree in a cluster.*

*Make the hedgehog prickles with a star tube.*

*Position the family together at the tree base.*

### THE SQUIRREL

*12* Colour 22g (³⁄₄oz) of modelling paste dark golden brown. Using the step photograph as a guide and 7g (¹⁄₄oz) of dark golden brown modelling paste, make the squirrel's body, twisting out two little legs at the front. Model two tiny teardrop-shaped back legs, then stick in position with the body on the tree branch. Model a rounded teardrop to make his head, and two tiny pointed

*Stick the squirrel onto the lower branch.*

### THE MOLE

*14* With the remaining brown sugarpaste, shape small pieces and arrange them in a pile to make the earth, pressing in the centre to create a dip ready for the mole to sit in. Colour 7g (¼oz) of modelling paste grey. To make the mole, first model two hands, making three cuts along the top of each and stick these in place. Then roll a teardrop shape with the remaining grey paste, to form a long muzzle. Indent the wide smile with the 1.5cm (½in) circle cutter, then dimple each corner with the end of a paintbrush. Stick on a small black ball for a nose and stick his head in place with the muzzle pointing upwards.

### THE MOUSE

*15* Colour 45g (1½oz) of modelling paste pale golden brown and a pea-sized amount pink. Using two tiny amounts, make the mouse paws, cutting three times along the top of each. Stick in position at the tree's mouth. Model a tiny teardrop-shaped head. For his ears, model two small balls with pink and press in the centre of each to indent, and shape a minute oval-shaped nose.

### THE BUNNIES

*16* To make the complete bunny, roll a long teardrop using 15g (½oz) of pale golden brown for his body. Split 7g (¼oz) of white into four pieces. With one piece, model a flattened teardrop for his tummy patch. With two more pieces, make his feet, cutting twice along the top to mark toes, then stick in position turning outwards. Put the last piece aside to make his tail and muzzle later. For his arms, split just under 7g (¼oz) of pale golden brown in half and roll sausages with rounded ends. Press each rounded end a little flat, and then make three cuts along the top of each. Stick these on the body and then place it against the cake using sugar glue.

*17* To make the bunny's head and ears, roll 7g (¼oz) of pale golden brown into a ball and stick onto the body, pinching gently either side at the top. Using a pea-sized amount for each, make two ears and indent down the centre of each with the side of a paintbrush. Stick in position using sugar glue, turning down the tip of one ear. With the piece of white modelling paste put aside, shape a flattened oval of white for his muzzle, indenting a smile as before, then indent down the centre with the back of a knife, and roll a ball tail. Shape a minute oval of pink for his nose. Using the remaining pale golden brown and white,

*Position one bunny disappearing into the tree.*

make the other bunny's bottom, tail and legs and stick these in place in a 'hole' at the base of the cake.

### FINISHING TOUCHES

*18* To finish, sprinkle a little each of red, dark green, black and brown dusting powders (petal dust/blossom tint) onto a sheet of kitchen paper. Using the medium paintbrush, pick up the dust on the brush, and then dust a little red onto the apples. Dust dark green onto the grass, around the base of the tree, the nest and on the leaves. Apply black dusting powder over the back of the mole's head, adding a little at a time, building up a darker shade at the back and fading out around his face. Apply brown dusting powder over the hedgehogs and a little over the grass and nest. Dilute a little black food colouring paste with a drop of water. Paint in the eyes of all the animals using a fine paintbrush.

*Position one bunny peeping around one of the tree's roots.*

# Sleepy Dragon

*Dragons don't always have to look fierce and breathe flames of fire. I decided on a kindly dragon here, captured asleep while on guard, with a contented smile after counting all his gold coins.*

## CAKE AND DECORATION
- One 1l (2 pints/4 cups) bowl-shaped cake and one 20cm (8in) round cake (see page 11)
- 30cm (12in) round cake board
- 1.85kg (3lb 11oz) sugarpaste (rolled fondant)
- Green, black and yellow food colouring pastes
- Icing (confectioner's) sugar in a sugar shaker
- 345g (11oz/1⅓ cups) buttercream
- Sugar glue
- Black, green, orange and yellow dusting powder (petal dust/blossom tint)
- Edible gold and silver lustre powder

## EQUIPMENT
- Small, sharp knife
- Large and small rolling pins
- Medium paintbrush
- Bone tool
- Small rose petal cutter
- Miniature circle cutter
- Sheet of kitchen paper

## CAKE AND BOARD

1 Colour 375g (12oz) of sugarpaste (rolled fondant) green. Roll out and cover the cake board completely, trimming any excess from around the edge, then put it aside to dry. Trim the crust from each cake and slice the tops flat where each has risen. Put the bowl cake on top of the round cake and trim the sides so that they slope down to the base. Cut out a wedge of cake to make the cave opening: cut from the base to 10cm (4in) in height and 5cm (2in) in depth, and remove the wedge (keep hold of this for later). Sandwich the layers together with buttercream on both cakes, then spread a layer of buttercream over the surface to help the sugarpaste stick.

*Spread buttercream over the surface of the cake.*

## THE CAVE

2 Colour 1kg (2lb) of sugarpaste grey using a touch of black food colouring paste. Roll out 750g (1½lb) of this and cover it over the cake, stretching out any pleats and smoothing downwards. Press the sugarpaste into the cave opening, pinching the edges. Trim excess from around the base and position on the cake board, slightly towards the back so that you leave room for the dragon. Mark the surface by pressing it with your hands, to create a rock effect.

## THE DRAGON

3 Colour 470g (15oz) sugarpaste pale yellow. Using 125g (4oz), roll out and cover the small piece of cake that you cut out in step 1, smoothing around the shape and tucking under, until the whole cake is completely covered. Stick the join together with sugar glue, then smooth gently with your fingers to remove it. Smooth upwards at the neck and stick in position against the cave using sugar glue.

*Cover the cave in grey and dragon in yellow paste.*

4 Using 170g (5½oz) of grey sugarpaste, shape different-sized rocks and arrange these around the cake, securing them with sugar glue. To make the dragon's tail, roll 60g (2oz) of pale yellow sugarpaste into a long, tapering sausage. Cut the rounded end straight, moisten with sugar glue, then

push up against the base of the dragon, looping the narrow end round and sticking against the side of the cave.

5 To make the dragon's head, roll 60g (2oz) of pale yellow into a ball. Pinch from just under halfway, all the way round to pull out the muzzle. Pinch all the way round at the opposite end to shape a neck, pulling it downwards. Indent the smile by rolling the back of a knife around the muzzle and dimple each corner by pressing in with the end of a paintbrush. Stick in position on top of the body, resting against the cave.

*Pinch out the dragon's muzzle and neck.*

6 Using 45g (1½oz) of pale yellow sugarpaste, model sausages in different lengths for the tummy scales. Stick one at a time down the dragon's front, tapering in size and smoothing along the length of each to make them little flatter. To make the dragon's wings, first split 7g (¼oz) of pale yellow sugarpaste in half. Model a flattened teardrop shape with one half, then pinch up at the full end to make three points. Press the side of a paint brush between each point to indent. Smooth the indentations wider at the full end using your finger. Make the opposite wing and stick in position with sugar glue.

7 Split 75g (2½oz) of pale yellow sugarpaste in half. To make a leg, take one piece and roll it into a sausage shape. Two thirds along the length, pinch all the way round to narrow it and round off a heel. Gently lift the foot and press in the centre to create a curve, rounding off the toe area. Make three cuts along the edge to

separate the toes and press gently to round these off. Make another leg and stick both in position, smoothing and slightly flattening the top of each leg.

8 To make the dragon's arms, split 30g (1oz) of pale yellow sugarpaste in half and roll each piece into a sausage shape. Pinch in the centre to round off the hands and press them to make them slightly flat. Make two cuts on each hand to create the fingers, then press gently to round them off. Using sugar glue to secure them, stick each arm in position, gently pressing at each shoulder to flatten.

9 Using 7g (¼oz) of pale yellow sugarpaste, model three pointed teardrops, tapering in size, to go on the back of his head. Stick in place and smooth the tip of each downwards. Using a pea-sized amount split in half, model two tiny teardrop shapes for ears, and press in the centre of each with the small end of a bone tool. With another

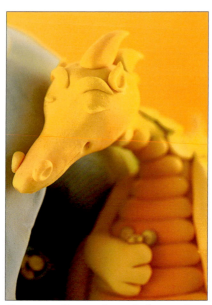

*Use two small pieces of paste for his nostrils.*

pea-sized amount split in half, model two small balls for his nostrils pressing in the centre of each with the small end of the bone tool and pushing up slightly to make it fuller at the top. Again using a pea-sized amount, model the eyebrows and eyes. Moisten the paintbrush with sugar glue, then paint over the eyes, smoothing the eyelids and removing any visible join.

*Stick the tapering tummy scales onto the front of the dragon with sugar glue.*

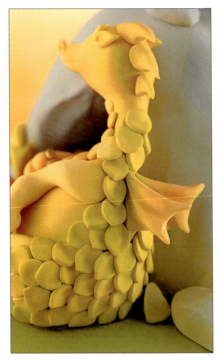

*Cover his back with teardrop-shaped scales.*

*10* With the remaining pale yellow sugarpaste, thinly roll out and cut teardrop-shaped scales using the small rose petal cutter. Stick them over the dragon's back, building up from the base, each layer overlapping the last. With trimmings, model the dragon's pointed tail end.

*Stick the treasure pots in and around the cave.*

## THE TREASURE POTS

*11* Using the black dusting powder (petal dust/blossom tint) and the medium paintbrush, brush into the cave opening a little bit of powder at a time – make it quite dense in the centre, fading out around the edges. To model the treasure pots, split 30g (1oz) of grey sugarpaste in half. To make the high necked pot, roll one piece into a ball, then pinch around the centre pulling up a neck and pinch around the top edge to create a rim. Split the remaining piece of grey sugarpaste in half again to make the two rounded pots; first shape a ball, then press into the top with your finger and pinch up a rim.

*12* To make the coins, roll out grey sugarpaste trimmings and cut small circles using the miniature circle cutter. Leave to set, then rub on gold lustre powder using your fingers. Rub silver lustre powder over the pots. Sprinkle green, orange and yellow dusting powder in groups on the kitchen paper. Using the medium paintbrush, brush on the orange dusting powder over the front of the dragon and around his head and on the tip of each wing. Stick some coins together in piles and place single coins into the pots. Arrange the pots into the cave opening, then scatter the rest of the gold coins around. Stick a few coins into the dragon's hand.

*Use a miniature circle cutter to make the coins.*

## FINISHING TOUCHES

*13* Use the medium paintbrush to apply green dusting powder around the base of the dragon's cave and over the rocks. Also, dust the dragon's scales, back of his head and tip of his tail. As a finishing touch, brush some yellow dusting powder onto the sleepy dragon to help blend the various colours together and to prevent harsh lines from occurring.

*Stick a few coins into the sleepy dragon's hands.*

*Brush dusting powder onto the dragon.*

# Snow White

*Snow White and the Seven Dwarfs is one of the most enchanting fairy tales. I decided to put her at the cottage window, with the wicked queen tempting her to bite into the poisoned apple.*

## CAKE AND DECORATION
- *25cm (10in) square cake (see page 11)*
- *25cm (10in) round cake board*
- *1kg (2lb) sugarpaste (rolled fondant)*
- *Green, yellow, black, brown, red and cream food colouring pastes*
- *Icing (confectioner's) sugar in a sugar shaker*
- *440g (14oz/1¾ cups) buttercream*
- *Sugar glue*
- *250g (8oz) modelling paste*
- *Two sugar sticks or lengths of raw, dried spaghetti*
- *Black food colouring pen*

## EQUIPMENT
- *Small, sharp knife*
- *Large and small rolling pins*
- *Flat-edged cake smoother*
- *3.5cm (1¼in) and 1cm (½in) square cutters*
- *A few cocktail sticks (toothpicks)*
- *A medium paintbrush*
- *Small pieces of foam sponge*
- *Miniature circle cutter*
- *Small blossom plunger cutter*

## CAKE AND BOARD

1. Colour 315g (10oz) of sugarpaste (rolled fondant) yellow-green using green food colouring paste with a touch of yellow. Roll out and cover the whole cake board, trimming any excess from the edge, then put aside to dry.

2. Trim the crust from the cake and slice the top flat where the cake has risen. Cut away a 2.5cm (1in) strip from one side of the cake. From this, cut a 5cm (2in) oblong piece for the bottom of the little shed on the side, and another piece of the same size for the shed roof. Cut a wedge from one side to make the shed's sloping roof. Sandwich the cakes together, cover them with a layer of buttercream and put them to one side.

3. Cut the cake into four pieces. Sandwich two of the pieces together. From another piece, cut wedges either side from the top, sloping down to the outside edge so that you are left with a triangular shape. Sandwich this on top of the others. Cut the remaining piece into two layers and sandwich them on either side of the roof, trimming to fit. Spread a layer of buttercream over the surface of the cake to help the sugarpaste stick.

## THE COTTAGE

4. Place the cake on the cake board. Roll out 100g (3½oz) of white sugarpaste and cut a piece to cover the back of the cake. Roll out another 100g (3½oz) and cut oblongs to fit the sides of the cake, leaving the roof uncovered. Roll out a further 100g (3½oz) and cut a piece to cover the front of the cake. Use a cake smoother to smooth the surface. From the front, trim out two squares using the large square cutter to make the window, and cut a doorway, removing the sugarpaste. Roll out 45g (1½oz) of sugarpaste and cover the front, sides and roof of the shed, trimming any excess from around the edge. Moisten with sugar glue and then press against the side of the cottage. With the smaller square cutter, cut a small doorway in the shed, removing the sugarpaste. Shape the corners by pressing with a cake smoother.

*Cut and stack the cakes to make a cottage.*

*Cut doors and windows in the sugarpaste.*

*Create the straw effect with a knife.*

5 Colour the remaining sugarpaste yellow. Roll out and cover the roof, smoothing the sugarpaste beneath and trimming any excess. Make cuts with a knife for a straw effect, and cut little pieces from around the edge, flicking them out. Cover the shed roof in the same way using the trimmings.

6 Model the chimney using 30g (1oz) of white modelling paste. Cut the bottom at an angle so that it will sit flush on top of the roof, then stick in position. Press into the top to indent. Using 60g (2oz) of paste, model small, flattened pieces of various sizes to create the stone-effect walls. Focus on the joins so that they are hidden, then stick them over the chimney and over the cake board to make the path.

7 Colour 65g (2¼oz) of modelling paste black. Roll out 7g (¼oz) of this thinly and cut an oblong shape to cover the window background. To make the panes, thinly roll out 7g (¼oz) of white modelling paste and cut two square

shapes with the larger square cutter. Cut four squares out of each of the window panes. Stick one on the left-hand side of the window while the other dries.

8 Colour 45g (1½oz) of modelling paste brown. Roll out 15g (½oz) and cut an oblong shape that is slightly smaller than the doorway width. Press in three vertical indents for the door panels and make the woodgrain pattern with a knife. With the trimmings, cut two more strips and mark them with woodgrain. Stick these strips across the door, then slot the door into position.

*Make the shed door out of brown paste.*

9 Using 15g (½oz) of brown modelling paste, make the window ledges, the rack of seven pegs on the side of the house and the shed door. Stick these in place with sugar glue. Roll a small sausage of brown modelling paste for the basket handle and texture using a knife. Bend it into a curve and leave to set. Put aside a minute amount of brown and then roll the remaining piece into a ball. Press in the centre and then pinch

up an edge all the way around to make the basket rim. Texture as before, then stick on the basket handle. Using a pea-sized amount of black modelling paste, roll two thin sausages and loop them round to make the door handles.

### THE APPLES AND CLOTHES

10 Colour 7g (¼oz) of modelling paste red. Split into three equally sized pieces. Using one piece, shape the top of Snow White's skirt and stick in position inside the window recess. To make the apple, roll the second piece into a ball and push a cocktail stick (toothpick) into the top to indent. Put aside the third piece until later. Model a stalk with the brown paste that you put aside earlier and stick the apple in position on the window ledge. To make the apple shine, apply a thick layer of sugar glue. Colour 7g (¼oz) of modelling paste green, make three more apples and stick them in the basket.

11 Model a long teardrop of 35g (1¼oz) black modelling paste for the queen's dress, pinching an edge around the base. Moisten a sugar stick, then push it down into the wicked queen's body to use as a support for the head. Split 7g (¼oz) of the black paste in half. Split one half again and model two sleeves out of it. Push the end of a paintbrush into the base of each to open up and make a hole for the hands to slot into. Stick in place using pieces of foam sponge to support the pose while the paste sets. With the second piece of black paste, shape Snow White's bodice. Press into the top to indent a curve for the neck, then stick in position.

### THE WICKED QUEEN

12 Colour just under 7g (¼oz) of white modelling paste grey by adding a touch of black and cream food colouring pastes. Split a pea-sized amount into two for the wicked queen's hands. For the hands, model a flattened teardrop and cut a thumb to one side. Make three cuts along the top, then gently twist each finger to a point. Pinch to make a wrist, moisten with sugar glue, then push into the end of a sleeve. To make the queen's head, first model a minute flattened ball for her

*Attach a rack of pegs to the side of the house.*

*Cut out the window panes with a square cutter.*

*Use a sugar stick to support the queen's head.*

*Modelled pieces needed for Snow White.*

the queen, but give her shorter fingers. Bend the arm halfway by pressing in the elbow and pinching out at the back. Twist the top of the arm to a point, stick into the hollowed out sleeves, and stick the hand in place resting it on the window sill. Repeat the process to make the other arm.

*16* Moisten a sugar stick and push into her neck, leaving about 1cm (½in) protruding to support the head. Model a tiny ball nose, then roll the remaining cream into an oval shape. Moisten the back of the head with glue, then push it into position. Stick on the nose. For the mouth, push the miniature circle cutter into the mouth area to create a smile. To dimple the corners, push the tip of a cocktail stick into each corner and lift gently.

*17* Model flattened pieces of black modelling paste and stick them onto Snow White's head to make her hair, building up the locks around the sides first. Use some of the remaining piece of red paste to model a tiny sausage for her hair bow,

looping it into position on the top of her head.

### FINISHING TOUCHES

*18* Roll out the rest of the red paste and cut all the blossom flowers using the plunger cutter. Stick the flowers in groups around the board. When the cake is dry, draw the eyes for the queen and Snow White with the black food colouring pen. Using sugar glue, stick the open window in position, supporting it with foam pieces until dry.

wart, then roll the remaining grey into a ball. Pinch out a long, hooked nose and cut a crooked smile. Moisten the end of the sugar stick with glue again, then gently stick the head in place, adding the wart to the side of her nose.

*13* Split 7g (¼oz) of black modelling paste in half. With one half, thinly roll out and cut a 2.5cm (1in) wide oblong shape to make the hood of the queen's cloak. Stick it around her head, pinching together at the back. With the second piece, thinly roll it out and cut her cloak. Roll the side of a paintbrush over the surface to create pleats, then stick the cloak around her shoulders.

### SNOW WHITE

*14* Colour a pea-sized amount of modelling paste yellow and make two puffed sleeves for Snow White, marking pleats in the top of each with a cocktail stick. Shape two minute flattened balls and push the end of a paintbrush down into each to make holes. Stick them in position.

*15* Colour just under 7g (¼oz) of modelling paste cream. Using half of this, model her neck and two arms. To make her neck, press the paste to flatten the chest area, then pinch around the top. To make an arm, roll a sausage of paste, rounding off one end for a hand. Make her hand as you did for

*Position Snow White on the window sill so that it looks as though she is leaning out.*

# Enchanted Castle

*It is easy to imagine a pretty castle, but an enchanted one has to be positioned high on a hill top, with a winding pathway up to it, secret tunnels and sparkling, twisting turrets reaching for the sky.*

### CAKE AND DECORATION
- *One 20cm (8in) round cake, one 15cm (6in) round cake and one 18cm (7in) square cake (see page 11)*
- *25cm (10in) round cake board*
- *500g (1lb/2 cups) buttercream*
- *1.5kg (3lb) sugarpaste (rolled fondant)*
- *Black, pink, brown and green food colouring pastes*
- *Icing (confectioner's) sugar in a sugar shaker*
- *Sugar glue*
- *Edible green and yellow dusting powder (petal dust/blossom tint)*
- *Edible sparkle powder*

### EQUIPMENT
- *Small, sharp knife*
- *Large and small rolling pins*
- *Template (see page 190)*
- *Medium and fine paintbrushes*
- *Large star piping tube (tip) or dinner fork*
- *Cake smoother*
- *Small blossom plunger cutter*

## COVERING THE CAKE

*1* Trim the crust from the cakes and slice the tops flat where they have risen. Put the smaller round cake centrally on top of the larger round cake and position them both on the cake board. For the castle, cut a 6cm (2½in) square from the corner of the large square cake. From the rest of the cake, cut an 11cm (4½in) circle. Trim around the top edge of this circle, cutting down and outwards to the base, then position it on top of the two round cakes slightly on one side, leaving a small ridge on the opposite side.

*2* Using buttercream, sandwich all the round cakes together to make the hill. Position cake trimmings around the cake board. Spread a layer of buttercream over all cakes to help the sugarpaste (rolled fondant) stick. Then put the castle cake aside until later. Colour 1.1kg (2lb 4oz) of sugarpaste pale grey using a touch of black food

*Use a sausage of sugarpaste to make the pathway.*

colouring paste. Roll 185g (6oz) of this into a long, tapering sausage and press it into position with the narrower end at the top, winding down the front of the cake. Smooth out the side edges so that they line up with the surface of the cake.

*3* Roll out 875g (1¾lb) of the pale grey sugarpaste and cover the cake completely, stretching out any pleats

*Stack the cakes up to make the hill and castle.*

*Cover the hill and the castle roof with grey paste.*

and smoothing down and around the overall shape. Pinch an edge along each side of the winding pathway and smooth along the ridges to create paths that wind around the cake. Press into the side of the cake repeatedly, smoothing downwards to create vertical ridges for the rock effect and trimming any excess away from around the base. Position the castle cake on top of the hill. Roll out 30g (1oz) of pale grey and cut a square to cover the top of the castle.

## THE CASTLE WALLS

Colour 220g (7oz) of sugarpaste pale dusky pink using pink food colouring paste with a touch of brown. Using 125g (4oz) of it, roll out and cut squares that are slightly higher than the castle sides and press them in position. Mark evenly along the top edge with the back of a knife. Cut out a small doorway in the front using the template (see page 190), removing the sugarpaste. Push in the tip of a knife to mark windows. Roll a long sausage of pale dusky pink, using 30g (1oz), and cut four turrets slightly higher than the castle walls and stick in place at each corner with sugar glue. Mark windows in these

as before. Colour 7g (¼oz) of sugarpaste brown. Roll out and cut a door using the template, then trim either side to narrow the width. Mark lines with a knife to make the wood panels, then mark woodgrain. Carefully slot the door into the doorway at the front of the castle.

## THE HILLSIDE DETAILS

Colour 90g (3oz) of sugarpaste green. Break it into different-sized pieces and texture by pressing the star piping tube (tip) repeatedly into the surface, tearing a rough edge. Stick these pieces onto the cake to make the grass. Colour 7g (¼oz) of sugarpaste black. For the tunnels, cut small openings in the hill, remove the sugarpaste, then fill the space by pressing in black paste.

*Make the pathway out of pebbles of various sizes.*

Using the remaining pale grey, model small flattened oval shapes to make steps and stick these against the cake, building up toward the tunnel openings, graduating them down in size. Model different-sized rocks, scattering these around the cake and securing with sugar glue. For the pebbles on the winding pathway and edging the doorway, knead a little dusky pink and pale grey together, then model tiny flattened pieces, sticking them in place with sugar glue.

*Use a star tube to texture the grass.*

*Use a knife to mark out wooden door panels.*

*Slot the castle door into the doorway carefully.*

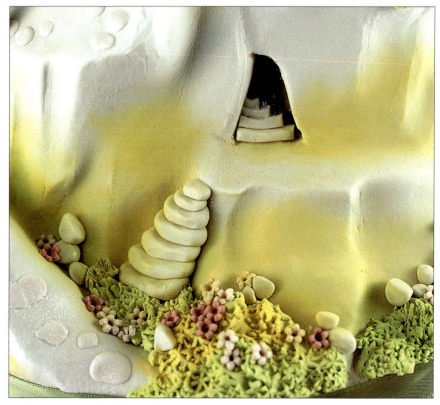

*Stick the grass onto the hillside with sugar glue.*

*Make a tower to go over the pathway.*

### THE CASTLE DETAILS

6 To make the large central turret on top of the castle, roll a ball using 30g (1oz) of pale dusky pink sugarpaste and pinch around the centre, pulling it up at the top. Lay the piece of paste down and press it on the work surface with a cake smoother to flatten the back and front. Cut the top and bottom straight, and stick it on top of the castle using sugar glue. Mark windows as before. With 22g (³⁄₄oz) of pale dusky pink sugarpaste, make five different-sized sausage-shaped turrets, sticking them in place with sugar glue. With the remaining pale dusky pink, make the pathway tower, cutting out a little doorway and marking windows as before. Then use sugar glue to stick this tower in position over the pathway about halfway up the hill.

*Brush sparkle powder onto the castle, concentrating mostly on the turret roofs.*

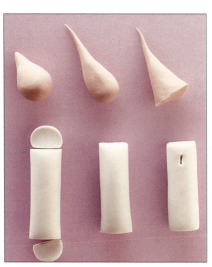

*Use dusky pink sugarpaste for the turrets.*

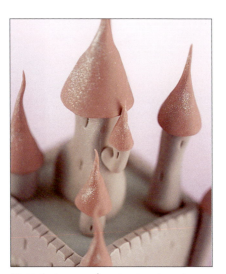

*Twist the turret roofs up to a tapering point.*

7 Colour the remaining sugarpaste dark dusky pink. Model all the different-sized turret roofs, twisting each up to a long, tapering point. Use all the pink trimmings to roll out and cut flowers with the blossom plunger cutter and then stick them randomly over the cake. With dark dusky pink sugarpaste, roll minute sausages of paste and loop round to make the door handles. When the cake is dry, dust the hill with green dusting powder (petal dust/blossom tint) using the medium paintbrush. Dust the grass with yellow dusting powder. Brush on the sparkle powder, adding a little more to the turret roofs than the rest of the cake.

# Snow Queen

*The Snow Queen is a delightful tale. She is beautiful, ice cold and quite enchanting. I hope I have managed to capture her as you imagine her to be.*

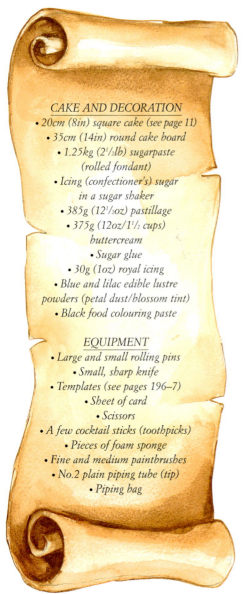

## CAKE AND DECORATION
- *20cm (8in) square cake (see page 11)*
- *35cm (14in) round cake board*
- *1.25kg (2½lb) sugarpaste (rolled fondant)*
- *Icing (confectioner's) sugar in a sugar shaker*
- *385g (12½oz) pastillage*
- *375g (12oz/1½ cups) buttercream*
- *Sugar glue*
- *30g (1oz) royal icing*
- *Blue and lilac edible lustre powders (petal dust/blossom tint)*
- *Black food colouring paste*

## EQUIPMENT
- *Large and small rolling pins*
- *Small, sharp knife*
- *Templates (see pages 196–7)*
- *Sheet of card*
- *Scissors*
- *A few cocktail sticks (toothpicks)*
- *Pieces of foam sponge*
- *Fine and medium paintbrushes*
- *No.2 plain piping tube (tip)*
- *Piping bag*

*Cut the sleigh side out of pastillage.*

*Stack the cakes up to make the sleigh shape.*

## THE SLEIGH

1 Roll out 500g (1lb) of white sugarpaste (rolled fondant) and cover the cake board. Using the large rolling pin, press down over the surface to indent it and then put it aside to dry. Roll out 170g (5½oz) of pastillage and cut a sleigh side piece using the template on pages 196–7 and a sharp knife. Make another sleigh side piece and leave them both to dry on a completely flat surface, preferably overnight.

2 Trim away the crust of the cake and slice the top so that it is flat. Cut it in half and cut away a slice measuring 4cm (1½in) from one end of one half. To make the sleigh, position the cakes one on top of the other, graduating in size, so that they line up at the back. Trim off the front edge of each cake to round it off and then trim a little from the edge on either side of the centre cake only.

3 Sandwich the cakes together with buttercream, then spread a thin layer over the surface to help the sugarpaste stick in place. The cake should stand no more than 13cm (5in) high so

that the sleigh sides fit perfectly. Roll out 140g (4½oz) of sugarpaste. Position the side of the cake down onto it and cut around it. Cover the opposite side in the same way. Position the cake on the board.

4 Roll a tapering sausage out of 15g (½oz) of sugarpaste and position on the top edge of the second layer of the cake to build up the queen's shoulders. Roll out 280g (9oz) sugarpaste and cut a long thin strip to cover from the front of the sleigh and down the back. Smooth ridges and ripples with your fingers.

*Use a rolling pin to apply the sugarpaste.*

*Make the queen's hair by rolling long teardrop shapes and attach in position with sugar glue.*

*Pinch out fingers and twist them to a point.*

of white sugarpaste. Stick them in place around the queen's head, covering from the base upwards and twisting up and around the back of the sleigh. Using two pieces of sugarpaste, each about the size of a large pea, make two hands, using the step photograph above as a guide, gently twisting each finger to a point. Stick them in position using foam sponge pieces to support them while they are drying.

### THE SNOW QUEEN

5 Using the collar template (see page 196), roll out 7g (¼oz) of sugarpaste and cut out the collar. To make the head, roll 22g (¾oz) into a rounded teardrop shape. Gently indent the eye area with your finger. Model a minute teardrop for the nose and stick in place with sugar glue, removing the join by smoothing with a cocktail stick (toothpick). Stick her head in place with the collar uppermost using a little sugar glue. Split 45g (1½oz) in half for the two sleeves. Roll a long teardrop shape and press into the wide end to open up the sleeve, pinching around the edge to widen it further as shown in the photograph above. Stick in position as each one is made, smoothing into the surface of the sugarpaste to remove the join on the outer side and pressing gently with your finger to indent.

6 Roll 45g (1½oz) of the paste into a thick sausage, then roll in the centre to create a dip for the foot rest at the front of the sleigh. Trim to fit at either end, sticking in place with glue.

7 To make the hair, roll long teardrop shapes, all of slightly different lengths, using 30g (1oz)

*Dilute black food colouring until it is dark grey, then paint her eyes and mouth.*

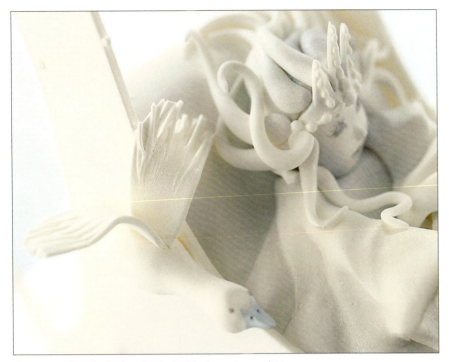

Pipe uneven lines for feathers for the birds' wings using royal icing.

## PUTTING THE CAKE TOGETHER

*10* Spread a thin layer of royal icing onto one side of the sleigh, then position a pastillage sleigh side against it. Hold for a few moments until it is secure. Stick the opposite side in place in the same way.

*11* Roll out the remaining pastillage and cut out four sets of birds' wings using the template (see page 196). Make cuts for feathers, then make a small centre crease by folding gently and stick wings onto each bird. Immediately place the birds on the cake, sticking them with royal icing, using a foam sponge support until dry.

## FINISHING TOUCHES

*12* With the remaining royal icing and the no.2 plain piping tube (tip), pipe different-sized dots to make the snowflakes over the cake and cake board. Pipe dots on the queen's crown and uneven lines for feathers on the bird wings. Dust the cake with blue and lilac edible lustre powders. Mix a little blue lustre powder (petal dust/blossom tint) with a drop of water and paint the beaks, then paint blue lustre powder onto the Snow Queen's lips.

## THE BIRDS

*8* Split 45g (1½oz) of the remaining pastillage into four pieces. To make a bird, roll one piece into a sausage and shape one end into a point. Pinch at the opposite end to shape the neck and round off the head. Gently pinch out a beak. Mark out either side of the beak using a cocktail stick. Make

Stick it in place with sugar glue. Dilute some black food colouring paste with a few drops of water until it is dark grey. Using the fine paintbrush, paint the Snow Queen's eyes and lips and the bird's eyes.

Make the birds out of pastillage.

small cuts for the tail feathers, then stroke them upwards. If you find the pastillage starts to set before you have finished modelling, slightly dampen your fingers. Make three more birds and set aside to dry.

## FINISHING THE QUEEN AND BIRDS

*9* Using the crown template on page 196, roll out a little of the pastillage trimmings and cut out the crown.

Dust the cake with blue and lilac edible lustre powders.

# Peter Pan

*Peter Pan and Wendy are well-loved characters from one of the most famous fairy tales. Sadly, it was impossible to create a flying Peter Pan, so I put him sitting cheekily on the roof instead.*

## CAKE AND DECORATION
- One 15cm (6in) and one 20cm (8in) square cake (see page 11)
- 30cm (12in) square cake board
- 1.85kg (3lb 10½oz) sugarpaste (rolled fondant)
- Navy blue, cream, black, brown, chestnut, bright green and mauve food colouring pastes
- Icing (confectioner's) sugar in a sugar shaker
- 500g (1lb/2 cups) buttercream
- 75g (2½oz) modelling paste
- Sugar glue
- Two sugar sticks or lengths of raw, dried spaghetti
- Edible gold lustre powder (petal dust/blossom tint)
- Edible gold paint

## EQUIPMENT
- Large and small rolling pins
- Small, sharp knife
- Small square cutter
- Cake smoother
- Template (see page 190)
- Fine and medium paintbrushes
- Kitchen paper
- Miniature circle cutter
- A few cocktail sticks (toothpicks)
- Small piece of foam sponge
- Small calyx cutter

## CAKE AND BOARD

Colour 440g (14oz) of sugarpaste (rolled fondant) navy blue. Roll out and cover the cake board completely, trimming any excess from around edge, then put aside to dry. To give them plenty of drying time, make the windows first. Roll out 7g (¼oz) of white modelling paste and cut six squares using the square cutter. Cut around the outer edge to make a window. Make another window and put them both aside to dry.

*Cut out the windows and leave aside to dry.*

Trim the crust from each cake and slice the tops flat where each have risen. Trim a 5cm (2in) strip from one side of the larger cake and put it to one side. Position the smaller cake centrally on top of the larger cake. Place the strip of cake on top, trimming off the length to fit – this off-cut will be used for the window later.

Trim on opposite sides of the roof to remove ridges and create the sloping sides. Fill gaps on the roof with trimmings. Slice at an angle at the back of the small off-cut of cake for the window, so it sits neatly against the roof cake. Trim a triangular-shaped roof for the window

*Trim and shape the cakes to make a roof.*

from trimmings. Sandwich all the layers together with buttercream, and sandwich on the window leaving a 2cm (¾in) gap from the base. Spread a layer of buttercream over the surface of the cake to help the sugarpaste stick, then position the cake on the cake board.

Colour the 1.4kg (2lb 12½oz) of sugarpaste cream. Roll out 155g (5oz) of it and cut a piece to cover the side of the cake. To create a smooth surface, rub with a cake smoother. Cover the opposite side in the same way.

## THE WINDOW

Thickly roll out 45g (1½oz) of cream sugarpaste and cut the window ledge so that it measures 9cm (3½in) in length. Thinly roll out 15g (½oz) and cut a piece to cover the front of the window only. Roll out 125g (4oz) and cover the window again, but this time cover the roof and sides, as well as the front. Cut out the window at the front measuring 5cm (2in) square and remove the sugarpaste to reveal the first sugarpaste covering. Dilute black food colouring paste with water

*Use a stippling action to paint in the windows.*

and paint the window recess a cloudy black using a stippling motion with the medium paintbrush.

### ROOF TILES AND FASCIA BOARDS

6 Use 625g (1¼lb) of cream sugar-paste to make the roof tiles on both sides of the cake. Roll out the sugarpaste a little at a time and cut 1.5cm (½in) wide strips to cover an area slightly wider than the side of the roof. Cut along the bottom edge to separate the tiles but leave the top joined. Stick in place with each layer overlapping the next, alternately lining up tiles. Cover both sides of the cake, then cover the window roof in the same way using 100g (3½oz) of cream sugarpaste.

*Stick the tiles to the roof before painting.*

7 Roll a 30g (1oz) sausage of cream sugarpaste and stick along the top of the roof. Press a little flat, then indent using the back of a knife. Edge the top of the window roof in the same way using 7g (¼oz) of cream sugarpaste. Thinly roll out a small piece of the cream sugarpaste trimmings and cut a thin strip for the top of the window. Roll out 7g (¼oz) of cream and cut strips for the wood-effect fascia board edging the window's roof. Mark wood lines with a knife. Make fascia boards for both sides of the cake using 60g (2oz) of cream sugarpaste, then roll out and cut the wood at each side using the template (see page 190), again marking wood lines.

*Stipple on brown and chestnut colouring.*

8 Protect the cake board from paint splashes by laying sheets of kitchen paper over it, right up to and around the cake. Dilute brown food colouring paste with a little water. Stipple over the surface of the roof in patches using the medium paintbrush. Paint over the fascia boards with brown, letting the colour seep into the scribed lines to highlight the wood effect. Dilute chestnut food colouring paste with water and stipple over the roof, covering it completely with colour. Leave to dry, then stipple on a third coat. (The tiles in the photograph above are shown on a work surface rather than the roof for clarity.)

*Paint the wood with diluted brown colouring.*

### THE CHIMNEY

9 Model the base of the chimney with 45g (1½oz) of cream sugarpaste and press onto the top of the roof smoothing it down on opposite sides. Roll out some cream sugarpaste trimmings and cut a square measuring 3cm (1¼in) to go on the top; stick in place with sugar glue. For the chimney pot, colour 7g (¼oz) of modelling paste chestnut. Model a small ball and press onto the top of the chimney. Roll a smaller ball, stick on top and press in an indent.

### WENDY

10 Take just under 7g (¼oz) of white modelling paste, put aside a pea-sized amount of it, then, with the rest, model a teardrop-shaped nightgown. Press down at the full end and mark pleats using the side of a paintbrush. Cut the base straight and stick it into the window recess.

11 Colour just under 15g (½oz) of modelling paste flesh-coloured using a touch of chestnut food colouring paste. Split 7g (¼oz) in half. Split one half in half again for her arms. To make an arm, roll the paste into a sausage shape with a rounded end. Press the rounded end flat to form a hand. Cut a thumb, slightly to one side, then make three cuts along the top to create her fingers. Twist each finger to lengthen. Pinch in halfway between her wrist and

*Position Wendy so that she is looking up at Peter.*

shoulder and pinch out at the back to mark her elbow. Stick in place with her hand resting on the windowsill. Repeat for the opposite side.

*12* Model the pea-sized piece into a flattened circle for her collar. Push a sugar stick down into her nightgown leaving 1.5cm (½in) protruding at the top to help hold her head in place. Model her head and nose using the remaining half of the flesh-coloured sugarpaste, and push this down onto the sugar stick, securing with sugar glue, turning her head to look towards Peter Pan. Indent her smile using the miniature circle cutter at an angle and dimple the smile using a cocktail stick (toothpick).

*13* For Wendy's hair, roll out a little chestnut modelling paste, cut thin strips and stick them over her head. Use the small piece of foam sponge to support the head in the pose until dry.

### PETER PAN

*14* Colour 7g (¼oz) of modelling paste brown, 7g (¼oz) dark green (using green with a touch of brown) and just under 15g (½oz) bright green. Split the dark green into three equal pieces – put one piece aside for later – and roll two pieces into tapering sausage shapes for legs. Indent at the back and pinch out at the front halfway on each to shape the knees.

Stick them in position either side of the window roof, with the top of each leg level with the top of the roof.

*15* For Peter's tunic, split 7g (¼oz) of the bright green paste in half. Model one half into the base of the tunic by pinching around the base to create an edge. Stick this over the legs and on top of the roof, pressing down at the waist to make a base for the belt. Model a small flattened ball of brown modelling paste and stick onto the tunic base for the belt. With the other half of the paste, make the top of his tunic. Split the remaining dark green in half and make two sleeves. Stick in position leaving a small gap for the hands to slot in.

*16* Model a flattened circle for Peter's collar using a pea-sized amount of brown modelling paste. Stick in place and push a sugar stick down through the top, leaving 1.5cm (½in) protruding at the top to help hold his head in place. With the remaining flesh-coloured sugarpaste, model his head, nose and two pointed ears, indenting them in the centre with the end of a paintbrush. Also make two hands from tiny flattened teardrop shapes, cutting thumbs and fingers as before.

*The modelled pieces of Peter Pan.*

*Use sugar glue to attach Peter to the roof.*

*17* Thinly roll out the remaining chestnut modelling paste and cut out two hair pieces using the calyx cutter. For the hat, model a flattened circle with the remaining bright green paste and fold over, pinching gently at each end. Open this up, and stick it onto the top of his head. Using white modelling paste, model a tiny feather making tiny cuts down either side of it with the knife. Indent in the top of the hat to make a small hole using a cocktail stick, then put the end of the feather into the hole using sugar glue to secure it.

### FINISHING TOUCHES

*18* To make the shoes using the remaining brown modelling paste, model two tapering teardrop shapes and pinch at the full end to shape the heels. Press into the top to indent holes for the legs to slot in and stick in place with sugar glue. Colour 7g (¼oz) of the modelling paste mauve. Thinly roll out and cut two strips to make the curtains at the window. Roll the side of a paintbrush over the surface to create pleats and stick in place with the windows that were made earlier.

*19* Dilute a little black food colouring paste with water and paint the eyes using the fine paintbrush. Dust the cake board and roof with the gold lustre powder (petal dust/blossom tint) then paint gold stars over the surface with edible gold paint.

# Whizzing Witch

*This cheeky moon is happy to have a friendly witch whizzing around it at high speed. The witch's cat is having trouble keeping up though and even the bats look dizzy!*

### CAKE AND BOARD

1 Colour 500g (1lb) of the sugarpaste (rolled fondant) dark blue. Roll it out and cover the cake board, trimming any excess, then put it aside to dry.

2 Trim the crust from each cake and slice the tops flat. Put them together to make a ball shape and trim any excess. Sandwich the cakes together with buttercream, then spread a thin layer over the surface to help the sugarpaste stick.

### THE MOON'S FACE

3 Use 75g (2½oz) of white sugarpaste to pad out the features. Using half the paste, model an oval shape for the nose and press this into position. Model two flattened balls for cheeks using 15g (½oz) of paste for each and press in place. With the rest of the paste, model tapering sausages for eyebrows, eyes and lips, and roll two small round pupils.

4 Moisten the facial features with sugar glue. Roll out the remaining white sugarpaste and cover the

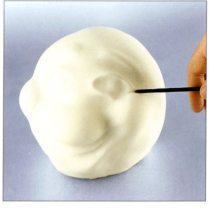

*Smooth around the features with a paintbrush.*

cake, pulling up a pleat at the back. Trim any excess and use sugar glue to stick the joins together – rub along the join to remove it. Trim excess from the base. Using the end of a paintbrush, smooth around the features to bring them out, then lift and position on the centre of the board.

### THE BROOMSTICK

5 First colour 15g (½oz) of modelling paste brown and use half to model the thatched end of the broomstick,

*Model the features and stick them onto the face.*

*Make the broomstick and stick it to the board.*

*Model the witch's body, legs, arms and head and assemble on the cake as each piece is made.*

8 Colour 45g (1½oz) of the modelling paste mauve. Shape it into a large teardrop and then pinch around the large end to widen it and make a ridge for the bottom of the dress. Place the two legs in position on either side of the broomstick and then put the dress on top, making room for the legs to pop out from underneath. To help support the head, moisten the sugar stick or raw spaghetti with a little sugar glue, then push this down into the top of the dress, leaving about 1–2cm (½–¾in) protruding.

9 Colour 7g (¼oz) of the modelling paste bright green. Put aside a minute amount for the cat's eyes, then split the remainder exactly in half. Roll a sausage shape, making it slightly fuller at one end than the other. Pinch the wide end to open the sleeve and then twist down to lengthen it so that it finishes in a point. Stick it in place with the sleeve opening resting at the side of the broomstick handle. Make the other sleeve in the same way.

10 To make the witch's head and hands, first colour 7g (¼oz) of the modelling paste cream. Roll three-quarters of it into a ball to make the head and then pinch out a crooked

marking the bristles with a knife. With the remainder, shape the centre piece, then roll a long sausage to make the handle. Mark along the handle with the back of a knife to create a wood effect. Assemble it on the cake board using sugar glue to secure it in place.

6 To make the witch's broomstick trails, brush glue in spirals over the cake board following the path that she might just have taken. Sprinkle the edible glitter onto this and leave to dry.

### THE WITCH

7 Colour just under 7g (¼oz) of the modelling paste yellow and a pea-sized amount red. Split the yellow into two pieces and roll tapering sausages to make the witch's stockings. Very thinly roll out the red and cut 10 small oblong shapes. Stick these evenly over the stockings, then gently roll each stocking on the work surface to inlay the red.

*Position the witch's legs either side of the broomstick and lean her forwards.*

nose. Smooth up the eye area and then pull gently at the chin, stroking it forward to make a point. Moisten the sugar stick and the top of the dress with sugar glue, then push the head into position. Shape two minute flattened balls of cream paste and stick one on the witch's nose, and the other on her chin.

*11* Split the remaining cream into two pieces. Shape a teardrop with one and flatten slightly. Cut the thumb, slightly to one side, then make three cuts along the top. Pinch and pull the thumb and fingers, twisting each to a point. Make the opposite hand and stick both in place with sugar glue.

*12* Colour 30g (1oz) of the modelling paste black. Thinly roll out 7g (¼oz) of it and cut out a cloak shape to drape over the witch's back. Roll the side of a paintbrush over the end of the cloak to thin and frill at the base, then stick it in place around her shoulders. Using a pea-sized amount for each, roll long, pointed teardrop shapes for her shoes and stick them in position, pointing upwards.

*13* Colour 7g (¼oz) of modelling paste orange. Thinly roll this out and cut strips for the witch's hair, sticking each strip in place as soon as it is made. Cut two smaller strips for around her face.

*14* For the witch's hat, roll 7g (¼oz) of black modelling paste into a rounded teardrop. Pinch around the larger end to create the hat rim, then pinch the top to a point and bend it round, sticking it in position with sugar glue. Carefully stick the hat in place on her head, again using sugar glue. Make two oval-shaped eyes with a minute amount of black.

### THE CAT

*15* Make the cat using 7g (¼oz) of black modelling paste. Using the photograph above as a guide, first model the body, twisting each leg out and rounding off the paws. Stick in place with one paw holding onto the end of the broomstick. Roll a small ball-shaped head and push the end of a

*Twist out the black paste to make the cat's legs.*

paintbrush into the mouth area to open it out. Stick on two tiny teardrop shapes for the muzzle and indent each with the tip of a cocktail stick (toothpick). With the green modelling paste that was put aside, model two tiny eyes. Colour a minute amount of modelling paste pale pink and make the nose. Shape two tiny pointed ears, two pupils and a sausage-shaped tail. Stick the tail on pointing upwards.

### THE BATS

*16* With the remaining black modelling paste make the tiny bats. To make the wings, shape a tiny tapering sausage shape and press flat. Cut out half circles along the bottom using the tip of the no.4 plain piping tube (tip). Cut a curve in the top using the wide end of the tube. Shape a

*Model bright white eyes for the bats.*

flattened ball-shaped body and make a curve at the base with the end of the tube. Make the white eyes with trimmings, adding black pupils, and also make two tiny ears. Make two more bats, sticking each in position as soon as it is made. To finish, dust the cake with edible sparkle powder (petal dust/blossom tint).

*Stick the bats over the moon's face.*

*Stick the cat on the end of the broomstick and bend its tail so that it is pointing upwards.*

# Busy Elves

*Little green elves are appealing subjects for a cake design. Fabled as enchanting creatures who like to keep busy and always help out when needed, here they are sprucing up their mushroom house.*

## CAKE AND DECORATION
- *25cm (10in) square cake (see page 11)*
- *25cm (10in) round cake board*
- *1.75kg (3½lb) sugarpaste (rolled fondant)*
- *Green, red, black, brown and cream food colouring pastes*
- *Icing (confectioner's) sugar in a sugar shaker*
- *440g (14oz/1¾ cups) buttercream*
- *Sugar glue*
- *220g (7oz) modelling paste*
- *Two sugar sticks or lengths of raw, dried spaghetti*

## EQUIPMENT
- *Large and small rolling pins*
- *Small, sharp knife*
- *Templates (see page 190)*
- *Fine paintbrush*
- *Miniature circle cutter*
- *A few cocktail sticks (toothpicks)*
- *Medium calyx cutter*

### THE CAKE BOARD
1 Colour 315g (10oz) of the sugarpaste (rolled fondant) light green. Roll this out and cover the cake board completely, trimming any excess from around the edge. Put aside to dry.

### THE MUSHROOM HOUSE
2 Trim the crust from the cake and slice the top flat. Cut the cake into nine equal pieces, by first cutting into three strips, then cutting each strip into three squares. Stack four squares together for the large mushroom, three for the medium-sized mushroom and two for the small mushroom. Trim off the four corners around the cakes and on the top to round them off. Sandwich the layers together using buttercream, then spread a layer over all the cakes to help the sugarpaste stick.

*Trim the corners away using a sharp knife.*

3 Roll out 500g (1lb) of white sugarpaste, carefully pick up and position around the large mushroom smoothing around the shape. Close the join with sugar glue, then smooth it out. Put the cake on its side and roll it on the work top to create a smooth surface.

Then position it on the cake board. Cover the remaining cakes in the same way, using 345g (11oz) of white sugarpaste for the medium-sized mushroom and 200g (6½oz) for the small one.

*Wrap white sugarpaste around each mushroom.*

4 Colour 345g (11oz) of sugarpaste red and put aside 7g (¼oz). Split the remaining sugarpaste into three equally-sized pieces to make the roofs, rolling them out into 15cm (6in) diameter. Smooth around the edges, then carefully lift and position one on top of each mushroom.

*Lay a red sugarpaste roof over each mushroom.*

Stretch and lift gently to create a wavy edge, bearing in mind where the windows are going to be cut.

### THE WINDOWS AND DOOR

**5** Using the templates (see page 190), cut out four windows from the mushrooms (one at the back) and a door and remove the sugarpaste cuttings. Colour 15g (½oz) of the sugarpaste black; thinly roll it out and cut the window shapes to fill the spaces. Colour 45g (1½oz) of the modelling paste brown. Using the 15g (½oz), roll out and cut the door, making it slightly smaller in width than the template. Mark three lines for the wood using the back of a knife, then mark the woodgrain. Carefully slot the door into position.

**6** Thinly roll out 22g (¾oz) of white modelling paste into a strip measuring around 28cm (11in) in length and cut different-sized V-shapes from one side of it only. Moisten around the base of a mushroom and stick this strip in position trimming to fit. Flick out some of the V-points away from the cake. Use a damp paintbrush to stop them breaking. Make two more strips as before for the other two mushrooms.

**7** Using the window frame template (see page 190), thinly roll out 7g (¼oz) of white modelling paste and cut out four window frames and slot in position. Using 30g (1oz), model two steps for the front door, a door handle and four window ledges. Stick different-sized white dots over the two highest mushroom roofs, pressing them flat.

*Cut out the details for each mushroom house.*

*The modelled pieces of the bucket.*

### THE BUCKETS

**8** Split 15g (½oz) of the brown modelling paste in half and make two buckets, indenting a dip in the top of each. Mark lines around the outside with the back of a knife and make small cuts for the woodgrain. Fill one bucket with some of the red sugarpaste, put aside, and make a tiny teardrop-shaped drip. Smooth some red sugarpaste onto the cake board to create a spill. Fill the other bucket with white sugarpaste, pinching it to a point. Using a pea-sized amount for each, roll two sausage-shaped handles, rounding off the end of each. Loop these around the buckets, and stick in place.

### THE ELVES

**9** Colour 30g (1oz) of the modelling paste dark green and 15g (½oz) light green. For the elves' legs, split just under 7g (¼oz) of the light green modelling paste into four pieces. Make one leg at a time, rolling the pieces into sausages. Thinly roll out and cut tiny strips of dark green modelling paste and stick over the surface of each sausage. Gently re-roll the legs to inlay the strips. Pinch up halfway for the knee and press in at the back to bend. Stick the legs in position on the cake as soon as they are made.

**10** Using pea-sized amounts of dark green modelling paste for each, make four shoes by rolling each into tapering teardrop shapes. Press in the wide end with the end of a paintbrush to indent a hole for the legs to slot in. Moisten with sugar glue, then press in position, curling up the toes.

**11** Split 15g (½oz) of dark green modelling paste in half. For each tunic base, model teardrop shapes and press into the wide end to open them up, pinching around to create edges. Stick these over the elves' legs, pressing the top flat to create the waists. Split 7g (¼oz) of dark green in half. Model two tunic tops, pinching at each shoulder and smoothing out a little cap sleeve. Stick in position using a touch of sugar glue. With the remaining light green paste, stick two balls of paste onto each tunic, then roll four thin sausage-shaped sleeves. Indent the end of each to create small holes for the hands to slot in. Push a sugar stick down into each of the elves' neck leaving 1.5cm (½in) protruding at the top to help hold their heads in place.

*The modelled pieces of one of the elves.*

*Position the top elf so that his bucket is tilting forwards to look like the paint is spilling out.*

base. With the remaining cream modelling paste, model oval-shaped noses and teardrop-shaped ears. Indent each ear with the end of a paintbrush and stick in position with their points uppermost.

### FINISHING TOUCHES

*14* Using half of the remaining brown modelling paste, make the paintbrush. Model the handle first, then cut a small oblong for the hairs and indent these by pressing in repeatedly with a knife. Stick the brush in position in the elf's hand. Place the remaining red sugarpaste onto the end of the paintbrush and down onto the roof surface, smoothing gently in order to remove the join.

*15* Thinly roll out the remaining brown modelling paste. Cut out four calyx shapes using the cutter and stick two each onto the elves' heads to make their hair. Dilute a little black food colouring paste with a drop of water and then, using a fine paintbrush, paint in their eyes.

*12* To make the hands, colour just over 7g (¼oz) of modelling paste cream. Split a pea-sized amount in half and model two teardrop shapes, pressing each flat. Cut the thumb, then fingers, across the top, keeping the cuts straight. Gently smooth each finger to round off and lengthen them slightly. Hold each wrist and pinch around to narrow and round off the hand. Moisten these with sugar glue and carefully stick into each sleeve of the elf that is painting the roof, turning one hand sideways ready to hold the paintbrush. Make another pair of hands and stick in position on the other elf so that it holds the white-filled bucket tipping forwards slightly.

### THE ELVES' HEADS AND FACES

*13* Put aside a pea-sized amount of cream modelling paste, then split the remaining piece in half. To make the heads, roll each piece into rounded teardrops. Indent smiles using the miniature circle cutter pressed in at an angle and dimple the smile using the tip of a cocktail stick (toothpick). Carefully push the heads onto the sugar sticks, securing with sugar glue at the

*Stick the paintbrush into position in the lower elf's hand.*

# Sunken Treasure

*I tried to capture a mysterious atmosphere when designing this shipwreck, which is seemingly lost forever at the bottom of the sea. It is a perfect cake for adventure-loving children of all ages.*

## CAKE AND DECORATION

- 25cm (10in) square cake (see page 11)
- 30cm (12in) round cake board
- 1.3kg (2lb 10oz) sugarpaste (rolled fondant)
- Cream, brown, black, green, yellow and rust food colouring pastes
- Icing (confectioner's) sugar in a sugar shaker
- 500g (1lb/2 cups) buttercream
- Sugar glue
- 230g (7½oz) modelling paste
- Edible gold and silver lustre powders (petal dust/blossom tint)
- Silver dragees
- Edible sparkle powder

## EQUIPMENT

- Large and small rolling pins
- Small, sharp knife
- Grater
- A few cocktail sticks (toothpicks)
- 1.5cm (½in), (2cm (¾in), 3.5cm (1½in) and miniature circle cutters
- Fine to medium paintbrush
- Foam sheet

## CAKE AND BOARD

1 Colour 440g (14oz) of the sugarpaste (rolled fondant) cream. Roll out a sausage using 45g (1½oz) and position it across the cake board, just over halfway. Roll out the remaining cream and cover the cake board completely. Indent over the surface by pressing down firmly with the large rolling pin and trim any excess from around the edge. Press the grater over the surface to create a textured sand effect. Put aside to dry.

*Use a grater to create a sand effect.*

2 Trim the crust from the cake and slice the top flat where the cake has risen. Cut the cake in half. One half is for the base of the ship; cut a layer in this piece and put it to one side. Cut two strips, both measuring 6cm (2½in) from the other half and position one at either end of the ship on top of the base. Cut a one-third layer from the remaining piece and place it on the centre of the ship to raise the height. Then cut a wedge to fit on top of the back of the ship. From the trimmings, cut two strips for steps, one wider than the other.

*Cut and trim the cake into the shape of a ship.*

3 Trim around the cake to shape the sloping sides, cutting down the corners on the back of the ship to about halfway, then trim them to round it off. Trim the sides at the front to a rounded point and do the same down and underneath to make the shape of the ship's bow. Then sandwich all the layers and pieces of cake together using buttercream as shown in the photograph above. Next, spread a layer of buttercream over the surface of the cake in order to help the sugarpaste stick in place.

## COVERING THE SHIP

4 Colour 90g (3oz) of sugarpaste black. Thinly roll out 45g (1½oz) of paste and cut a piece to cover the centre of the cake and up the inside at the front. Colour 750g (1½lb) of the sugarpaste brown. Using 90g (3oz) of this, cut out strips to cover the front of each of the steps, marking wood lines with a knife. Lay the top steps in the same way, making each piece slightly wider than the cake it is covering. Cut strips measuring 1.5cm (½in) from 155g

*Use a knife to create a wood effect.*

*The pieces of the ship's railing.*

### SEABED DETAILS

9 Colour 60g (2oz) of modelling paste pale grey. Use just under 7g (¼oz) to model the anchor, first roll a tapering teardrop for the centre. Roll a small sausage and press into each end with the end of a paintbrush to mark holes. Roll another sausage, tapering at both ends, and bend this around into a curve. Pinch up two, tiny, pointed sausages and stick these on either side of the anchor. Model

(5oz) of brown sugarpaste, marking wood grain as before, and cover the top of the cake, starting at the back of the ship.

5 Using 500g (1lb) of brown sugarpaste, cut strips to cover the sides of the cake – make a few at a time and cut them all in different lengths. Cover from the top of the cake first, keeping the corners at the back at the top half only.

6 To help tip up the cake slightly, apply some strips underneath on one side only. At the joins, indent holes using the tip of a cocktail stick (toothpick). For portholes, cut out circles on both sides of the cake using the larger circle cutters and remove the sugarpaste. Cut holes in the ship, removing the sugarpaste, and cut the ends of the planks so that they look splintered. Thinly roll out the remaining black paste and fill all the spaces. Position the cake on the cake board supporting the far side of the ship on the large sugarpaste strip.

7 Colour 140g (4½oz) of modelling paste brown. Using 15g (½oz) of it, model the base of the large broken mast, cutting the end to create splinters. Roll a smaller piece for the broken top part of the mast. Make a smaller broken mast, using 7g (¼oz) of the paste. Mark the surface of each and put aside to dry.

8 To make the railings, using 30g (1oz) of brown modelling paste, roll 26 pea-sized balls and edge the top of the ship (leave some spaces so it looks damaged – see picture on page 85). Indent slightly into the top of each ball to create a recess, then model 20 long oval shapes and stick in position. Roll out 30g (1oz) and cut strips for the rail, marking wood lines and splinters as before. Curl the railing around at the front.

*The components of the anchor.*

*Attach the anchor to the side of the ship using sugar glue.*

two small flattened balls and stick onto the base and centre of the anchor. Model another, slightly larger flattened ball and stick this onto the top. Cut a hole from this with the miniature circle cutter. Leave to dry, preferably on a sheet of foam.

10 Using 45g (1½oz) of pale grey paste, model different-sized rocks and stick over the board. Split 7g (¼oz) into two pieces, one larger than the other. Roll out the smaller piece and cut two plates using the larger circle cutters. Place on the foam sheet, then indent in the centre of each using the 1.5cm (½in) circle cutter. Mark small holes using the end of a paintbrush. Model the pitcher with the larger piece, indenting into the top to open up using the end of the paintbrush, then pinch up a rim. Put it all aside to dry.

11 Split the remaining brown modelling paste in half. Make the two barrels marking wood lines as you did before. Thinly roll out the remaining pale grey trimmings and cut out strips to make the banding. Indent small holes in the banding using the tip of a cocktail stick.

12 Colour 15g (½oz) of modelling paste cream. Split 7g (¼oz) of it in half. Roll a long sausage with

*The pieces of the barrel.*

*Paint rust patches onto the barrel banding.*

*Position the rope so that it is draping over the top of the ship and down the sides.*

one half and indent lines at an angle using a cocktail stick for a rope effect. Drape this around the top of the ship and down the side. With the other half, model a small pitcher as before, and a small bottle. The small bottle is made by sticking a smaller ball on top of a larger ball and indenting the top using the end of a paintbrush. Roll out the remaining cream and cut out all the coins.

13 Colour 7g (¼oz) of modelling paste green. Thinly roll out small pieces to make the seaweed, and stick these between the stones and against the ship using sugar glue. Stick a small piece coming out of a porthole. Split the remaining modelling paste in half colouring one half yellow and the other rust. With the yellow half, make two fish indenting their fins with the side of a cocktail stick and their eyes with the tip.

## FINISHING TOUCHES

14 Stick the masts in place using sugar glue. Roll out the rust modelling paste and cut strips for around the base of each mast to hold them in place. Indent holes around the top edge using the end of a paintbrush.

15 Carefully rub silver lustre powder (petal dust/blossom tint) over the surface of the anchor, plates, pitcher and barrel strips. Brush silver onto the rust strips at the base of each flag pole and over the fish. Rub gold lustre powder onto the small pitcher, bottle and all the coins. Position on the cake board with some gold coins sprinkled on top of the cake.

16 Dilute rust food colouring paste with a little water and paint flecks onto the fish, and patches on the barrel banding and anchor. Sprinkle silver dragees randomly over the cake board and press some into the cake board covering. Dust the whole cake with edible sparkle powder.

# 12 Dancing Princesses

*With a round cake in the centre and 12 cup cakes decorated like princesses, all the little guests can take a princess home, leaving the small round cake for the adults. But I know which I would prefer!*

### CAKE AND DECORATION
- One 15cm (6in) round cake, 12 cup cakes (see page 11)
- 30cm (12in) round cake board
- 375g (12oz/1½ cups) buttercream
- 1.6kg (3lb 3½oz) sugarpaste (rolled fondant)
- Peach, orange, golden brown, egg yellow, green, mauve, blue and black food colouring pastes
- Icing (confectioner's) sugar in a sugar shaker
- Sugar glue
- 575g (1lb 2½oz) modelling paste
- 12 sugar sticks or lengths of raw, dried spaghetti
- 250g (8oz) royal icing
- Peach and yellow dusting powders (petal dust/blossom tint)

### EQUIPMENT
- Large and small rolling pins
- Small, sharp knife
- Cake smoother
- Single curve serrated crimping tool
- Bone tool
- Small pieces of foam sponge
- 8cm (3in) scalloped circle cutter
- No.1 plain piping tube (tip)
- Piping bags
- Scissors
- Fine and medium paintbrushes

## MAIN CAKE AND BOARD

1 Trim the crust from the round cake and slice the top flat. Position it on the centre of the cake board. Spread a layer of buttercream over the surface to help the sugarpaste (rolled fondant) stick in place. Split each cup cake in half and fill them with a layer of buttercream. Then spread the remaining buttercream over the surface of each cake as before.

*Cut the cup cakes in half and fill with buttercream.*

2 Colour 1kg (2lb) of sugarpaste pale peach. Moisten around the cake board edge with sugar glue. Roll out 800g (1lb 10oz) of the paste and cover the cake and cake board, trimming any excess from around the edge. To create a smooth surface, rub gently with a cake smoother. Crimp around the edge of the cake board using the crimping tool. If you haven't used this tool before, practise first on some sugarpaste trimmings. Squeeze the prongs together gently until they are just a little open. Press vertically into the sugarpaste and squeeze until nearly closed. Release gently and lift out in one movement. Then put the cake aside to dry.

*Use a crimping tool to make the border.*

## THE CUP CAKES

3 Colour 200g (6½oz) of sugarpaste mid-peach, 200g (6½oz) dark peach, 200g (6½oz) orange and, along with the remaining pale peach, split each of the four colours into three equally-sized pieces. Roll each piece out and use it to cover the cup cakes. Smooth the sugarpaste around each cake, tucking it underneath. Mark several pleats at the base of each cup cake in order to create a puff-ball effect skirt.

*Mark pleats for a puff-ball effect skirt.*

### THE PRINCESSES' BODIES

Colour 345g (11oz) of modelling paste mid-peach. Using 200g (6½oz) of it, thinly roll out and cut 12 scalloped circles using the cutter. Stick in position with one on top of each skirt. Split 90g (3oz) into 12 pieces. Model each piece into an oval-shaped body, and stick in position pinching gently to narrow the waist. Push a sugar stick down through each of the princesses' bodies to help hold their heads in place. Thinly roll out the mid-peach trimmings that are left over and then cut out thin strips with small 'v' shapes cut from both ends to make the ribbon belts. Stick these in place so that they cross over at the back of the princesses' waists.

To make the sleeves, split 30g (1oz) of mid-peach modelling paste into 24 pieces. Roll each into a ball, stick in place on the shoulders to make a sleeve, then press in with the large end of a bone tool to indent a hole for the arms to slot in, pushing up gently to round off at the top.

Colour 170g (5½oz) of modelling paste cream using a touch of golden brown food colouring paste. Split 35g (1¼oz) into 24 pieces for the arms. To make an arm, roll each piece into a

sausage shape, rounding off the end to make the hand. Press the hand a little flat. Cut a small thumb, slightly to one side, then press into the palm to round off. Indent the elbow one third of the length from the top by indenting at the front and pinching out at the back. Stick in position, pushing gently into the sleeve. Arrange the arms so that they stretch out, turning each hand slightly to make it look as though the princesses are holding hands when they come to be positioned around the cake. If necessary, use foam pieces to hold them up while they are drying or rest them on top of the skirt.

### THE PRINCESSES' FACES

Split 125g (4oz) of cream modelling paste into 12 pieces. Model oval-shaped heads and push each gently down onto the sugar sticks, securing them at the base with sugar glue. Stick tiny ball noses onto the centre of each face. Colour 30g (1oz) of modelling paste pale peach. Split another 30g (1oz) of the paste in half and colour one half dark peach and one half orange. Using half of the

pale peach paste and the remaining mid-peach, dark peach and orange pastes, split all four colours into three equally-sized pieces.

### THE HATS

To make the hats, model cone shapes and indent into the base of each to create a dip so that they sit neatly in place on the princesses' heads. Stick in position with sugar glue, slightly towards the back of the head, holding for a few moments until secure. To make the scalloped edging for each hat, model pea-sized balls of pale peach modelling paste and press flat. Cut in half and arrange five half-circles around the base of each hat, securing with sugar glue.

Thinly roll out all the remaining pale peach modelling paste and cut out two circles using the scalloped circle cutter. Cut each circle in half, then cut each half into three pieces to

*The pieces of each princess.*

*Position the arms so that it looks as though the princesses are holding hands.*

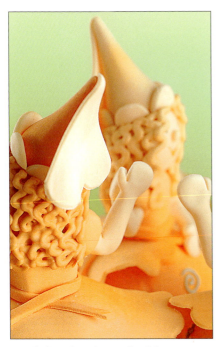

*Attach the veils to the top of each hat.*

*Use different shades of golden brown for the hair.*

small hole in the tip. Pipe hair onto two of the princesses, making wavy strands from the hat rim, down over her back and shoulders. Pipe the hair on the remaining princesses using the different shades of golden brown royal icing.

### FINISHING TOUCHES

*11* Split the remaining royal icing five ways and colour them mauve, blue, green, orange and egg yellow. Using the no.1 plain piping tube (tip), pipe different patterns onto all the princesses' skirts. Dilute the black food colouring paste with a drop of water and paint each of the princesses' eyes. Dilute some peach food colouring paste and paint their lips. When the cake is completely dry, dust randomly over the cake with yellow dusting powder (petal dust/blossom tint). To finish, dust a little peach powder over their cheeks.

make 12 triangular-shaped veils in all with three scallops along the bottom edge. Stick these onto each of the hats.

### THE PRINCESSES' HAIR

*10* Split 155g (5oz) of royal icing six ways. Colour these different shades of golden brown. Add a touch of egg yellow to one to make a yellow golden brown. Put one of the colours into a piping bag and cut a

*Pipe the hair with royal icing.*

*Dust the princesses with dusting powders.*

# Pixie Teapot House

*To make a family of pixies, I decided on a half-buried teapot for a house, with a curtain covered doorway and the teapot handle as a wood store. Cheeky little ginger-haired pixies complete the scene.*

## CAKE AND DECORATION
- *2l (4 pints/10 cups) bowl-shaped cake (see page 11)*
- *35cm (14in) round cake board*
- *1.2kg (2lb 6½oz) sugarpaste (rolled fondant)*
- *Black, cream, brown, red, green, yellow, blue, orange, mauve and golden brown food colouring pastes*
- *Icing (confectioner's) sugar in a sugar shaker*
- *375g (12oz/1½ cups) buttercream*
- *Sugar glue*
- *170g (5¾oz) modelling paste*
- *4 sugar sticks or lengths of raw, dried spaghetti*
- *22g (¾oz) royal icing*
- *Green dusting powder (petal dust/blossom tint)*

## EQUIPMENT
- *Large and small rolling pins*
- *Small, sharp knife*
- *Cake smoother*
- *Fine and medium paintbrushes*
- *Templates (see page 190)*
- *Small firm bristle paintbrush*
- *Scissors*
- *Ivy leaf cutters*
- *A few cocktail sticks (toothpicks)*
- *Medium and large calyx cutters*
- *Miniature circle cutter*
- *Small and medium petal cutters*
- *No.4 & no.1 plain piping tubes (tips)*
- *A few piping bags*

### CAKE AND BOARD

Roll out 500g (1lb) of sugarpaste (rolled fondant) and cover the cake board completely, trimming any excess from around edge, then put aside to dry. Trim the crust from the cake and slice the top flat where the cake has risen. Cut a slice from the front of the cake to create a flat area for the doorway. Trim a smaller piece to make the back for the teapot base. Cut a layer in the cake and sandwich back together with buttercream. Spread a layer of buttercream over the surface of the cake to help the sugarpaste stick.

*Spread buttercream over the shaped cake.*

Roll out 500g (1lb) of sugarpaste and cover the cake completely, smoothing around the shape and trimming any excess from around the base. Carefully pick up and place on the centre of the cake board. Rub the surface with a cake smoother to produce a smooth surface. Smooth ridges around the base of the teapot. Dilute some black food colouring paste with a little water. Stipple the colour over the doorway with

*Stipple black colour in the doorway.*

the medium paintbrush, making the colour deeper in the centre to create shadow when the curtain is positioned.

### THE TEAPOT HOUSE

Colour 75g (2½oz) of modelling paste cream. Using 30g (1oz), roll and cut out the curtain using the template (see page 190). Roll over the surface using the side of a paintbrush to create pleats, then stick in position, trimming to fit. Leave an opening on one side and gently pull the curtain away from the cake surface to make room for the pixie to be stuck behind.

To make the spout, roll 90g (3oz) of sugarpaste into a long teardrop shape. Indent into the top of the narrow end to create an opening using the end of a paintbrush, then pinch around the edge to shape. Bend at the base, and stick against the side of the teapot and on the cake board using sugar glue to secure it. For the handle, roll 45g (1½oz) of white sugarpaste into a sausage measuring 20cm (8in) in length.

Press down with a cake smoother to create a flattened surface, bend around and stick in position on the opposite side of the teapot. Smooth both ends of the handle into the surface of the teapot to remove any joins.

5 For the teapot rim, roll out the remaining white sugarpaste into a long sausage and stick around the edge of the teapot, trimming any excess from each end. Dilute some brown food colouring with a little water, until it is quite translucent. Using the firm bristle paintbrush, stipple the brown colour over the cake board. Concentrate colour around the teapot, stippling less at the edge of the cake board to create a fading effect. Colour 7g (¼oz) of modelling paste pale grey using a touch of black food colouring paste. Model different-sized ovals, press them flat and stick onto the cake board around the doorway.

*Stick a sausage-shaped rim around the doorway.*

6 Colour 15g (½oz) of modelling paste pale brown. Roll it out and cut little strips to make pieces of wood. Put some aside for later, then stick the rest in a pile at the bottom of the handle. Roll 7g (¼oz) of cream modelling paste and using the template (see page 190) cut out the wood store roof. Stick it in place using sugar glue. Model a little nail for the wood store roof. With pea-sized amounts of white modelling paste, make five mushroom stalks, and thinly roll out and cut two patchwork pieces. Stick one onto the door curtain and one onto the wood store roof. Colour 7g (¼oz) of modelling paste red. Split into three different-sized pieces and model the mushroom tops. Stick on minute

flattened balls of white to make the spots, then stick onto the stalks. Stick these in place beside the spout.

7 To make the daisies, model six pea-sized amounts of white modelling paste into little flattened circles. Cut around the edge of each with scissors to make the petals. Indent the centres by pressing in with the end of a paintbrush. Colour 15g (½oz) of the modelling paste yellow and roll minute balls to make the centre of each flower. Texture the surface of each with the tip of a cocktail stick (toothpick) and put aside to dry. Make another patch for the door curtain and two more mushrooms, sticking them in place with sugar glue.

8 To make the ivy, thinly roll out 7g (¼oz) of white modelling paste and cut out different-sized ivy using the ivy cutters. Bend each one and put them aside to dry. Roll a long, very thin sausage of white modelling paste for the ivy stalk and stick on the side of the teapot curling it upwards.

**FATHER PIXIE**

9 To make the pixies, first colour 15g (½oz) of modelling paste green, 7g (¼oz) blue, 7g (¼oz) orange and a small ball mauve. For the father pixie, split 7g (¼oz) of the green into four pieces. Using two pieces, make two legs, pinching at the ankles to round off the feet. Pinch each foot to lengthen them and indent underneath each to make the foot arches. Halfway from the ankle to the top of the leg, push in at the back and pinch out at the front to mark the knees. Stick in position so that the pixie is sitting on the teapot handle, with one leg slightly forward and crossing over the other.

10 Model the third piece of green to shape his body and stick this onto the legs, making sure it is completely straight and well balanced. Split just under 7g (¼oz) of the cream modelling paste in two, making one piece larger than the other. Split the smaller piece in half for the arms. To make an arm, roll the paste into a sausage, rounding off the end to make the hand. Press the hand a little flat, then cut a thumb on one side. Make three cuts

*The modelled pieces of the father pixie.*

along the top to separate the fingers. Gently twist each finger to lengthen, then press in the palm to round off. Pinch in halfway to indent the elbow and pinch out at the back. Make another arm, then stick both in position holding a small pile of the wood.

11 With the fourth piece of green, model a teardrop shape and push the full end down onto the work surface. Roll an edge all the way round, keeping the centre full and high. Position the large calyx cutter over the top and cut out the hat. Indent underneath and hollow it out using the end of a paintbrush, then curl up the calyx points. With trimmings, thinly roll out and cut two calyxes, one for his collar and cut up the other to make the base of the tunic. Stick on the collar, then stick on all the tunic pieces.

12 Push a sugar stick down through the top of the body, leaving about 1cm (½in) protruding to help hold the pixie's head in place. Using the larger piece of cream, first model an oval-shaped nose, then roll the rest into a rounded teardrop for his head. Push gently down onto the sugar stick, securing the head at the base with sugar glue. Indent the smile by pushing in the miniature circle cutter at an angle and

*Position the father pixie sitting on the teapot handle.*

*Stick daisies around the blue pixie.*

dimple the smile using the tip of a cocktail stick, then stick on the nose.

### BLUE GIRL PIXIE

*13* To make the girl pixie holding the daisies, split 7g (¼oz) of the cream paste in half. Split one half into four pieces for the arms and legs, and model as before. Make a nose and head as before using the other half. Split 7g (¼oz) of the blue paste in half. Model an oval-shaped body using one half and stick in position on the cake board with the legs. From the other half of blue, thinly roll out and cut five petals using the small petal cutter and stick around the base of the pixie. Stick her arms in place.

*The components of the blue girl pixie.*

*14* Roll the remaining blue paste into a teardrop shape. To make the flower hat, push the end of a paintbrush into the full end. Make five small cuts all around the edge, remove the paintbrush, then pinch out the petals. Thinly roll out a pea-sized amount of green and cut a small calyx collar. Stick this in place, then insert a sugar stick as before. Carefully stick on the head, nose and flower hat. Stick the daisies around her and place one in her hand.

### THE REST OF THE PIXIES

*15* Using the remaining coloured modelling paste, make the yellow pixie to go on the roof in the same way as you made the blue girl pixie, only slightly bigger and using the larger petal cutter for her dress. Assemble her on the cake as each piece is made. Make the pixie at the door and the pixie at the front in the same way as the father pixie but slightly smaller.

### FINISHING TOUCHES

*16* Dilute some blue food colouring with a little water. Using the fine paintbrush, paint a wavy line around the doorway and base of the teapot. Then paint the flower design on top of the teapot

Pipe the pixies' curly golden brown hair.

17 Dust the ivy with green dusting powder (petal dust/blossom tint) and scratch the veins on using the tip of a sharp knife. Stick the leaves in place along the stalk using royal icing. Dust green over the board, concentrating more colour around the teapot.

18 To make wings, thinly roll out white modelling paste and cut an ivy shape using the large cutter. Cut in half. Cut out a pattern using the tips of the piping tubes, then stick onto a pixie with a dab of royal icing. Repeat for the other. Colour the remaining royal icing golden brown. Using a piping bag with a small hole cut in the tip, pipe the curly hair.

Cut the pixie wings with an ivy leaf cutter.

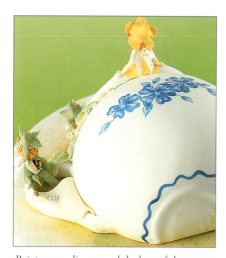

Paint a wavy line around the base of the teapot.

using the template (see page 190). Paint dots on the wood store roof patch. Dilute some red food colouring and paint the patches onto the door curtain. Finally, dilute some black food colouring and paint the stitches on each patch on the teapot and all the pixies' eyes.

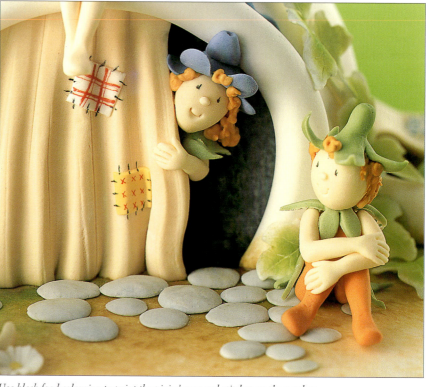

Use black food colouring to paint the pixies' eyes and stitches on the patches.

# Sleeping Beauty

*There were so many ways I could have made Sleeping Beauty. Eventually, I decided on a dark wood-effect bed with crowns, gave her chestnut hair and completed the look with dusky colours.*

## CAKE AND DECORATION
- 30cm (12in) square cake (see page 11)
- 35 x 25cm (14 x 10in) oblong cake board
- 470g (15oz) pastillage
- 1.5kg (3lb) sugarpaste (rolled fondant)
- Pink, brown, cream, jade green, blue and black food colouring pastes
- Icing (confectioner's) sugar in a sugar shaker
- 345g (11oz/scant 1½ cups) buttercream
- Sugar glue
- 75g (2½oz) royal icing
- Edible sparkle powder (petal dust/blossom tint)

## EQUIPMENT
- Templates (see page 192–3)
- Large and small rolling pins
- Small, sharp knife
- 3.5cm (1¼in), 2.5cm (1in) and 1.5cm (½in) square cutters
- Fine and medium paintbrushes
- Foam sheet
- Scissors
- A few cocktail sticks (toothpicks)
- Miniature circle cutter
- Two piping bags
- Small pieces of foam sponge

## THE BED DETAILS

1 To ensure plenty of drying time, make the headboard, footboard and bedframe first before you begin on the cake itself. Roll out 75g (2½oz) of pastillage and cut the headboard using the template on page 192. Take another 15g (½oz) of pastillage, roll it out and cut the two headboard centrepieces, then cut a small square from the top and bottom of each using the smallest square cutter. Make the footboard and its centrepieces in the same way using 75g (2½oz) of pastillage and the template on pages 192–3.

2 Roll out 60g (2oz) of pastillage and cut two strips to make the bedframe using the template on page 106. Roll out another 30g (1oz), cut small squares with the smallest square cutter and stick them along the bedframe strips with sugar glue, and on the headboard and footboard on one side only. Cut out an additional eight small squares and put them aside to dry. Thickly roll out 155g (5oz) of pastillage and cut the four bedposts using the template on page 192.

## THE ROSE STAND

3 Take 22g (¾oz) of pastillage. To make the pole, break off a piece and roll it into a long sausage measuring 9cm (3½in). Thickly roll out the rest of the pastillage and cut three squares, one with the large square cutter and two with the medium square cutter. Stick a medium-sized square on top of the larger square to create the base of the rose stand, then press in the centre with the end of a paintbrush to create a hole making sure it is as wide as the pastillage pole, and indent the underside of the remaining square, so it will fit on top of the pole, but do not assemble yet. Roll the pastillage trimmings into a ball for the top of the rose stand.

## PAINTING THE PASTILLAGE

4 Dilute some brown food colouring paste with water. With the medium paintbrush, paint a thin coat over all the pastillage pieces on one side only. Paint in one direction, letting the bristles on the paintbrush pull through the diluted food colouring to create a striped wood effect. Do not go back over the areas you have painted as this will cause the food colouring to lift off. This coat

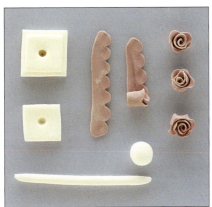

*The components of the rose stand.*

*Apply two thin coats of colour to the pastillage.*

may dry patchy. Leave for 10 minutes to dry, then paint on another thin coat. Place the pastillage pieces on the foam sheet to dry completely, preferably overnight.

### THE CAKE BOARD

5 Colour 685g (1lb 6oz) of the sugarpaste (rolled fondant) dusky pink using pink food colouring paste with a touch of brown. Roll out 440g (14oz) and cover the cake board, trimming any excess from around the edge. Make small cuts at either end to create a frill. Cut out small diamond shapes along the edge, following the frill, using the square cutter, then put the cake board aside to dry.

### THE BED

6 Trim the crust from the cake and slice the top flat. Cut the cake exactly in half and put one piece on

*Trim to round off the top two sides only.*

top of the other. Trim off 5cm (2in) from the length, then trim to round off the top two sides only. Using buttercream, sandwich the pieces together and spread a layer over the surface of the cake to help the sugarpaste stick. Roll out 345g (11oz) of the white sugarpaste and cover the cake completely, trimming off any excess from around the base. Lift carefully and position on the cake board.

7 Split 125g (4oz) of white sugar-paste in half. Roll into two oval shapes, then pinch up four corners on each oval to make two pillows. Stick onto the bed using a little sugar glue pressing down to flatten slightly where Sleeping Beauty's head will rest. Using royal icing to stick in place, position the two bed frame strips against the cake sides. Colour 125g (4oz) of sugarpaste pale pink. Thinly roll out and cut a 20cm

*Use a cocktail stick to mark the pattern.*

(8in) square for the bed cover. Lift this carefully and position it over the bed. Mark a pattern using the tip of a cocktail stick (toothpick) over the surface.

8 Colour 155g (5oz) of the sugarpaste jade green. Thinly roll out 7g (¼oz) of this and cut strips to edge the top and bottom of the bedcover. Take 15g (½oz) more, roll it out thinly and cut strips to go along the sides of the bedcover, marking pleats with the back of a knife. To create the scalloped edge, press gently between each marked line and pull downwards, then stick each strip in position with sugar glue.

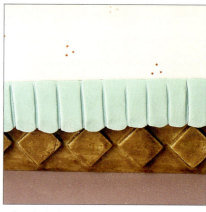

*Edge the bedcover with strips of jade green paste.*

### SLEEPING BEAUTY'S DRESS

9 Split 7g (¼oz) of dusky pink sugarpaste in half and roll it into two sausage shapes for legs. Stick them onto the bedcover with sugar glue flattening each a little. To make the skirt, thickly roll out 185g (6oz) of dusky pink sugarpaste into a triangular shape. Mark pleats from the top using the side of a paintbrush. Cut the top straight at the waist, then stick it over the legs, letting the dress drape down over the side of the bed. Mark a line across the bottom of the dress using a knife to create a border and indent a pattern using the cocktail stick. Using 22g (¾oz) of dusky pink sugarpaste, model the top of her

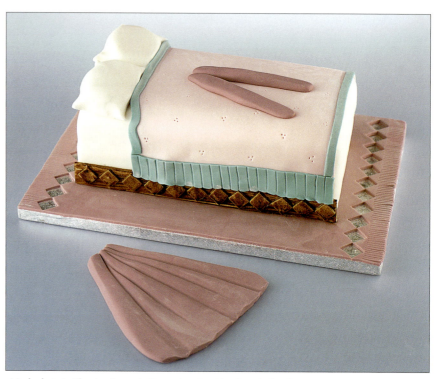

*Mark pleats in Sleeping Beauty's dress using the side of a paintbrush.*

*Stick Sleeping Beauty's top and arms in place with sugar glue.*

dress, indenting with your finger to create a dip where her chest would be. Mark lines and indent the pattern as you did with her skirt. Thinly roll out and cut a strip of paste to make her belt and stick this in position around her waist.

10 To make her sleeves, split 22g (¾oz) of dusky pink sugarpaste in half and roll two long teardrop shapes. Pinch each end to create pointed sleeves, then push in the end of a paintbrush to make holes for the hands to slot into. Pinch the sleeves halfway at the back and indent at the front to bend each elbow. Mark pleats at the shoulders using the side of a paintbrush, then stick the arms in position on the bed using sugar glue. Mark a border edging each sleeve, and mark a pattern as before.

## HER HEAD, FACE AND HANDS

11 Colour 30g (1oz) of the sugarpaste cream. Model a small flattened ball and stick it into the dip of Sleeping Beauty's dress to make her chest. Roll out and cut a tiny strip of dusky pink sugarpaste and use it to edge around the top of her dress. Roll 22g (¾oz) of cream sugarpaste into an oval shape to make her head and stick it in position, resting on the pillow. Indent her eyes, eyelids and smile using the miniature circle cutter pressed in at an angle. Stick a tiny ball in the centre of her face to make her nose. Using two pea-sized amounts of cream sugarpaste for her hands, model teardrop shapes

and press them flat. Cut thumbs on opposite sides of the two teardrops, then three straight cuts along the top to separate her fingers. Gently twist and smooth each finger to lengthen it. Pinch gently at the wrists to round off the hands and create a point that slots into each sleeve. Stick one of her hands in place draping off the end of the bed and the other resting on her dress.

## FINISHING TOUCHES

12 Thinly roll out 22g (¾oz) of white sugarpaste and cut two strips for skirt panels, slightly wider at the base. Mark down the edges using a knife, then stick them in position with sugar glue. Mark the pattern along the edge and at the base of the dress using the tip of a cocktail stick. Use the remaining dusky pink sugarpaste to make the roses (see page 97): roll thin sausages and press them slightly flat, scallop one edge by pressing in with your finger and pulling downwards, roll it up and pinch at the base, then stroke out the petals. Make 10 roses and put aside to dry.

*Pipe her chestnut brown hair around her face and down onto her shoulders.*

*13* Colour the remaining royal icing chestnut brown using brown food colouring with a touch of pink. Put the royal icing into a piping bag and cut a small hole in the tip. Pipe long, wavy strands of hair over her head, building up from the pillow to the top of her head. Assemble the rose stand using the brown royal icing to stick it together. Put this aside and leave it to dry completely using pieces of foam sponge for support. Using dabs of brown royal icing, stick the headboard and footboard in position with the painted side against the bed, and the bedposts either side of each. Press these gently in position and take care that they are completely straight.

*14* Using 7g (¼oz) of pastillage, model four small balls for the top of the bedposts, then split the remaining piece in half and shape into ovals and stick on the centre of the headboard and footboard at the top. Take another 7g (¼oz) split into two pieces, one larger than the other, and roll into balls. Stick the larger ball onto the centre of the headboard with the smaller one on the footboard.

*15* Thinly roll out the remaining pastillage and cut out the crowns for the bed, one at a time, using the template on page 192. Moisten with sugar glue, then wrap around the ball shape, smoothing the join closed.

Pastillage dries very quickly, so if the crowns crack before you have time to apply them, just cut out the triangles and stick them on individually. Using diluted brown food colouring paste, paint the unpainted sides of the headboard and footboard. Stick the centre panels and small squares in place. Paint all the unpainted headboard and footboard pieces as before.

*16* When the rose stand is dry, stick on all the roses using the remaining brown royal icing. Split 125g (4oz) of jade green paste into 16 equally-sized pieces. Model into oval

*Stick the roses on the stand with royal icing.*

shapes and mark the surface to create pleats using the side of a paintbrush. Pinch each end to a point and stick in place, draped around the headboard and footboard.

*17* Use the remaining jade green sugarpaste to make the bow for the rose stand. Thinly roll out and cut two strips, making them both wider at one end than the other. Cut a 'v' shape in each wide end and mark pleats with the side of a paintbrush. Stick these against the rose stand pole. Model a square-shaped centre tie, then model teardrop shapes for the bow, indenting pleats as before. Stick this in position using sugar glue, then stick the rose stand in place by the side of the bed.

*18* Split the remaining sugarpaste in half and colour one half pale blue and the other pale dusky pink. Using both colours, as well as the jade green and pale pink trimmings, roll

*Use trimmings to fill squares on the board.*

out and cut squares to fill in the spaces on the cake board. Mark the surface of each with the tip of a cocktail stick.

*19* Dust Sleeping Beauty's eyelids with sparkle powder (petal dust/blossom tint) and dust sparkle on the dress and panel borders. Dilute black food colouring paste with a few drops of water then, using the fine paintbrush, paint on very faint eyelashes.

*Use the remaining pastillage to make crowns to go on top of the headboard and footboard.*

# Genie

*I nearly put this genie on a magic carpet, but then decided to keep it simple and create a cloudy effect on the cake board. Using two basic bowl-shaped cakes, this genie can be decorated in next to no time.*

## CAKE AND DECORATION

- One 1l (2 pint/5 cup) and one 625ml (1¼ pint/3 cup) bowl-shaped cakes (see page 11)
- 25cm (10in) round cake board
- 1.7kg (3lb 6oz) sugarpaste (rolled fondant)
- Mauve, yellow, brown, jade green and black food colouring pastes
- Icing (confectioner's) sugar in a sugar shaker
- Pink dusting powder (petal dust/blossom tint)
- 375g (12oz/1½ cups) buttercream
- Sugar glue

## EQUIPMENT

- Large rolling pin
- Small, sharp knife
- Medium paintbrush
- Cake smoother
- 1.5cm (½in) circle cutter

### CAKE AND BOARD

1. Colour 470g (15oz) of sugarpaste (rolled fondant) mauve. Roll out 315g (10oz) and cover the board, trimming excess from the edge. Using a paintbrush, dust the board with pink dusting powder (petal dust/blossom tint), concentrating the colour in patches, then put aside to dry.

2. Trim the crust from each cake and slice the tops from each where they have risen. Cut a layer in the large cake. Trim a curved recess for the facial area from the front of the small cake.

*Cut out a recess for the genie's face.*

Using buttercream, sandwich the layers of the large cake together, then spread a layer of buttercream over the surface of both cakes to help the sugarpaste stick.

3. Colour 825g (1lb 10½oz) of the sugarpaste yellow. Roll 90g (3oz) into a long, tapering teardrop shape and press the full end against the base of the large cake, smoothing the sugarpaste in line with the surface of the cake to remove any ridges. Roll out 440g (14oz) of the

*Attach a tapering trail to the larger cake.*

sugarpaste and cover the cake completely, smoothing around the shape and tucking the sugarpaste underneath. Use a cake smoother to create a smooth surface. Place on the cake board and curl the tapering piece of paste round at the front. Roll out 280g (9oz) of yellow sugarpaste and cover the small cake, trimming excess from around the base. Trim around the edge of the face to outline the turban and smooth to round off. Press gently into the front of the turban to indent it slightly. Stick the cakes together with sugar glue.

*Cover the cakes with yellow sugarpaste.*

## THE FACE

4 Colour 315g (10oz) of sugarpaste light brown. Roll 45g (1½oz) into an oval shape. Press down onto the work surface, making the edge of the oval shape flatter, then press this onto the facial area, smoothing it into the recess. Indent the sugarpaste slightly at the eye area using your finger.

5 Model a pea-sized amount of white sugarpaste into a flattened oval shape, then cut in half. Stick them onto the face to make the eyes. Model two tiny pupils using brown paste. Roll two tiny tapering sausage shapes for under each eye, and stick them in position curving around the eye. Model a small ball nose and stick onto the centre of his face, pushing upwards to make it fuller at the top.

*Use pale jade for the edge of his waistcoat.*

## THE WAISTCOAT

6 To make the genie's waistcoat, thinly roll out the remaining mauve sugarpaste and cut an oblong piece measuring 10 x 40cm (4 x 16in). Moisten his body with sugar glue. Roll up one end

*Roll a mauve waistcoat around his body leaving a gap at the front.*

*Stick the strip of jade in place with sugar glue.*

of the paste, stick it in position at the front, then unroll the waistcoat around his body and trim away any excess leaving a gap at the front. Colour 7g (¼oz) of sugarpaste pale jade. Thinly roll this out and cut a strip to edge the waistcoat. Moisten around the waistcoat with sugar glue, then stick the strip in position.

## THE ARMS AND HANDS

7 Split the remaining brown sugarpaste in half. To make an arm, roll a sausage with one half and indent in the centre to mark the elbow by pinching all the way round. Indent twice more either side of the elbow to shape a muscle at the top and the wrist at the opposite end. Press the rounded end under the wrist a little flat and cut a thumb slightly to one side, then cut three times along the top to create fingers. Twist each finger to lengthen it and remove ridges. Indent nails by pressing in with the end of a paintbrush. Make the opposite arm and stick both in position, pressing the shoulders firmly in place with the arms crossing over at the front.

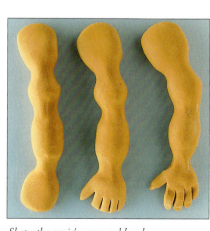

*Shape the genie's arms and hands.*

*Stick his moustache and beard on with sugar glue.*

### THE LAMP

*9* Make the genie's lamp with 7g (¹/₄oz) of yellow sugarpaste. First, roll it into a teardrop shape and then pull out the point and twist it upwards in order to make the lamp's spout. Indent into the top to mark the lid by pressing in gently with the circle cutter. With the remaining yellow sugarpaste, model a little handle for the

*Model the genie's lamp with yellow sugarpaste.*

### FACIAL DETAILS

*8* Colour the remaining sugarpaste black. Roll two small pupils and press onto the centre of each eye. Model tiny sausages of paste and stick edging the top of each eye. Using pea-sized amounts, model two eyebrows. Split 15g (¹/₂oz) of black paste in half. Model two tapering teardrop shapes for his hair and stick them onto the front of his turban. Split 22g (³/₄oz) in half and shape his moustache, sticking it in position right under his nose, curling the ends upwards. Model the beard using the remaining black and stick it in position, making a small dip in the centre to mark the genie's mouth. Using the mauve and jade green trimmings, model a mauve teardrop shape to go on the front of his turban and stick on a jade green flattened ball.

side, a flattened circle for the base, and roll two small balls to make the lid handle on the top.

Position the lamp on the cake board in front of the genie, securing it in place with sugar glue. Roll out the genie's trail of smoke into a tapering sausage shape and stick the narrow end onto the spout. Smooth with your fingers to remove the join so that it looks as though the genie has just appeared out of the lamp.

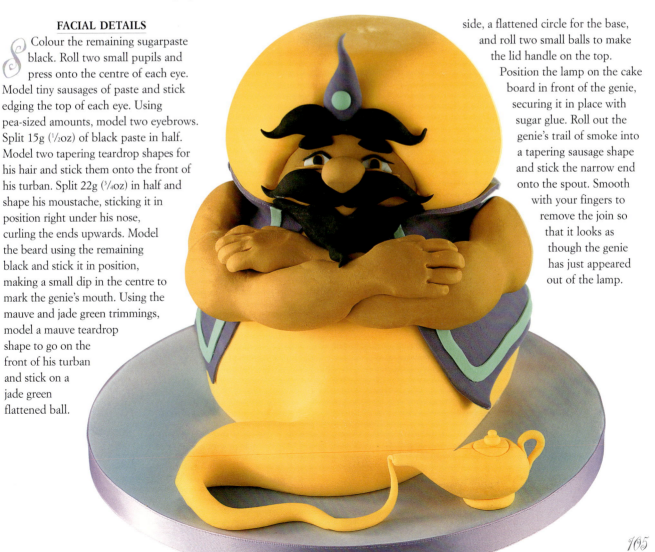

# Sugar Plum Fairy

*The Sugar Plum Fairy is the fairy queen from the enchanting ballet,* The Nutcracker Suite, *so I dressed her properly, and as prettily as all little ballerinas on their own first nights.*

## CAKE AND DECORATION
- *20cm (8in) round cake (see page 11)*
- *35cm (14in) petal-shaped cake board*
- *1kg (2lb) sugarpaste (rolled fondant)*
- *220g (7oz/1 scant cup) buttercream*
- *Pink, cream and brown food colouring pastes*
- *Icing (confectioner's) sugar in a sugar shaker*
- *90g (3oz) modelling paste*
- *Sugar glue*
- *Sugar stick or length of raw, dried spaghetti*
- *Pink, lilac and mother of pearl edible lustre powders (petal dust/blossom tint)*

## EQUIPMENT
- *Large and small rolling pins*
- *Sharp knife*
- *Garrett frill cutter*
- *A few cocktail sticks (toothpicks)*
- *Fine and medium paintbrushes*
- *Miniature circle cutter*
- *Large and small blossom plunger cutters*
- *Small piece of foam sponge*

## CAKE AND BOARDS

1 Roll out 500g (1lb) of sugarpaste (rolled fondant) and cover the cake board completely, trimming any excess away from around edge. Then put it aside to dry.

2 Trim the crust from the cake and slice the top flat where the cake has risen. Trim around the base, cutting at an inwards angle. Cut three triangular shaped wedges out of the top of the front half of the cake. To give height to the back of the dress, position these cut-out wedges on the top of the back half of the

*Cut and position the cake wedges for the skirt.*

cake. Using buttercream, sandwich the wedges in place, then spread a layer of buttercream over the surface of the cake to help the sugarpaste stick.

3 Thinly roll out 220g (7oz) of white sugarpaste and cover the cake, smoothing around the shape and trimming any excess from base. Do not worry if this covering looks untidy because it will all be covered later. Position the cake on the centre of the board.

## THE FAIRY'S SKIRT

4 Colour 60g (2oz) of sugarpaste deep dusky pink using pink food colouring paste with a touch of brown. Thinly roll out 7g (¼oz) and cut a frill using the Garrett cutter. Gently roll the side of a cocktail stick (toothpick) over each scallop to thin and frill. Cut the

*Use a Garrett cutter to make the skirt frills.*

frill open and, using sugar glue, stick this around the base of the cake. Make more frills, building them up around the cake, adding 15g (½oz) of white sugarpaste to the remaining dusky pink after each layer to create a toning effect.

*Build up layers of frills around the cake.*

*Back view of the Sugar Plum Fairy.*

indent her palm. Bend halfway up the arm to make the elbow, and pinch at the back to shape it. Stick in position, pressing the shoulder firmly. Make the opposite arm.

8 Roll a tapering sausage using 7g (¼oz) of dusky pink sugarpaste and press it flat. Make a mark down the centre by pressing down with the side of the paintbrush. Moisten it at the back with sugar glue and then wrap it around the back of the ballerina, around her shoulders, and finishing at the front of her bodice to hide the join.

### THE FAIRY'S HEAD

9 For the head, roll 22g (¾oz) of cream modelling paste into a rounded teardrop shape. Slightly flatten the face, then push it down onto the sugar stick, securing it with sugar glue. Push the tip of a cocktail stick into the centre of the face to use as a guide. Mark the eyes slightly above and either side of this centre guide by pushing the miniature circle cutter in at an angle to indent semi-circles. For the eyelids, use the miniature circle cutter again to mark a fainter semi-circle from the outside corner to halfway across each eye. Using a minute amount of cream sugarpaste, roll two tiny teardrops for her ears,

5 Roll out 155g (5oz) of white sugarpaste and cut a 20cm (8in) circle for the top of the skirt. Using the end of a paintbrush, roll the side into the surface to mark indentations and thin and frill the edge. Lift carefully and position the skirt on top of the frills, smoothing around the shape. Then secure it in place with sugar glue.

### THE FAIRY'S BODY

6 Use 22g (¾oz) of white modelling paste to make the bodice, pinching gently to thin the paste at the shoulders. Colour 60g (2oz) of the modelling paste cream. Using just over 7g (¼oz), shape the shoulders, and pinch and smooth at the top to create the neck. Stick the shoulders onto the bodice using a touch of sugar glue and then attach this to the centre of the cake. Slightly moisten the sugar stick with sugar glue and then carefully push it down through the neck and bodice to provide support. This may cause the neck to bulge, so smooth the neck upwards, over the sugar stick and trim away any excess.

7 Split just over 7g (¼oz) of cream modelling paste into two equally-sized pieces. To make an arm, roll one piece into an 8cm (3in) long sausage. Pinch at one end to round off a hand, then press it down to flatten it slightly. Cut a thumb on one side, then make three cuts across the top to separate her fingers. Twist each finger gently to lengthen it, then

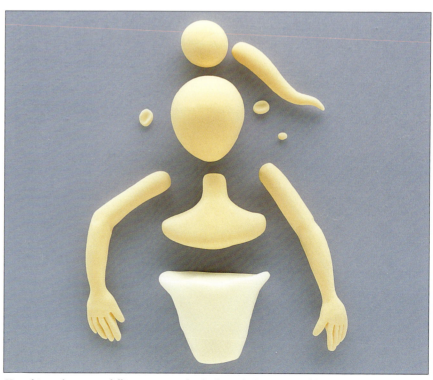

*Use white and cream modelling paste to make the fairy's bodice, arms and head.*

108

*Use a fine paintbrush to paint the fairy's delicate facial features and hair.*

*Make flowers with the blossom plunger cutters.*

indenting the centre of each with the end of a paintbrush, and a little ball nose. With a ball of cream modelling paste, model the bun for the top of her head, then roll a long teardrop-shaped pony tail, sticking it in place with sugar glue.

*10* Dust her eyelids with lilac lustre powder (petal dust/blossom tint). To make her cheeks blush, rub on a little pink dusting powder. Dilute the brown food colouring paste with some water. Using a fine paintbrush, paint her hair, and faint eyebrows and eyelashes. If they still look too heavy, wash your brush and lift off any excess colour. Paint her lips with a little diluted pink colouring paste.

### THE FAIRY'S BALLET SHOES

*11* Split 7g (¼oz) of cream modelling paste into two and use these to model two pointed-toed feet. First roll a thick sausage out of one, then make a twist a third of the way along to shape the ankle. Pull the remaining part down, shaping the arch of her foot. Make the other foot and then with pale pink trimmings cut thin

ribbons to stick around the ankle to make the ballet shoe laces. Dust the feet with pink dusting powder to outline the ballet shoes, then carefully stick in position with sugar glue – make the shoe at the back of the cake with the heel facing upwards so that the ballerina is doing the splits.

### FINISHING TOUCHES

*12* Using dusky pink trimmings, roll out and cut blossom flowers using the large and small blossom plunger cutters. Each flower is

cut, then pressed into foam to give it more shape. Stick blossoms around the ballerina's bun for her crown, a flower on her bodice and the remaining flowers in groups around the cake board. With the white trimmings, roll tiny ball shapes to make the flower centres and her earrings.

*13* Dust the skirt from the waist with pink dusting powder. Rub the mother of pearl dusting powder around the edge of the dress as well as around the edge of the cake board.

*Position her ballet shoes either side of the dress.*

*Make a crown for the fairy out of blossom flowers and dust her dress with pink dusting powder.*

# Dragon Castle

Dragons are always rather frightening in mythology, so I designed this one to appeal to someone older. Although I'm sure that smaller children would love the thrill of this scary beast.

## Cake & decoration

(See pages 11,20–1 for recipes and cake chart)
18cm (7in) and 20cm (8in) round cakes
25cm (10in) round cake board
440g (14oz/1 3/4 cups) buttercream
1.25kg (2 1/2lb) sugarpaste (rolled fondant)
Cream, black, orange, green and brown food colouring pastes
Icing (powdered) sugar in a shaker
Sugar glue
625g (1 1/4lb) modelling paste
Red and green powder food colourings
Edible gold powder

## Equipment

Plain and serrated kitchen knives
4cm (1 1/2in) and 5cm (2in) circle cutters
Large rolling pin
Small glue brush
1cm ( 1/2in) square cutter
Templates (see page 198)
A few cocktail sticks
Pieces of foam sponge
Medium paintbrush
New small flexible scourer
Dusting brush

## Castle

1 Trim the crust from both cakes, level the tops and cut a layer in each. Cut the smaller cake in half and place one half on top of the larger cake. Trim around the cake, creating sloping sides, and place on the cake board. From the remaining half, cut three circles, two using the 4cm (1 1/2in) cutter and the third with the 5cm (2in) cutter, and sandwich the two smaller circles together with buttercream to make the tall tower. Sandwich all layers together *(see a)* and spread a thin layer of buttercream over the surface of all cakes to help the sugarpaste (rolled fondant) stick.

2 Colour 1kg (2lb) of sugarpaste dark cream, kneading until the colour is marbled and nearly blended. Put the two tower cakes aside. Roll out and cover the cake and cake board completely, smoothing around the shape, then trim excess from around the

a

edge. For a rock effect, slice a very thin piece of sugarpaste from the surface of the covering in small amounts around the cake sides, taking care not to cut too deep and reveal the cake underneath (see b). Indent at the front to make a recess for the winding steps.

## Towers and doors

3 Colour 250g (8oz) of sugar-paste pale cream. Roll out 220g (7oz) and cut strips to cover around the sides of both towers, smoothing the joins closed. To remove the joins completely, rub gently in a circular motion with a little icing sugar on your fingertips. To cover the tops, roll out 30g (1oz), place the top of each tower down onto it and cut around. Stick each tower onto the cake using a little sugar glue.

4 Cut out a doorway in each tower using the templates. Colour 7g (¹/₄oz) of modelling paste black, thinly roll out and cut pieces to fill both. Reserve the trimmings for later. Colour 265g (8¹/₂oz) of modelling paste pale cream. Roll out 45g (1¹/₂oz) and cut strips to fit around the top of each tower, 2cm (³/₄ in) in depth. From the top of each, cut out small squares with the 1cm (¹/₂in) square cutter. Mark slits for windows using the tip of a knife, then stick around the top of each tower, smoothing the join closed. Mark longer windows on the towers.

5 With 125g (4oz) of pale cream modelling paste, and using the step photograph as a guide (see c), make four different-sized towers, marking slit windows on each as before. Indent little doorways and fill with black modelling paste trimmings. Colour 75g (2¹/₂oz) of modelling paste deep cream. Make four different-sized pointed roofs using 60g (2oz), then stick onto the top of each tower.

6 With pale cream trimmings, roll two sausages to edge the top of each doorway, rolling each thinner in the centre and bend halfway. Thickly roll out 60g (2oz) of pale cream modelling paste and cut the stepped archway using the template (see page 198). For the steps winding down the front of the cake, cut little strips graduating in size using 7g (¹/₄oz) of pale cream, and stick in place. With the remaining pale cream, make the doorstep and cut strips for the arches, bend round and re-cut the ends so they sit against the cake sides. With trimmings, model some oval-shaped stones for around the base of the castle. Make some more, using the deeper cream, and cut little strips for windowsills.

## Dragon

7 Colour 250g (8oz) of modelling paste orange. For the dragon's body, roll 100g (3¹/₂oz) into a tapering sausage, 35cm (14in) in length. Immediately stick in place, winding around the castle with the neck end resting on top of the small tower and leaving room for the head. Shape the dragon's head

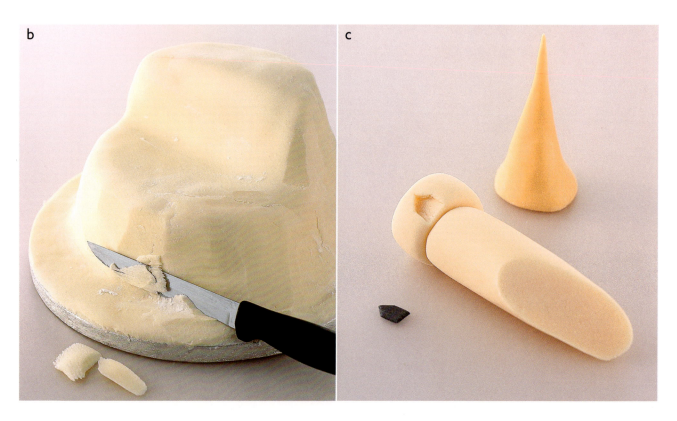

using 22g (³/₄oz) of orange modelling paste, cutting his mouth open with a knife. Wedge a small piece of foam into the mouth until set. Using the step photograph as a modelling guide (see d), model all the facial features. Remove the piece of foam before applying the teeth and rub gently at each join to remove. To make the fans either side and at the back of his head, indent into flattened teardrop shapes using the paintbrush handle, then pinch up little points in between. Colour 15g (¹/₂oz) of modelling paste green. Using a tiny amount with a little black modelling paste, make his eyes.

8 Split 7g (¹/₄oz) of orange modelling paste into three pieces. Shape the triangular point for the end of his tail with one piece, indenting twice with the paintbrush handle. Make the arms with the other two pieces. First, roll into sausages, rounding off one end. Cut twice into the top and pinch out three claws. For feet,

split another 7g (¹/₄oz) in half and roll into sausage shapes. Bend each half way and press one half flat, pinching out a heel at the back. Cut twice at the end of each foot and pinch out three claws. Using 7g (¹/₄oz) of orange, shape different-sized, flattened oval shapes for scales and stick over the dragon's back, with the larger scales down the centre.

## Dragon's wings and trees

9 Split the remaining orange modelling paste in half and use for the two wings. To make the wings, use the template and step photograph (see e). Use the handle of the paintbrush, rolled over the surface, to indent the ridges. Stick each wing in place, holding for a few moments until secure, or use small pieces of foam sponge to support until dry. Colour the remaining modelling paste brown and, with the remaining green, make six trees in different sizes, texturing the green by rolling over the scourer.

## Magical touches

10 Mix red and green powder colours separately with a little icing sugar. Dust red over the dragon, keeping the colour more concentrated centrally down his back. Dust a little green powder colour onto the cake board, around the base of the trees. Randomly dust the whole cake and dragon with gold powder.

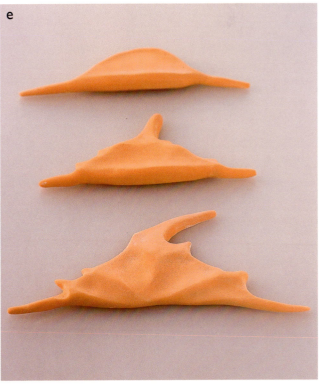

d

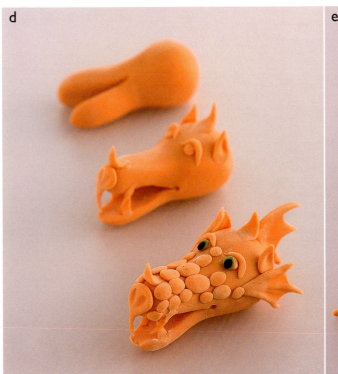

e

# Rock Monster

I nearly put this trio of elfins camping down for the night beside a friendly rock monster. But I thought I would make it a little scary, so they all became dinner instead!

## Cake & decoration

(See pages 11, 20–1 for recipes and cake chart)
10cm (4in), 15cm (6in) and 20cm (8in) round cakes
35cm (14in) round cake board
1.75kg (3½lb) sugarpaste (rolled fondant)
Blue, black, brown, cream, green and egg yellow food colouring pastes
Icing (powdered) sugar in a shaker
470g (15oz/scant 2 cups) buttercream
Sugar glue
140g (4½oz) modelling paste
Dark green and egg yellow powder food colourings
Edible sparkle powder

## Equipment

Large rolling pin
Plain and serrated kitchen knives
Small glue brush
A few cocktail sticks
Fine paintbrush
Pieces of foam sponge
Dusting brush

## Cake board and cake

1 Colour the sugarpaste (rolled fondant) blue/grey using a touch each of blue and black food colouring pastes. Roll out 500g (1lb) and cover the cake board completely, marking an uneven surface by pressing with the rolling pin, then trim excess from around the edge. Trim the crust from each cake and level the tops. Cut the top edge from the two larger cakes and stack one on top of the other. Trim the small cake to round the top, then cut into the sides to create an uneven surface. Position on top of the other cakes, slightly towards the back.

## Rock monster

2 To shape the mouth, remove a wedge from the top of the second cake and trim a curved line at the front to round off a full bottom lip (see a). Place the cake on the board, slightly towards the back. Use

a

cake trimmings to fill out around the base of the cake. Sandwich the layers together with buttercream, then spread a layer over the surface of the cakes to help the sugarpaste stick. For the rock feet, make two piles of cake trimmings and spread completely with buttercream, filling any gaps.

3 Roll out 875g (1$\frac{3}{4}$lb) of blue/grey sugarpaste and cover the cake completely, smoothing the paste into the mouth recess and around the shape. Trim excess from around the base and press the knife around the edge to curve it under. Roll out 90g (3oz) and cover the two remaining feet cakes, trim excess around the base and then position on the cake board.

4 For the rock hands, split 125g (4oz) of blue/grey sugarpaste in half and shape into rounded teardrop shapes. Curve each round slightly and stick against the sides of the rock, near the corners of the mouth. Split 30g (1oz) and model angular rocks for arms. Using 100g (3$\frac{1}{2}$oz), model different-sized angular rocks and stick in position around the cake, piling a few on top of his head. Using the step photograph as a guide (see b) and the blue/grey trimmings, model all the shapes to build up his facial features, colouring his pupils a slightly darker shade of grey.

5 Colour 7g ($\frac{1}{4}$oz) of modelling paste dark brown. Roll different-sized twigs for the fire and three twigs for the backpacks, marking the surface of each with a knife. Arrange the fire twigs in a circle at the front of the cake board. Put aside the twigs for the backpacks to allow to dry.

## Elfins

6 To make the elfins, first colour 45g (1$\frac{1}{2}$oz) of modelling paste cream. For bodies, split just under 7g ($\frac{1}{4}$oz) in half and model two oval shapes. Stick one on top of each rock hand, filling the recess. Colour pea-sized amounts of modelling paste green. Roll out into triangle shapes and indent pleats with a cocktail stick (toothpick) for tunics, sticking the point of the triangle over one shoulder.

7 To make the heads, using the step photograph as a guide (see c), roll 7g ($\frac{1}{4}$oz) for each into oval shapes and then pinch out long noses. Push the end of a paintbrush into each mouth area and move up and down to open them wide. Colour a minute piece of modelling paste black and shape four tiny oval-shaped eyes. Edge the top and bottom of each eye with tiny tapering sausage shapes. For ears, model teardrop shapes using pea-sized amounts, and indent in the centre of each. Pinch the ears at the pointed end to lengthen, then stick in place level with the nose.

b

c

**8** Colour just over 7g (¹/₄oz) deep cream and a pea-sized amount deep golden brown, using brown with a touch of egg yellow. Model tiny teardrop shapes for hair and eyebrows. For arms, use just under 15g (¹/₂oz) of cream modelling paste, split into four equal pieces, and the step photograph as a modelling guide (see d). Stick the arms in place as each is made, bending into position and, if required, use foam pieces for support until completely dry.

**9** Using the remaining cream, model little sausage-shaped legs, making the eaten elfin's legs longer, pinching a knee half way on each. Colour 45g (1¹/₂oz) of modelling paste brown. Split 22g (³/₄oz) into six equal sized pieces. To make a shoe, first roll a long teardrop shape and pinch up at the full end. Hollow this out slightly by pinching up a rim. Mark little pleats, using a cocktail stick, and indent by pinching underneath to shape the arch of the foot.

Make all the shoes and stick in place as each are made.

## Backpacks

**10** To make a backpack (see e), shape 7g (¹/₄oz) of brown modelling paste into a teardrop. Press down onto the pointed end to indent, pushing up excess either side. Pinch this excess up, twist each to a point and wrap around the end of a backpack twig. Thinly roll out the remaining brown for mats and, using the knife, score two oblong shapes measuring 5 × 8cm (2 × 3in) on the surface. Carefully tear out the oblong shapes – this will create a ragged edge but keep neat lines. Fold one over and roll up another and stick in position on the cake board. With trimmings, make some more twigs for the fire.

**11** Colour 7g (¹/₄oz) of modelling paste pale brown and, using the remaining dark cream, make two further backpacks as before.

## Camp fire

**12** For the fire, colour the remaining modelling paste egg yellow, kneading until streaky, then shape into a teardrop. Cut into the pointed end with a knife to shape flames and pull each up, tearing off the excess paste. Stick the flames in position on the centre of the fire twigs.

## Magical touches

**13** Mix dark green and egg yellow powder food colourings separately with a little icing (powdered) sugar. Brush green colour around the cake board and rocks, and egg yellow colour around the surrounding area of the fire to create fire glow. Brush the whole cake with edible sparkle powder.

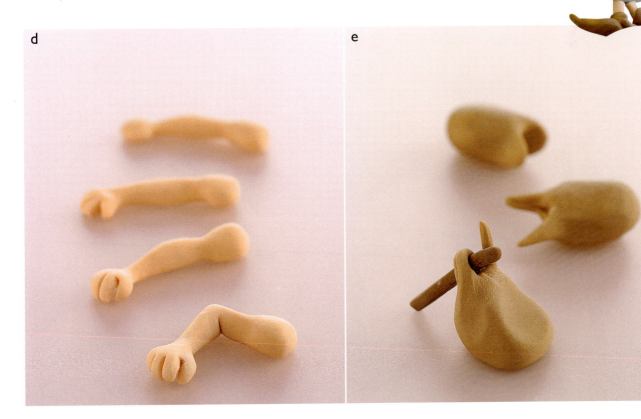

d

e

# Emerald City

I made lots of jewel-coloured fairies to show how different they all could be, but choosing just one jewel in a birthstone colour would beautifully personalize this cake.

## Cake & decoration

(See pages 11, 20–1 for recipes and cake chart)
3 x 15cm (6in) round cakes
25cm (10in) round cake board
1.875kg (3¾lb) sugarpaste (rolled fondant)
Mint green, red, blue, violet, egg yellow, golden brown, brown and black food colouring pastes
440g (14oz/1¾ cups) buttercream
Icing (powdered) sugar in a shaker
Sugar glue
75g (2½oz) modelling paste
12 sugar sticks
Green, red, blue, violet, silver, gold and clear green edible glitters
90g (3oz) royal icing

## Equipment

Large rolling pin
Serrated and plain kitchen knives
Miniature and 5cm (2in) circle cutters
Length of thread
Ruler
Cake smoother
Templates (see page 198)
A few cocktail sticks
Small daisy and star cutters
6 paper piping bags
Fine and medium paintbrushes
Pieces of foam sponge

## Cake board and cake

1 Colour the sugarpaste (rolled fondant) green. Roll out 315g (10oz) and cover the board. Press the rolling pin into the surface to indent ridges. Trim excess from around the edge, then put aside to dry. Trim the crust from each cake and slice the tops flat. Cut a layer in two of the round cakes and sandwich all four layers together with buttercream. Cut out four circles from the third cake, using the 5cm (2in) circle cutter. Sandwich together to make the two towers, trimming each to a total height of 12cm (5in) (see a). Spread buttercream over the surface of the cakes.

2 Roll out 100g (3½oz) of green sugarpaste and place the top of the large cake down onto it. Cut around, lift and put back on its base. Measure around the cake, using the length of thread, and cut to size. Measure the depth of the cake with a ruler. Roll out

a

410g (13oz) of green and cut an oblong using these measurements. Sprinkle with icing sugar to prevent sticking, roll up from one end, position against the cake and unroll around the sides (see b). Trim excess from join and glue together. To remove the join completely, rub gently with a little icing sugar. Position the cake on the cake board, slightly towards the back, and rub the surface with a cake smoother. Cover the two tower cakes in the same way using 315g (10oz) of green sugarpaste.

3 To make the structural wall for the large cake, roll out 410g (13oz) of green sugarpaste and cut an oblong measuring 38x20cm

b

(15x8in). Measure 14cm (5½in) from the bottom on the left-hand side and cut at an angle straight across to the top corner on the right-hand side. Moisten the cake with sugar glue, place the shortest side against the front and smooth around the cake. The highest point at the back will be a little floppy at first: just keep smoothing it back into place until it begins to firm. If the edges are uneven, use a cake smoother to push them back.

4 Using the template (see page 198), cut out a doorway in the front, removing the structural wall piece only. Thinly roll out this piece of paste and cut out the door. Stick in position and mark holes using the tip of a cocktail stick (tooth-pick). Roll out trimmings and cut two strips for steps, the bottom step slightly thicker than the top. Model a small door handle.

5 Using the remaining green sugarpaste, make the walls for the two towers, using the template

(see page 198), and stick in place as before. Using a knife, mark crosses for windows and indent into each corner with the end of a paint-brush (see c). Using sugar glue, stick each tower in position, checking that the top tower is sitting completely straight.

## Fairies

6 Each fairy is built up flat until the hair is piped. Colour 15g (½oz) of modelling paste green, and then 7g (¼oz) each for red, blue, violet and egg yellow, with 7g (¼oz) white. Put aside half of the green until later.

7 To make a fairy (see d), split the respective coloured modelling paste in half and use one half to shape the dress. First, model a teardrop shape and press to flatten slightly. Indent radiating lines using the paintbrush handle and smooth along the bottom to thin and frill. With the remaining half, roll out and cut a collar and crown using the daisy cutter, then cover

c

to prevent drying. Cut a star and stick to the top of a sugar stick to make the wand. Model the remainder into four teardrop shapes for wings, with two slightly larger, and press flat.

8 Paint sugar glue over the bottom of each fairy's dress, wings, crown and wand, and sprinkle with glitter. Split 22g (³/₄ oz) of modelling paste into six equally sized pieces. Colour each a different skin tone using golden brown and brown food colouring pastes. Split each piece in half and roll into a ball-shaped head. Indent a smile using the miniature circle cutter, pressed in at an angle, then dimple the corners using the tip of a cocktail stick. Model a tiny ball nose for each.

9 Using the remaining skin tone modelling paste, make two legs and two arms with each shade. To make a leg, roll the paste into a thin sausage and bend one end round to shape the foot. Pinch out a heel at the back and press either side of the foot to narrow and lengthen. Pinch gently underneath to indent the arch of the foot. Pinch around the ankle and then stick in position.

10 To make an arm, roll the paste into a thin sausage, rounding off one end for the hand. Press the hand to flatten slightly and then stick the arms in place with the collar on top. Push a sugar stick down through the dress, leaving a little protruding to help hold the head in place. Make a small hole in the base of each head, using a cocktail stick, and press onto the sugar stick, securing at the base of the head with a little sugar glue.

11 Stick each fairy in place on the castle, using dabs of royal icing. Hold each for a few moments until secure. Split the royal icing into six and colour light blonde and dark blonde using a touch of egg yellow food colouring paste, pale golden brown, and the remaining three different shades of brown. Put the coloured icings into piping bags and cut a small hole in the tip. Pipe the hair by waving the bag gently from side to side to create waves and curls, then place on their crowns. Stick the fairies' wands in place.

## Magical touches

12 Using the remaining green modelling paste, roll into balls and roll in green glitter while they are soft, so the glitter will stick to the surface (see e). Stick together in groups of three and use to decorate around the top edges. Finally, brush a tiny amount of the clear green glitter all over the cake.

13 When the cake is dry, dilute black food colouring paste with a little water and carefully paint the eyes on the fairies using the fine paintbrush.

d

e

# Ramshackle Village

A little cobbled street where trolls live in odd dwellings, all misshapen and rickety, is the last place where you would expect to find treasure. But that is exactly why it's buried there!

## Cake & decoration

(See pages 11, 20–1 for recipes and cake chart)
25cm (10in) square cake
30cm (12in) hexagonal cake board
1.65kg (3lb 5oz) sugarpaste (rolled fondant)
Cream, black, brown and chestnut food colouring pastes
Icing (powdered) sugar in a shaker
345g (11oz) modelling paste
440g (14oz/1³⁄₄ cups) buttercream
Sugar glue
2 sugar sticks
Edible gold glitter
Edible gold powder

## Equipment

Large and small rolling pins
Plain and serrated kitchen knives
Ruler
Sheet of card for templates
Templates (see page 199)
Small glue brush
Medium paintbrush
A few cocktail sticks
2.5cm (1in) square cutter
1.5cm (³⁄₄in) circle cutter
Pieces of foam sponge
Dusting brush

## Cake board

**1** Colour 1.09kg (2lb 3oz) of sugarpaste (rolled fondant) stone using cream colouring paste with a touch of black. Roll out 375g (12oz) and cover the board, trimming excess from the edge. Cut templates 1cm (¹⁄₂in) larger than the base of each house (see cutting diagram on page 199) and position on the cake board. Score around the front of each as a guide for the cobbles. Trim out a little hole at the front of the cake board. Colour 60g (2oz) of sugarpaste black and fill, using a small piece *(see a)*. Using stone sugarpaste trimmings, model piles and group around the hole. Model a large pile, then chop up some more trimmings into small crumbs and put aside. Colour 60g (2oz) of modelling paste dull brown using brown and black food colouring pastes, 155g (5oz) brown and 60g (2oz) chestnut brown. To make the cobbles, roll out 45g (1¹⁄₂ oz) of each and cut into squares. Stick onto the cake

**a**

board, following the guiding lines. Reserve some cobbles to edge around each house.

## Dwellings

2 Trim the cake crust and slice the top flat. Using the cutting diagram (see page 199), cut out the shapes to assemble the dwellings. To assemble the largest dwelling, put the three larger squares, one on top of the other. Trim the slanted roof shape equally either side, cutting down and taking off the top edge of the second layer. Trim the front and back of the house to slope inwards. For the medium dwelling, put the 8x7cm (3x2³/₄ in) cake on top of the 7x6.5cm (2³/₄ x2¹/₂ in). Trim either side at the top and then turn one trimming over and use to give height and create the angled roof. The small oblong dwelling is turned upright with an angled roof trimmed. Trim down each side to curve slightly inwards.

3 Sandwich all layers together with buttercream, then spread a layer over the surface of each cake to help the sugarpaste stick. Colour 500g (1lb) of sugarpaste dull brown using brown and black food colouring pastes. With 15g (¹/₂ oz), pad the top of each roof at either end. Thinly roll out black sugarpaste and cover the window and door areas (see b). Using 625g (1¹/₄ lb) of stone sugarpaste, cover all sides of the two large houses by rolling out and placing the sides down onto it and cut around. Close joins with sugar glue, then rub gently with a little icing sugar to remove completely. For the smallest dwelling, roll out a strip to cover around all sides and close the join at the back. Mark little cracks and imperfections over the surface of all three cakes. Cut out all the misshapen doors and windows, exposing the black areas underneath.

4 Roll out 170g (5¹/₂ oz) of dull brown sugarpaste and cut a piece to cover the roof area on the largest cake. With 125g (4oz), cover the other two roofs the same way. Thinly roll out the remaining dull brown sugarpaste, a little at a time, and cut out 2.5cm (1in) squares for the roof tiles. Roll the handle of the paintbrush along the bottom edge of each to thin and frill. Build up over the roof, overlapping each layer (see c).

5 Thinly roll out black sugarpaste and stick on patches for the dormer windows on the roof and front of the largest dwelling, and either side of the smallest. Thickly roll out 45g (1¹/₂ oz) of stone sugarpaste even thicker at the top and cut the roof dormer using the template. With 15g (¹/₂ oz), make the dormer for the front using the template. Split 7g (¹/₄ oz) of stone sugarpaste in half and make the two small dormers for the smallest house. Cover the top of each with roof tiles. With the remaining stone sugarpaste, model three chimneys, indenting the top to hollow out.

b

c

**6** For the shutters and doors (see d), roll out 60g (2oz) of brown modelling paste and indent lines over the surface using a ruler. Scratch lines for wood grain using a cocktail stick (toothpick). Mark an outline for all the shutters and doors, and tear to create a ragged edge. Using 15g ($^1$/2 oz), model logs and twigs, and make the wooden spade using 7g ($^1$/4 oz). To make the spiked club, roll a small sausage handle, then roll a ball. Indent a hole underneath and stick in the handle. Indent holes, using the end of a paintbrush, for the spikes.

## Trolls

**7** For the trolls (see e), first colour 15g ($^1$/2 oz) of modelling paste stone, 22g ($^3$/4 oz) cream and the remaining piece grey. For the shoes, split just under 7g ($^1$/4 oz) of dull brown in half and model into teardrops. For the trousers, shape a flattened sausage with 7g ($^1$/4 oz) of brown. Make a cut to separate legs, smoothing to remove ridges. Stick onto the shoes and lay the figure

flat. Model a flattened circle, using just under 7g ($^1$/4 oz) of stone for the top. Split 7g ($^1$/4 oz) of stone paste in half and make two sleeves, hollowing out the end of each. Thinly roll out the remaining dull brown and, using the template for the costume (see page 199), score around the paste, then tear out the shape. Stick both pieces over the top of his body. Use a sugar stick to help hold the head in place.

**8** Roll a ball head using 7g ($^1$/4 oz) of cream and pinch out a long nose. Mark a smile using the circle cutter, then dimple the corners using a cocktail stick. Smooth along the smile with the glue brush to open the mouth. With pea-sized amounts, make the two ears, indenting the centre by rolling the paintbrush handle into each. Model two tiny black oval eyes. Stick the spiked club in place.

**9** Make two hands (see page 177, step 12 and e). Curve the hand round and stick into the

sleeve. Put the troll upright and support with foam. Roll out grey paste and cut strips of different lengths for hair. Stick over his head with the shorter lengths around his face. For the club spikes, model tiny teardrop shapes and stick into the holes, points facing outwards.

**10** Make the troll in the window with only one arm, made from grey paste, holding a long teardrop of cream paste in one hand. Stick his head in the window recess and make hair using chestnut paste. With grey trimmings, cut small strips for hinges on doors and shutters, indenting holes with a cocktail stick.

**11** Arrange remaining cobbles around each house and sprinkle the crumbs. Model the sack with dull brown paste and fill with gold glitter. Moisten the large cream pile and small teardrop in the window troll's hand with sugar glue and sprinkle with gold glitter. Brush the cake with gold powder.

d

e

# King Neptune

I have always imagined King Neptune to have a kindly face and be a father figure to all the sea creatures, riding the waves with galloping seafoam horses in a chariot of shells.

## Cake & decoration

(See pages 11, 20–1 for recipes and cake chart)
10cm (4in) and 20cm (8in) round cakes
30cm (12in) round cake board
410g (13oz) modelling paste
Icing (powdered) sugar in a shaker
280–300g (9–9$^1$/$_2$oz) royal icing
440g (14oz/1$^3$/$_4$ cups) buttercream
1.25kg (2$^1$/$_2$ lb) sugarpaste (rolled fondant)
Pink, navy, cream and black food colouring pastes
Sugar glue
Green and yellow powder food colourings
Confectioner's varnish or 2.5ml ($^1$/$_2$ tsp) white vegetable fat
Edible gold sparkle powder

## Equipment

Plain and serrated kitchen knives
Large rolling pin
Small glue brush
Fine paintbrush
No. 4 plain piping tube (tip)
Template (see page 199)
Pieces of foam sponge
2–3 piping bags
Medium/large firm bristle paintbrush
Dusting brush

## Trident and carriage

1 Make King Neptune's trident first, using 7g ($^1$/$_4$ oz) of modelling paste. Roll two-thirds into a sausage measuring 12cm (5in) for the handle. Shape the rest into a tapering sausage and bend into a horseshoe. Roll a long pointed centre and shape two flattened circles, one slightly larger. Assemble using royal icing, then leave to dry. Colour 7g ($^1$/$_4$ oz) of modelling paste pale pink. For the carriage base, knead half into 170g (5$^1$/$_2$ oz) of white modelling paste until streaky, then roll into a long tapering sausage. Moisten along the length with sugar glue, then roll up into a spiral from the narrow end. Press down on the full end to create a seat area.

## Shells

2 For shells (see a), knead a pea-sized amount of pink into 45g (1$^1$/$_2$ oz) of modelling paste, leaving a little streaky, and split into seven pieces. To make a

a

shell, roll one piece into a teardrop shape and press down to flatten. Mark radiating lines with the paintbrush handle, then press either side to re-shape. Stroke out around the top edge to thin and frill. Cut the surface, using a knife held flat, and press underneath to curve round.

## Cake and cake board

3 Trim the crust from each cake and slice the tops flat. Cut a layer in each cake, put one on top of the other and sandwich the layers with buttercream. To create waves, cut different-sized wedges from the top edge of both cakes, turn over and sandwich to the top surface (see b), protruding a little from the edge. Position the cake on the board and spread a layer of buttercream over the cake surface.

4 Colour 1.25g (2$\frac{1}{2}$lb) of sugarpaste (rolled fondant) mid blue using navy colouring. Roll out and cover the cake and cake board completely, smoothing

around the shape, then pinch each wave, pulling gently downwards.

## Seafoam horses

5 To make the seafoam horses, split 30g (1oz) of white modelling paste in half and make two teardrop-shaped bodies. To make the heads, split 22g ($^{3}/_{4}$oz) of white and model into ball shapes, pinching out a muzzle on each. Cut smiles with the end of the piping tube, indenting the corners with the tip of a cocktail stick. Indent nostrils with the end of the paintbrush. Stick on tiny flattened circles for eyes and a tiny tapering sausage for each eyelid. For the ears, split a pea-sized amount into four and model into teardrops. Indent in the centre of each using the paintbrush handle. Cut the rounded end straight and position.

6 For the horse legs, split 7g ($^{1}/_{4}$oz) of white modelling paste in half and roll into sausages. Flatten the end of each and pinch half way to mark the knees. For

hooves, stick a pea-sized amount on the end of each, pinching to straighten the sides. Assemble on the cake (see c), sticking together with royal icing. Stick the carriage on top of the cake without the shell decoration.

## King Neptune

7 Colour 90g (3oz) of modelling paste cream, putting just under 22g ($^{3}/_{4}$oz) aside. To make King Neptune, roll the remainder into a tapering sausage and press down to flatten slightly. Pinch in a little at the waist and press either side to mark hipbones. Mark details on his torso using the paintbrush handle and a cocktail stick. Pinch at the top to shape a neck. Moisten the carriage with sugar glue and stick King Neptune on the seat, supported by the carriage. Mark scales on him using the No. 4 plain piping tube (tip), pressed at an angle over the surface.

8 Roll a ball-shaped head with 7g ($^{1}/_{4}$oz) of cream modelling

b                                                    c

paste and using the step photograph as a guide (see d), stick on tiny facial details including two tiny flattened white pieces for eyes, and mark wrinkles and an open mouth using a cocktail stick. Stick onto the body with a generous amount of royal icing (none will show when the beard and hair are piped) and hold for a few moments until secure. For his crown, knead small amounts of pink and white together until marbled. Roll out and cut his crown using the template. Make cuts into each point, bend and stick onto the top of his head.

9 Using pea-sized amounts of cream modelling paste for the tail fins, model each into flattened teardrop shapes. Press around the outside edge to thin and frill, then stick in place. For arms, split the remaining cream in half and, using the photograph as a modelling guide (see e), make two arms, one at a time, and stick them in place using pieces of foam sponge for

support. Stick the trident in King Neptune's hand.

10 Colour 30g (1oz) of royal icing grey, mixing it until streaky. Put it into a piping bag and cut a small hole in the tip. Pipe King Neptune's beard, moving the piping bag from side to side to create waves. Pipe the moustache and the eyebrows, and finally the hair curling down his back with shorter curls framing his face.

11 Pipe a thick line of white royal icing along the edge of each wave for foam. Dampen the firm paintbrush with water and draw the brush from the royal icing, diluting it and creating lines. Do the same effect around the tail fins. Paint the excess royal icing on the brush over the shell carriage and then stick all the shells in place using dabs of royal icing.

12 Pipe large curls over the horses for their manes and for the sea foam around them.

Pipe extra foam along the edge of each wave. Roll four thin sausages of white modelling paste for reins and stick into the King's hands, with the ends attached to the back of each horse.

## Magical touches

13 Dilute green and yellow powder colourings with a little icing (powdered) sugar. Brush green over the King's tail and fins, fading out with a little yellow. Brush the cake and trident with a little green colour.

14 To give the sea a shiny effect, brush on 2–3 coats of confectioner's varnish, allowing each coat to dry for a few minutes before applying the next, or brush with a little white fat (shortening).

15 Dilute black food colouring paste with a little water and paint the eyes using the fine paintbrush. To finish, randomly dust the whole cake with the edible gold sparkle powder.

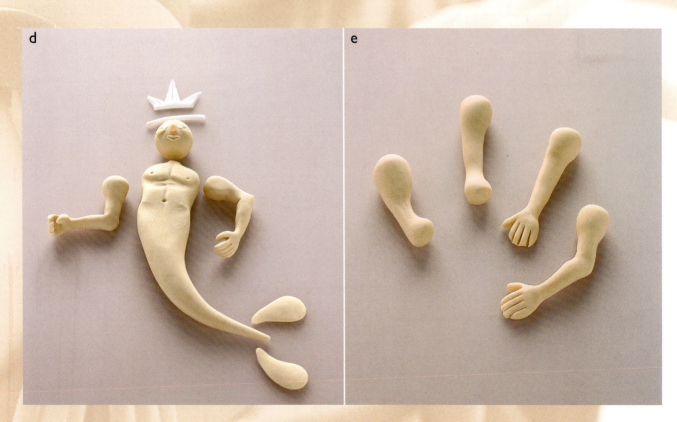

d

e

# Wizard Owl

White owls always look a little more mystical than others, so I made a snowy owl wizard reading spells from his chair of wisdom, which is made completely from books.

## Cake & decoration
(See pages 11, 20–1 for recipes and cake chart)
25cm (10in) square cake
30cm (12in) round cake board
2kg (4lb) sugarpaste (rolled fondant)
Navy blue, chestnut, black and yellow food colouring pastes
Icing (powdered) sugar in a shaker
410g (13oz/1²/₃ cups) buttercream
Sugar glue
315g (10oz) modelling paste
Edible gold powder

## Equipment
Large rolling pin
Plain and serrated kitchen knives
Ruler or similar straight edge
Cake smoother
Small glue brush
Medium paintbrush
A few cocktail sticks
Template (see page 200)
Pieces of foam sponge
1cm (¹/₂ in) and 1.5cm (³/₄ in) circle cutters
Dusting brush

## Cake board

1 Colour 375g (12oz) of sugarpaste (rolled fondant) navy blue and knead until streaky. Roll out and cover the cake board completely, trimming excess from around the edge, then put aside to dry.

2 Trim the crust from the cake and slice the top flat. Cut the cake *(see a)* as in the cutting diagram (see page 200). Take off 1cm (¹/₂ in) from the depth of both owl layers and put them together. Trim to round the body shape and then sandwich the layers together with buttercream. Spread all the cakes with buttercream to help the sugarpaste stick.

## Chair of wisdom

3 Colour 1.5kg (3lb) of sugarpaste stone using a touch each of chestnut and black food colouring paste. Roll out 90g (3oz) and cut a strip to cover

a

around three sides of the seat book. Indent pages by pressing in with a ruler.

4 To make the book cover, measure the book, roll out 265g (8½oz) and cut an oblong to fit around the cake. Position the cake on the right-hand side of the rolled-out sugarpaste and flip over the left-hand side, pressing the cake smoother along the edge to straighten or trim any excess (see b). Smooth the binding until it curves round. Mark a line on the top by pressing in with a ruler. Position the cake centrally on the cake board.

5 Make two sugarpaste books, one for the seat and another for a support for the back of the chair. Thickly roll out 280g (9oz) of sugarpaste and cut two oblong shapes measuring 6 × 10cm (2½ × 4in). Mark pages as before around three sides of each. Roll out 170g (5½oz) and cut covers for both, slightly larger than the pages, then

wrap around the pages, sticking with sugar glue. Mark the binding as before, then set aside. Cover the cake for the chair back as previous instructions and position on top of the seat, level with the back, securing with sugar glue. Stick the two sugarpaste books in position on the chair.

6 With the remaining stone sugarpaste, cover the two cakes for the book arms in the same way and stick in position, leaning slightly inwards. Cut little cracks in the books using a knife. Roll out trimmings and cut strips for the binding on all books.

## Wizard Owl

7 Roll out the remaining white sugarpaste and cover the owl's body, smoothing the sugarpaste down and stretching out any pleats. Trim away excess sugarpaste from around the base of the body. Indent over the surface to mark feathers using the paintbrush handle (see c).

8 To make the head (see d), roll 125g (4oz) of modelling paste into a ball. Shape a flattened teardrop, using 22g (¾oz), and stick the point on the centre of the owl's face, then smooth up and over the top of his head. Pinch up ears either side and stroke the eyebrow area to lift and flatten slightly. Indent each eye area by pressing in with your finger.

9 Colour a pea-sized amount of modelling paste yellow, split into two and model two flattened circles for eyes. Use two pea-sized amounts to make eyebrows. Take care when positioning his eyebrows. Although he has quite a serious expression, if the eyebrows are positioned too low over his eyes, this will result in his face looking unfriendly. Split 7g (¼oz) of white in half and make the teardrop-shaped cheeks. Roll five small teardrop shapes and stick the points together for his beard. Using the paintbrush, mark lines to give texture around his eyes and

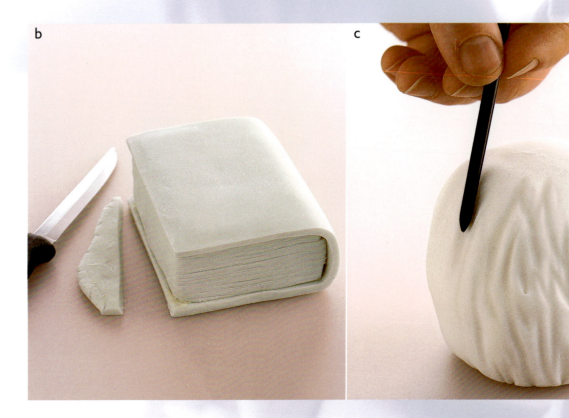

b

c

cheeks, and then stick the head onto the body.

## Cloak

10 Colour 90g (3oz) of modelling paste navy blue. Thinly roll out 60g (2oz) and cut a cloak, using the template (see page 200). Roll the paintbrush over the surface to create pleats, and then stick around the owl's shoulders. Lift the owl and stick him in position on his chair. Slot a small piece of foam either side of the cloak to hold it open ready for the wings.

## Scroll and wings

11 For the scroll, thinly roll out 22g (³/4 oz) of white modelling paste and cut a strip measuring 4 x 15cm (1 1/2 x 6in). Stick against the owl and chair, curling over at the top and rolling it up a little at the bottom. Split 30g (1oz) of modelling paste in half and, using the step photograph as a guide (see e), make the two wings, marking feathers along the

bottom edge with the paintbrush handle. Carefully slot the wings in position on the body, securing them with sugar glue.

## Hat and face

12 To make the Wizard Owl's hat, roll the remaining navy blue modelling paste into a teardrop shape and pinch out a rim around the full end. Stick on top of his head, twisting up the point. Model two tiny dots of white for the eye highlights and put aside.

13 Colour the remaining modelling paste black. For his beak, model two teardrop shapes using pea-sized amounts. Indent into one for the bottom part of the beak. Stick them together, then stick onto the owl's face and stroke downwards slightly. Edge around each eye with very thin uneven sausages of black and model two flattened circles for pupils. Stick the highlights in the same position on each eye.

## Glasses

14 Roll out the remaining black modelling paste and cut out two circles using the larger circle cutter. To make hoops for the glasses frame, cut out another circle from the centre of each using the smaller cutter. Leave to set for a few moments and then stick each hoop in place against his beak and cheeks. Roll long pointed claws using the black modelling paste trimmings, bend them to shape and stick in place.

## Magical touches

15 Paint stars with sugar glue over the hat and cake board, a few at a time. When they are tacky, brush with the edible gold powder. When the cake is completely dry, brush more gold powder randomly over the cake and cake board using the dusting brush.

d

e

# Labyrinth

With its towers, tunnels, secret doors and a maze of walkways, these cute little brightly coloured gnomes must be dizzy trying to find their way to the castle in the centre.

## Cake & decoration

(See pages 11, 20–1 for recipes
and cake chart)
25cm (10in) square cake
35cm (14in) square cake board
2kg (4lb) sugarpaste (rolled
fondant)
Cream, black, brown, violet, blue,
raspberry and green food
colouring pastes
845g (1lb 11oz) modelling paste
440g (14oz/1³/₄ cups) buttercream
Icing (powdered) sugar in a shaker
Sugar glue
6 sugar sticks
Lilac powder food colouring

## Equipment

Large and small rolling pins
Plain and serrated kitchen
knives
Fine paintbrush
Small glue brush
Miniature and 1.5cm (³/₄ in) circle
cutters
2.5cm (1in) square cutter
A few cocktail sticks
Pieces of foam sponge
Dusting brush

## Cake board and towers

1 Colour 750g (1¹/₂ lb) of sugarpaste (rolled fondant) dark cream. Roll out 500g (1lb) and cover the cake board completely, then trim excess from around the edge. Using your hands, mark an uneven surface, then put aside to dry.

2 Colour 440g (14oz) of modelling paste pale cream and use to model all the towers (see a). They are all shaped from a sausage shape that tapers at one end with both ends cut straight. The large central tower on top of the cake is 100g (3¹/₂ oz). The three surrounding ones are 30g (1oz) for one and 15g (¹/₂ oz) each for the remaining two. Shape a small square tower using 22g (³/₄ oz), cutting at an angle each side at the top for the sloping roof. Split the remaining pale cream paste into eight and model the towers around the outside wall. Indent windows using the paintbrush handle.

a

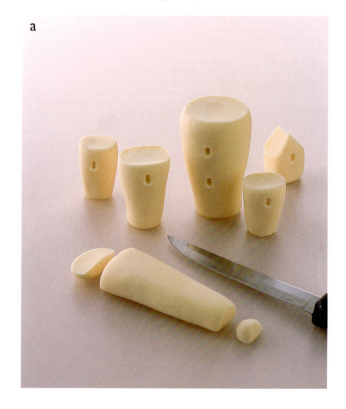

## Labyrinth

**3** Trim the crust from the cake and slice the top flat. Cut a 2.5cm (1in) strip from one side of the cake and cut this strip into three lengths. Sandwich together with buttercream to make the smaller square cake. Remove a further 2.5cm (1in) strip from the longest side of the larger cake to make it square. Cut a layer in the large square and sandwich back together with buttercream. Place centrally on the cake board. Spread a layer of buttercream over the surface of both cakes to help the sugarpaste stick.

**4** Roll out the remaining dark cream sugarpaste and cover the top of both square cakes, trimming excess from around the top edge. Place the small square cake centrally on top of the larger cake. Colour 1.25kg (2½lb) of sugarpaste pale cream. Roll out 875g (1¾lb) into a strip to fit around the large cake, measuring 8cm (3in) in depth. Dust with icing (powdered) sugar and roll up. Place one end against the large cake and unroll the sugarpaste around the cake, trimming away excess at the join (see b). To remove the join, stick together with sugar glue, and then rub gently to close. Cover the smaller square cake in the same way using 200g (6½oz), cutting the strip with a depth of 6cm (2½in).

**5** Cut out all the windows around the cake and on the cake board, using the round and square cutters. Colour sugarpaste trimmings black, thinly roll out and cut out shapes to fill each window (see c).

**6** Thickly roll out and cut strips measuring 2.5cm (1in) in height for the two walls on top of the large cake, using the remaining cream sugarpaste. Stick in position with gaps ready for the little doors, and on the inner wall and double gates at the front. Colour 60g (2oz) of modelling paste brown and use to make all the doors, shutters and gates, marking lines in the surface with the back of a knife for planks and using the blade to score a wood grain effect (see d). Using the cream trimmings, roll out and cut the doorsteps and strips to edge the windows and doors. Shape different-sized oval shapes and stick onto the surface of the labyrinth, pressing each flat. Colour 7g (¼oz) of modelling paste pale grey and model the sausage-shaped bars, indenting in the centre of each to narrow, and make all the hinges and door handles.

**7** Colour 75g (2½oz) each of modelling paste mauve and pale mauve using a touch each of violet and blue, and another 75g (2½oz) violet, then use to make all the tower roofs. Model into teardrop shapes first, then roll the point long and thin. Pinch around the full end to indent underneath and create an edge. Stick the wall tower roofs in place supported by the top edge of the wall.

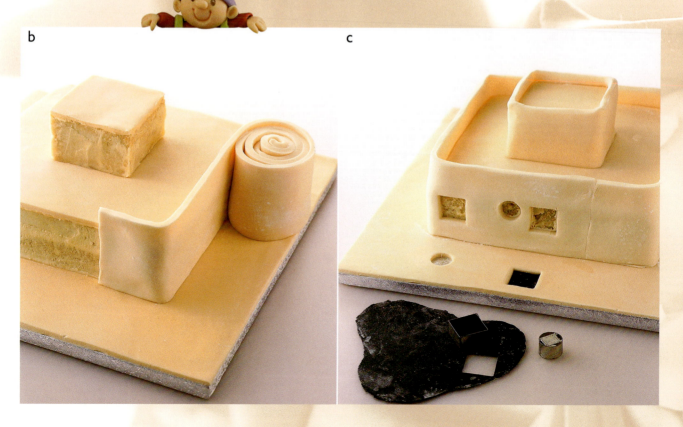

b

c

## Gnomes

**8** To make the gnomes (see e), first colour 7g ($^1/_4$ oz) of modelling paste pale blue, 7g ($^1/_4$ oz) deep violet, 15g ($^1/_2$ oz) raspberry, 15g ($^1/_2$ oz) green, 15g ($^1/_2$ oz) pale violet, 7g ($^1/_4$ oz) deep cream and 22g ($^3/_4$ oz) flesh, using cream food colouring paste with a tiny touch of raspberry. Each gnome is built up on the cake as each piece is made, all in different poses. The instructions that follow will make the gnome that is positioned at the front of the labyrinth, standing at the doorway.

**9** Using pea-sized amounts of pale blue, model oval shaped shoes first, pinching around the centre to narrow and press into the top to flatten ready for the trousers. Split the raspberry modelling paste into five pieces and shape one into a flattened square for trousers. Cut down the centre to separate the legs, smooth out all the ridges and then stick onto the shoes.

**10** Split the remaining white modelling paste into three pieces. Using one piece, make a top with two sausage-shaped sleeves, indenting into the end of each with the end of the paint-brush. Thinly roll out deep violet and cut two strips for braces, then stick a tiny green ball for a button onto the end of each, indenting in the centre with the end of the paintbrush. Push a sugar stick down through the top, leaving a little protruding to help hold the head in place. Split the flesh paste into seven pieces. Six are for all the heads, with the seventh making all the hands, noses and ears. Shape each head into an oval and stick lengthways over the sugar stick, securing at the base. Indent a smile using the miniature circle cutter pressed in at an angle, then dimple the corners using a cocktail stick (toothpick).

**11** To make the hat, split the green modelling paste into four pieces and shape one into a teardrop shape. Pinch up at the point to lengthen and indent into the full end to hollow out and pinch a rim. Model tiny oval shapes for the nose and two ears, then indent into each ear using the end of the paintbrush. For hands, split a pea-sized amount of flesh in half and shape into flattened teardrops. Cut a thumb on one side and two cuts along the top to separate three fingers on each, then stick into the sleeves. Using the remaining modelling paste, make all the other gnomes in various poses.

## Magical touches

**12** When the cake is dry, dilute a little black food colouring paste with water and paint the gnomes' eyes and tiny eyebrows using the fine paintbrush. Mix lilac powder colouring with some icing sugar and brush around the base of the cake.

d

e

# Pirate Dreams

Most children read under the covers with a torch and wonderful adventures are dreamed. For would-be swashbucklers, this ship-styled bed is afloat on a sea, flying the skull and crossbones.

## Cake & decoration

(See pages 11, 20–1 for recipes and cake chart)
20cm (8in) square cake
35cm (14in) round cake board
625g (1¼lb) modelling paste
Dark brown, dark blue, red, black, cream, yellow and golden brown food colouring pastes
Icing (powdered) sugar in a shaker
315g (10oz/1¼ cups) buttercream
1.34kg (2lb 11oz) sugarpaste (rolled fondant)
Sugar glue
45g (1½ oz) royal icing
Sugar stick
Yellow powder food colouring
Edible silver powder
Confectioner's varnish or white vegetable fat

## Equipment

Large and small rolling pins
Plain and serrated kitchen knives
Templates (see page 200)
1.5cm (¾ in) and 2.5cm (1in) square cutters
Miniature and 1.5cm (¾ in) circle cutters
A few cocktail sticks
Foam sheet and foam pieces
Bone tool
Fine and medium paintbrushes

## Headboard and bed

1 Colour 440g (14oz) of modelling paste brown. Roll out 155g (5oz) and cut the headboard and footboard using the templates (see a). Cut two circles from the footboard for the cannon holes. Thickly roll out another 155g (5oz) and cut four strips for the posts, measuring 15cm (6in) in length. Cut four squares from trimmings, using the smaller square cutter. Measure the side of the cake, roll out the remaining brown and cut two strips to fit the length, measuring 4cm (1½ in) in height. Mark the wood grain by scratching the surface with a cocktail stick, then put to dry on a foam sheet. Roll a long sausage for the flagpole, using 7g (¼ oz) of white modelling paste, and leave to dry.

2 Trim the crust from the cake and level the top. Cut the cake in half and put one on top of the other. Trim the two ends so they slope inwards towards

a

the base, then trim off the top edge around the cake. Sandwich the layers together with buttercream, then spread a layer over the surface to help the sugarpaste (rolled fondant) stick. Roll out 375g (12oz) of sugarpaste and cover the cake, trimming excess from the base. Colour 500g (1lb) of sugarpaste deep blue and roll out and cover the cake board, trimming excess from around the edge. Position the cake on the board. To indent a sea effect, mark the board with a bone tool and smooth ripples around each corner (see b). Make small dips where the bedposts will be.

3 Stick the two bed sides against the base of the cake. Colour 235g (7½oz) of sugarpaste blue and 170g (5½oz) deep blue. Using 60g (2oz) of blue, model a pillow, pinching up four corners, and stick onto the bed, taking care not to go over the edge. Model another pillow with 60g (2oz) of white sugarpaste, indent in the centre

and mark pleats with the paint-brush handle. Thickly roll out the remaining blue and dark blue sugarpaste and cut squares using the larger square cutter. Pinch each square to soften the edges, then build up a chequered pattern to make the quilt (see c).

## Boy pirate

4 Colour 30g (1oz) of modelling paste red. To make the pyjama bottoms, roll 22g (¾oz) into a fat sausage and press a little flat. Make a cut three-quarters of the length to separate legs, then smooth out ridges on either side. Flatten the end of each and pinch half way to shape the knees (see d). Bend and stick in position at the end of the bed. Roll out a little red, cut an oblong for the book cover and indent down the centre using the back of a knife. For pages, thickly roll out 7g (¼oz) of white paste and cut an oblong slightly smaller than the cover. Mark pages around the sides, indent down the centre and stick on the pillow.

5 Colour the royal icing brown and use to stick the head-board and footboard in place with the posts. Shape just over 7g (¼ oz) of white modelling paste into a teardrop shape for the pyjama top and indent around the full end to hollow out slightly. Press the point flat. Colour 45g (1½ oz) of modelling paste black. Thinly roll out a little, cut a square, using the larger square cutter, and stick onto the pyjama top. Split 7g (¼ oz) of black modelling paste in half and roll sausage-shaped sleeves. Bend half way and pinch out an elbow, then stick in position with one wrapped around the bedpost. Using a pea-sized amount of red, model a flattened circle for a collar and split another pea-sized amount to make two cuffs, indenting into the end of each with the end of a paintbrush. Model two pea-sized cuffs for the trousers, indenting as before. Push a sugar stick down into the body, leaving a little protruding to help hold the head in place.

b

c

6 Colour 15g (¹/₂ oz) modelling paste cream. Roll two-thirds into a ball-shaped head and press down onto the sugar stick, securing at the base with sugar glue. Mark the centre of the face using the tip of a cocktail stick (toothpick), and use as a guide for the mouth and eyes. Push the end of the paint-brush into the mouth and pull down slightly. Indent closed eyes using the miniature circle cutter pushed in at an angle. Mark tiny eyelashes in each corner and little eyebrows using the tip of a cocktail stick. Stick on a tiny ball nose and model two oval-shaped ears, indenting into the centre of each with the end of a paintbrush. Stick the ears in place. Colour 7g (¹/₄ oz) of modelling paste pale yellow and model different-sized flattened teardrops for the hair.

7 Colour a marble-sized piece of modelling paste grey. Make the cutlass (see e) using the step photograph as a modelling guide. Rub with silver powder and then

set aside. Split the remaining cream modelling paste into four pieces, with two slightly larger, and make two hands and two feet. To make a foot, model a small sausage with a larger piece and pinch up an ankle, shaping the heel. Pinch in the centre to arch the foot and stick in place. For hands, see page 173, step 8. Pinch around the wrist and slot into the end of the sleeve, securing with glue. Wrap the fingers around the cutlass handle and secure against the bedpost. Using a pea-sized amount of red, make tassels.

8 Colour 15g (¹/₂ oz) modelling paste pale golden brown and make the teddy, using half for the teardrop-shaped body. Model a little red flattened circle for the collar and teardrop-shaped ties. Assemble him against the foot-board, sticking with dabs of royal icing. Roll out white and cut the waistcoat using the template. Use just over 7g (¹/₄ oz) of black to make both pirate hats, one larger than the other. Indent on the

underside so they sit neatly on the heads, then turn up the two ends. Model a tiny nose and eyes.

## Magical touches

9 With the remaining black, model two cannons, three cannon balls and the torch. Roll out and cut a flag, using the template (see page 200). With black and red trimmings, model flattened circles for the top. Using the templates and the remaining white modelling paste, make all the skull and crossbones, smoothing the paste into the surface to inlay. Stick the flagpole in place using royal icing. Dust radiating lines of yellow powder from the torch for the torchlight and rub silver powder onto the end of the torch. Paint 2–3 coats of confectioner's varnish over the cake board, leaving each coat to dry for a few moments before applying another or, alternatively, rub the surface with white fat. Dilute black colouring with a little water and paint lines over the book pages for the print.

d

e

# Wizard's Helpers

I imagined how a wizard's table would look in the middle of the night and thought of these two naughty pranksters mixing potions. It is surprisingly simple to capture their cheeky looks.

## Cake & decoration

(See pages 11, 20–1 for recipes
and cake chart)
20cm (8in) square cake,
10cm (4in) and 15cm (6in) round
cakes
30cm (12in) square cake board
1.75kg (3$^1$/$_2$ lb) sugarpaste (rolled
fondant)
Cream, black, mauve, brown, green
and orange food colouring pastes
Icing (powdered) sugar in a shaker
440g (14oz/1$^3$/$_4$ cups) buttercream
Sugar glue
280g (9oz) modelling paste
2 sugar sticks
15ml (1tbsp) clear piping gel
Edible gold powder
Edible gold glitter

## Equipment

Large rolling pin
Serrated and plain kitchen knives
6cm (2$^1$/$_2$ in), 4.5cm (1$^3$/$_4$ in) and
3.5cm (1$^1$/$_4$ in) circle cutters
Ruler or straight edge
Small glue brush
Ball or bone tool
Pieces of foam sponge
A few cocktail sticks
Templates (see page 199)
Medium and large sable
paintbrushes

## Cake board and cake

**1** Colour 500g (1lb) of sugarpaste (rolled fondant) stone using a touch each of cream and black paste. Roll out 440g (14oz) and cover the cake board. Press the rolling pin and your hands over the surface to create ridges. Trim excess from around the edge, reserve trimmings, then set aside to dry. Trim the crust from each cake and slice the tops flat. Cut a 5cm (2in) strip from the square cake; the resulting oblong cake will make the book. Cut a layer in this oblong cake and sandwich back together with buttercream. For the hat, put the smaller round cake on top of the larger, with the 6cm (2$^1$/$_2$ in) circle cutter centrally on the top. Trim down the sides from the circle cutter to the edge of the base of the large cake, creating the smooth sloping sides of the hat. Sandwich using buttercream, then spread a layer over the surface of all the cakes (see a). Colour 750g (1$^1$/$_2$ lb) of sugarpaste pale mauve. To give

**a**

height to the hat and help create the pointed top, model a teardrop shape of sugarpaste, using 75g (2¹/₂oz) of pale mauve, and press the full end onto the top of the hat, smoothing down around the join until it is level with the cake surface.

## Book

2 Roll out the remaining stone sugarpaste and cut a strip to cover around three sides of the oblong cake. Using the ruler or straight edge, mark lines to create the book pages, then pinch an edge at each corner. Colour 500g (1lb) of sugarpaste pale brown and roll out. Spread a little buttercream on the underside of the oblong cake and place down on the front of the rolled-out sugarpaste, leaving an exposed edge (see b). Trim to fit at least 38cm (15in) in length, then immediately flip the remaining sugarpaste over the top of the cake. Position the cake on the cake board. This may disturb the sugar-paste covering, so press

the length of the ruler against the edges to re-straighten or carefully re-trim any excess. Press down to mark a line for the binding using the length of the ruler and move gently backwards and forwards to flatten either side of the marked line. Roll out trimmings and cut two thin strips for the binding and stick in place with sugar glue.

## Wizard's hat

3 The hat covering and rim are made separately. To cover the hat, roll out 500g (1lb) of pale mauve sugarpaste and dust with icing sugar before rolling up. Position the sugarpaste against the side of the cake with excess at the top, then unroll around the cake, covering it completely. Trim excess from the join at the side and base. Smooth up the excess at the top and mould into the pointed top part of the hat (see c), tapering it to a point and securing at the side with a little sugar glue. Glue, press the join closed and rub gently with a little icing sugar to remove the

join completely. Secure the hat cake on top of the book cake using a little buttercream or sugar glue.

4 Roll out the remaining pale mauve sugarpaste into a circle measuring 20cm (8in). Cut away a circle from the centre, leaving a hat rim measuring 5cm (2in). Moisten around the base of the hat with sugar glue, then lift the hat rim over the top of the cake and secure at the base. To make the hatband, thinly roll out the trimmings and cut a strip measuring 41 x 2.5cm (16 x 1in). Cut the hatband along both sides at an angle, making a ragged edge, and stick around the base of the hat, crossing it over at the back.

## Bottles

5 Colour 100g (3¹/₂oz) of modelling paste grey and 60g (2oz) green. Use 45g (1¹/₂oz) of grey to make the spilt bottle. Model a small ball and press into the centre with a ball or bone tool to indent, making the bottle rim.

b

c

Roll the remainder into a ball and stick on the rim, and then stick the bottle in place on its side, up against the book. With just under 15g ($^1/_2$ oz) of green modelling paste, roll into a sausage, tapering at either end. Pinch in the centre to pull up a little to fill the pot opening, smoothing the lengths unevenly against the cake board surface. With pea-sized amounts, model little teardrop splashes, sticking one onto the bottle rim with the others pressed on the cake board. For the large green bottle, shape the remaining green modelling paste into a ball and pinch gently to indent the neck of the bottle, keeping a rounded top. Press the ball or bone tool into the top to open it up, creating the rim. To make the little dish, colour 15g ($^1/_2$ oz) of modelling paste orange and roll just under 7g ($^1/_4$ oz) into a ball. Press in the centre with your finger to indent and smooth round in a circular motion for a dip, then stick in position on the book cake.

## Imps

**6** Colour 45g ($^1/_2$ oz) of modelling paste brown and just over 7g ($^1/_4$ oz) mauve. Each imp is built up in place on the cake (see d for modelled shapes). To make the trousers for the first imp at the front, roll the remaining orange into a sausage shape, keeping the centre part fuller. Bend the two ends forward to make the legs, pinching gently to shape each knee, then pinch up the centre, smoothing the front flat. Stick onto the spilt bottle using small pieces of foam sponge to support each leg while drying. For the second imp, use the mauve paste and shape as before. Stick in place on the book, supporting with foam sponge between the legs until dry.

**7** For the tunic, shape 7g ($^1/_4$ oz) of brown modelling paste into a teardrop and cut the top and bottom flat. Mark a line down the centre and crease lines with a knife. Push in gently to indent the arm sockets either side at the top.

Using trimmings, thinly roll out and cut a tiny square pocket, indenting tiny stitches with the tip of a cocktail stick (toothpick), then shape three tiny flattened circular buttons. Push gently on the underside to indent, then stick the tunic onto the legs. Repeat for the second imp.

**8** Colour 7g ($^1/_4$ oz) of modelling paste stone as before and split into four pieces. Roll into sausage shapes, slightly narrower at one end, making the sleeves. Indent into each end to hollow out. Bend each half way, marking elbows, and stick in place using foam pieces for support. For each collar, split 7g ($^1/_4$ oz) of brown in half, shape two flattened circles and stick in place. To help support their heads, push a sugar stick down through each collar, leaving 2cm ($^1/_2$ in) pro-truding. For their shoes, split just under 7g ($^1/_4$ oz) of brown into four pieces and model each into a

d

e

long teardrop. At the full end, pinch around the top to shape an ankle and heel. Roll out pea-sized amounts of brown and cut out the top part using the template (see page 199--). Stick the shoes in place with the top wrapped around and joining the leg to the shoe, using foam for support.

9 Colour 30g (1oz) of modelling paste pale green and a minute piece black. Roll 7g (¼oz) of pale green into a ball-shaped head (see e) and pinch out a long nose, curving it downwards slightly. For the mouth area, thinly roll out a tiny piece of brown paste and stick just underneath the nose. The chin and bottom lip are tiny pale green sausages, each tapering to points at either end. Curve around and stick in place, edging the mouth area, and use the glue brush with a little sugar glue to blend each end in line with the surface. Roll a tiny pale green tapering sausage for the top lip and make two even smaller to shape the top of each eye. With

the tip of a knife, mark wrinkles at the corner of each eye. Split a pea-sized amount in half and shape into teardrop shapes for the cheeks, again smoothing in the points using the glue brush. With black, roll two minute tapering sausages for each eye then, using a cocktail stick, pull down a little, making the pupils. Make the second head as before.

10 Split the remaining brown in half and model teardrop-shaped hats, hollowing out each full end so they sit comfortably. For the ears, roll four pea-sized amounts of pale green into long teardrop shapes and indent down the centre with the ball or bone tool. Stick in place with each pointing outwards. Push each head down onto the sugar stick and secure with sugar glue.

11 Split the remaining pale green into four pea-sized pieces. To make hands, model teardrops and press flat. Cut thumbs to the side at the pointed end, then cut twice

and twist to make three fingers. Pinch wrists and stick into the sleeves.

## Magical touches

12 Roll out the remaining grey paste and cut two circles using the 4.5cm (1¾in) circle cutter (see f). From the centres, cut out circles using the 3.5cm (1¼in) circle cutter, and use the hoops for the frames. Cut a 4cm (1½in) strip, bend round and cut each end to join the frames. Stick on the board. Using the template (see page 199), cut out the frame arms and position.

13 Fill the dish and top of the bottle with piping gel, creating some drips on the rim and over the cake and board. Sprinkle a little glitter over the gel. Paint stars over the hat with sugar glue and, when tacky, brush on gold powder (see g). Paint glue onto the book corners and brush with gold. Edge with tack holes, indented with the tip of a cocktail stick. Brush gold over the cake and board.

f  g

# Baby Dragon

Although this cake was initially made with smaller children in mind, anyone would fall in love with this baby dragon's cute expression and big blue eyes.

## Cake & decoration

(See pages 11, 20–1 for recipes and cake chart)

3 × 625ml (1 1/4 pint/3 cup) bowl-shaped cakes

35cm (14in) round cake board

1.875kg (3 3/4 lb) sugarpaste (rolled fondant)

Mauve, blue, black and green food colouring pastes

Icing (powdered) sugar in a shaker

315g (10oz/1 1/4 cups) buttercream

Sugar glue

Edible mauve sparkle powder

Edible purple glitter

## Equipment

Large rolling pin

Plain and serrated kitchen knives

Ball or bone tool

Small glue brush

Paintbrush

A few cocktail sticks

Pieces of foam sponge

Dusting brush

1 Colour 625g (1 1/4 lb) of sugarpaste (rolled fondant) pale mauve. Roll out 500g (1lb) and cover the cake board completely. Press the rolling pin over the surface to create ripples, then trim excess from around the edge and put aside to dry. Trim the crust from each cake and slice the tops flat. Cut a layer in one of the larger cakes, sandwich back together with buttercream, then place centrally on the cake board for the dragon's body. Trim the second larger cake to make the rounded end a little more pointed for the large eggshell. Spread a layer of buttercream over the surface of all the cakes to help the sugarpaste stick.

### Eggshells

2 Roll out the remaining pale mauve and place the two eggshell cakes down onto it. Cut around, covering the top of each. Colour 500g (1lb) of sugarpaste blue. Roll out 315g (10oz) and cover the largest eggshell cake (see a). Leave 2.5–4cm (1–1 1/2 in)

a

excess around the edge, lift and put on its side. Cut a ragged edge, smoothing the points down towards the inside. Cover the smaller eggshell cake in the same way using the remaining blue. Reserve some of the pieces cut from the edge of the eggshell to decorate the cake board. With trimmings, shape different-sized flattened ovals to decorate the outside of each. Cut cracks, using a knife, and put the shells aside.

## Baby dragon

3 Colour a pea-sized amount of sugarpaste black and put aside for later with two pea-sized amounts of white sugarpaste. Colour the remaining sugarpaste green. Roll out 185g (6oz) and cover the dragon's body, trimming excess from around the edge. Using the knife, press around the bottom edge to tuck under. Shape the neck, using 60g (2oz). Roll a sausage, tapering to a point, for the tail using another 60g (2oz) and bend up. Stick both against the

dragon's body (see b). To make the head, roll 155g (5oz) of green sugarpaste into a ball and indent to round off the muzzle. Stick onto the neck with the head turned slightly. Indent the open mouth using the small end of a ball or bone tool. Using 7g ($^1/_4$oz), model facial features. Make two pointed ears and two flattened oval-shaped eyelids, smoothing the centre of each to indent. Model a pointed horn for the muzzle, two eyebrows and two pea-sized nostrils, indenting the centre of each with the small end of a ball or bone tool, slightly off centre.

4 Using 7g ($^1/_4$oz) of green, model the point for the end of his tail. Make a small hole in the bottom and stick in place using sugar glue. Model different-sized flattened oval shapes for scales using 60g (2oz) of green. Stick all over his back, neck and tail, hiding the joins. Keep the larger scales central down his back, with smaller ones either side (see c). For eyes,

stick on two white flattened oval shapes; use blue trimmings for the iris and then finish with black pupils. To make the wings, split 30g (1oz) of green sugarpaste in half. Model a teardrop shape and, from the full end, pinch up a point. Pinch another point in the centre and then indent in the direction of each point, using the paintbrush handle. Make the second wing, stick in place and support until dry.

5 Split the remaining green into four pieces. To make legs, roll sausages and indent in the centre. Press to flatten, then cut twice in one end to separate claws. To position the eggshell cakes, stick a back leg on the dragon first and bend, sticking the leg and foot together. Moisten the base of the foot with sugar glue, then stick the eggshell cake in place, holding until secure. Wedge some shell pieces underneath for support and scatter a few over the board. Brush the cake with mauve sparkle powder and sprinkle glitter onto the wings.

b

c

# Hocus Pocus

I just had to make three witches dancing around the cauldron as I have two sisters; so to me, these witches are called Debbie, Dawn and Jackie. Husbands are in the pot, of course!

## Cake & decoration

(See pages 11, 20–1 for recipes and cake chart)
2 × 1 litre (2 pint/5 cup) bowl-shaped cakes
30cm (12in) petal-shaped cake board
1.17kg (2lb 5$^1$/$_2$ oz) sugarpaste (rolled fondant)
Turquoise, yellow, mauve, black, green, cream, orange and blue food colouring pastes
Icing (powdered) sugar in a shaker
680g (1lb 5$^3$/$_4$ oz) modelling paste
280g (9oz/1 generous cup) buttercream
Sugar glue
Edible silver powder

## Equipment

Large rolling pin
Serrated and small/medium plain kitchen knives
Star cutters in various sizes
Small glue brush
Paintbrush
Template (see page 201)
A few cocktail sticks
Pieces of foam sponge

## Cake board and cake

1 Split 375g (12oz) of sugarpaste (rolled fondant) into three pieces and colour turquoise, yellow and mauve. Knead the three colours together until streaky. Roll out and cover the cake board completely, trimming excess from around the cake board edge. Cut out star shapes with the different-sized star cutters, removing the sugarpaste. Colour 60g (2oz) of modelling paste yellow and roll out to the same depth as the cake board covering. Cut out stars and slot into the spaces on the cake board (see a).

2 Trim the crust from each cake and slice the tops flat. Slice a little off the bottom of each to create a flat area and then sandwich the two cakes together with buttercream to form the cauldron shape. Spread a layer of buttercream over the cake surface.

a

3 Colour 750g (1¹/₂ lb) of sugarpaste pale grey. Roll out and cut an oblong measuring 48 × 18 cm (19 × 7in). Dust with icing (powdered) sugar and roll up. Position against the cake, then unroll the sugarpaste around the cake (see b), trimming excess from the join. To remove the join completely, moisten with sugar glue, then rub gently in a circular motion with icing sugar on your fingertips. Smooth around the top of the cauldron, creating a rim (see c). For the silver effect, rub a little edible silver powder over the surface. Lift the cake and position centrally on the board.

4 Colour 45g (1¹/₂ oz) of sugarpaste green. To make the bubbling potion in the cauldron, roll 22g (³/₄ oz) into five different-sized balls and position randomly inside the top. Roll out 15g (¹/₂ oz) and cover completely, trimming excess. With the remainder, roll different-sized bubbles and scatter over the top.

## Witches

5 To make the witches, first colour 140g (4¹/₂ oz) of modelling paste mauve, 125g (4oz) green, 90g (3oz) cream, 60g (2oz) orange, 155g (5oz) blue and 22g (³/₄ oz) pale blue. To make a dress, roll 90g (3oz) of mauve into a long teardrop shape and roll to flatten a little, keeping it slightly thicker at the narrow end. Mark pleats radiating down from the top using the paintbrush handle, then cut a ragged edge. Stick onto the side of the cauldron with the top level with the cauldron rim (see d). For sleeves, split 15g (¹/₂ oz) of mauve modelling paste in half and roll into long teardrop shapes. To open up each sleeve, push into the full end with your finger to indent and then pinch down the long tapering sleeve, rolling it gently between your fingers. Moisten at the shoulder and along the rim of the cauldron with sugar glue, then stick in place, holding until secure. Mark tiny stitches with the tip of a knife. With trimmings, cut a small square

pocket, stick in place and then mark stitches around the edge. To make the collar, roll a pea-sized amount of green modelling paste into a tapering sausage shape and stick around the top of the dress, crossing over at the front. Thinly roll out 7g (¹/₄ oz) of green and cut out a cloak using template (page 201). Gently fold to create pleats and stick in place.

6 For a head, roll 22g (³/₄ oz) of cream modelling paste into a ball and gently pinch out a long nose. Just underneath the nose, draw a semi-circle for a mouth using a damp paintbrush. Move the brush backwards and forwards along the semi-circle, pushing in a little deeper each time. This will push out a rounded bottom lip. Stick the head in position, making sure it is well balanced and supported by the collar and the cauldron rim. Thinly roll out 15g (¹/₂ oz) of orange modelling paste

b

c

for hair and cut into small strips measuring 2.5–4cm (1–1 1/2 in) in length. Build up the hair, leaving the top uncovered, finishing with smaller strips either side of her face. With orange trimmings, model minute flattened circles to decorate the dress patch.

7 Press a 7g (1/4 oz) ball of blue paste flat and smooth around the edge to thin and frill, then stick onto the top of her head, making the hat rim. Roll 15g (1/2 oz) of blue into a teardrop, tapering to a long point, then cut the full end straight. Stick onto the hat rim and bend the point around. To complete the hat, thinly roll out mauve modelling paste trimmings and cut a hatband.

8 Roll a minute ball of cream paste and stick on a wart. For hands, split just under 7g (1/4 oz) of cream in half. With one half, shape a teardrop shape and press down to flatten. From the pointed end, cut a thumb on one side. At the point, make three cuts to separate

four fingers and twist each to a long point. At the full end, twist gently creating a long wrist, which will slot into a sleeve. Moisten inside a sleeve with sugar glue, then add the hand, holding until secure. Make a second hand, cutting a thumb on the opposite side.

9 For the striped stockings (see e), twist pea-sized coloured sausages of modelling paste together, one pair orange and green, another mauve and green, and the last pair orange and blue. Make one stocking at a time. First, roll contrasting pea-sized amounts into sausages and stick together. To prevent cracking, moisten your hands slightly, then twist the sausages until the colours spiral. Roll gently to inlay, then taper each slightly at one end for the ankle.

10 Using the remaining coloured modelling paste, make two more witches, spacing them evenly dancing around the cauldron. One witch has a blue

dress, orange collar and cloak, pale blue hair, purple hat and orange hatband, while the other has a green dress, mauve collar and cloak, blue hair, and orange hat with a pale blue hatband. Cut the cloaks in half, instead of folding, and position either side of each dress. The patches are left plain, with one indented with a tartan pattern using the back of a knife.

11 Put a pea-sized amount of white modelling paste aside, then colour the rest black. Put aside a tiny amount of black for eyes, then split the remainder into six pieces to make all the shoes, following the step photograph as a guide (see e). Stick a stocking into the top of each and secure in position, using foam to support. Using white modelling paste, shape flattened oval shaped eyes and stick in position. Roll out and cut minute squares of white for teeth. With black, shape tiny flattened pupils and stick in place on the bottom of each eye.

d

e

# Star Castle

A magical castle in the sky isn't complete without a pretty princess. I made her blonde with lots of curls, but she could be a look-alike for your very own little princess.

## Cake & decoration
(See pages 11, 20–1 for recipes
and cake chart)
25cm (10in) square cake
25cm (10in) round cake board
1.325kg (2lb 10½oz) sugarpaste
(rolled fondant)
Blue, cream, yellow, black and red
food colouring pastes
Icing (powdered) sugar in a shaker
440g (14oz/1¾ cups) buttercream
Sugar glue
170g (5½oz) modelling paste
10–15ml (2–3 tsp) royal icing
Edible silver paint

## Equipment
Large rolling pin
Plain and serrated kitchen
knives
11cm (4½in), 8cm (3in) and 4cm
(1½in) circle cutters
Length of thread
Ruler
Cake smoother
Small glue brush
2.5cm (1in) square piece of card
Fine and medium paintbrushes
Template (see page 201)
1.5cm (¾in) square cutter
A few cocktail sticks
Paper piping bag
Various star cutters

## Cake board and cake

**1** Knead a little blue colouring paste into 315g (10oz) of sugarpaste (rolled fondant) until streaky. Roll out and cover the cake board. Trim the crust from the cake and slice the top flat. Cut the cake exactly in half. From one half, cut two circles using the 11cm (4½in) circle cutter and sandwich together to make the base of the castle. From the remaining half, cut two 8cm (3in) circles and sandwich together for the second tier of the castle, and then two further circles measuring 4cm (1½in) for the third tier (see a). Cut a little from the depth of both small circles and sandwich together, making their total height 7cm (2¾in). Spread each cake with buttercream to help the sugarpaste stick.

**2** Colour 500g (1lb) of sugarpaste blue. To cover the top of the largest cake, roll out 75g (2½oz), place the top of the cake down onto it and cut around.

**a**

Measure around the cake, using the length of thread, and cut to size. Measure the depth of the cake and add another 1cm (½ in). Roll out 410g (13oz) of blue sugarpaste and, using the two measurements, cut out the strip of sugarpaste to cover around the largest cake. Sprinkle with icing sugar to prevent sticking, roll up and place the sugarpaste against the side, and unroll around the cake (see b). Trim any excess from the join and stick together with sugar glue. To remove the join completely, sprinkle with icing sugar and rub gently with your fingertips. Create a smooth surface by rubbing gently with a cake smoother.

3 Place the cake centrally on the cake board. Fold the card in half and push the fold into the covering to indent windows. Push the end of the paintbrush into the top and bottom of each. Cut out the doorway at the front using the template (see page 201). Smooth around the top with your fingertip.

Colour 7g (¼ oz) of sugarpaste deep blue, thinly roll out and cut the door. Reserve the trimmings for later. Thickly roll out the remaining blue sugarpaste and cut a circle measuring 8cm (3in). Cut two steps, one larger, from the circle and assemble at the base of the doorway.

4 For the second tier, colour 315g (10oz) of sugarpaste a slightly paler shade of blue than the bottom tier, and use 235g (7½ oz) to cover the top and sides of the 8cm (3in) circle cakes as before. Stick centrally on the top of the bottom tier, making sure that the cake is level and sitting straight. For the dormer window at the front, thickly roll out 30g (1oz) and cut a 6cm (2½ in) square. Cut another square from the centre and indent at each corner with the end of a paintbrush. Slice off the top at an angle to help shape the roof and stick in place. Thinly roll out the deep blue trimmings and cut a square to fill the window.

5 Colour 100g (3½ oz) of sugarpaste a paler shade of blue than the second tier. Roll out and cover the 4cm (1½ in) circle cakes as before, marking a window at the front, and stick in place with sugar glue. For the fourth tier, colour 30g (1oz) of modelling paste palest blue and roll into a sausage. Cut the top and bottom straight, mark a small window using the tip of a knife, and stick in place. Check that all tiers are level and sitting straight.

## Towers and clouds

6 To make all the towers (see c), roll the remaining pale blue sugarpaste into different-sized sausages, cutting the top and bottom of each straight. Cut the piece of card down to measure 1.5cm (¾ in) square and mark a window in each as before. Colour the remaining sugarpaste mid blue. Thinly roll a tiny sausage and loop into the door handle, finishing with a tiny ball at the top. Roll out 7g (¼ oz) and cut a strip for the roof

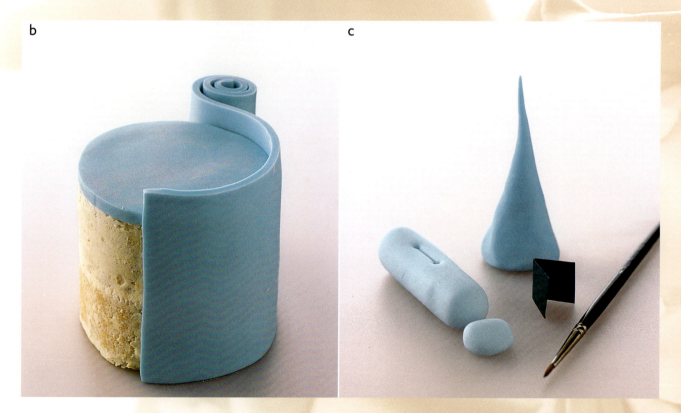

b

c

of the dormer window. Use the remaining mid blue sugarpaste to make all the different-sized roofs. Each roof is made from a teardrop shape, rolled with a tapering point and an edge pinched around the base which hollows out slightly underneath. The very top tower roof is made with 22g ($^{3}/_{4}$ oz). Stick the towers in place with a small ball of sugarpaste at the bottom, then stick a roof on top.

7 For the clouds, roll 22g ($^{3}/_{4}$ oz) of white modelling paste into a sausage, tapering at either end, and roll over the surface to flatten slightly. Stick against the base of the castle and curve round on the cake board. Paint a line of sugar glue around the castle, where the long cloud will spiral round, and leave until tacky. Roll 45g (1$^{1}/_{2}$ oz) of modelling paste into a thin tapering sausage, roll the surface as before, then carefully pick up and, following the glue line, press the edge of the rolled-out strip against it. Hold in place until secure.

## Princess

8 Colour a marble-sized piece of modelling paste cream. To make the princess (see d), model her head, a tiny ball nose, her chest from a sausage with a pinched-up neck and two hands. To make hands, see page 137, step 11. Pinch around the wrist and then gently curve each hand round by pressing gently into each palm. Stick her head and chest area in place, holding for a moment. Colour 60g (2oz) of modelling paste pale blue. Split 7g ($^{1}/_{4}$oz) in half and roll into a cone for her hat, cutting the bottom at an angle to fit around the back of her head. Stick in place onto her head, resting against the dormer window roof. To make the hat rim, roll a pea-sized amount of paste into a teardrop shape. Flatten, then cut in half and stick the pieces either side of her head.

9 With the remaining piece, model one sleeve, pinching around the end to hollow out slightly for the hand to slot in

easily and roll down to a point. Make a tiny sausage for the top of her dress, pinching along the length to thin and frill. Stick one hand into the end of the sleeve, with the other resting against the window base. Colour royal icing pale yellow and, using the piping bag with a small hole cut into the tip, pipe curly hair by gently squeezing out the icing, waving the bag gently from side to side.

10 Thinly roll out the remaining white modelling paste and cut a triangular hat scarf. Indent pleats by rolling the paint-brush handle over the surface and then stick in place. From the trimmings, cut a small square handkerchief. Roll out the remaining blue paste, cut out different-sized stars and stick around the cake and board. Paint the stars using edible silver paint (see e). When the cake is dry, dilute a little black and red paste separately with a little water, and paint her eyes and lips.

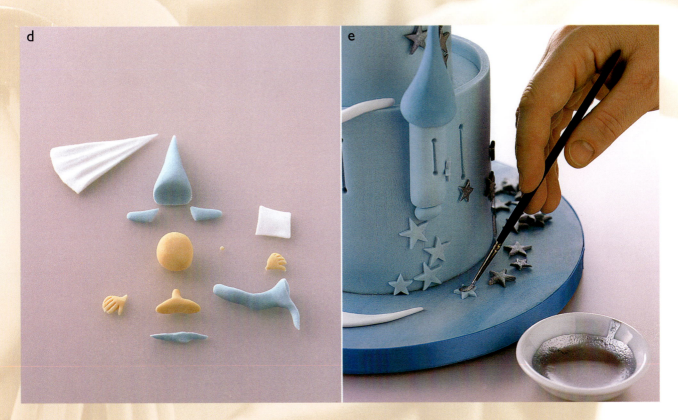

d

e

# Golden Pegasus

Magical Pegasus is the golden winged flying horse from Greek and Roman mythology. I have put him dancing amongst the clouds and stars in a sparkling, midnight blue sky.

## Cake & decoration

(See pages 11, 20–1 for recipes and cake chart)
10cm (4in), 15cm (6in) and 20cm (8in) round cakes
35cm (14in) round cake board
1.75kg (3½lb) sugarpaste (rolled fondant)
Navy blue food colouring paste
Icing (powdered) sugar in a shaker
250g (8oz) modelling paste
Sugar glue
15g (½oz) royal icing
440g (14oz/1¾ cups) buttercream
Midnight blue sparkle powder
Edible gold powder
Edible gold glitter

## Equipment

Large rolling pin
Cake smoother
Plain and serrated kitchen knives
Small glue brush
Pieces of foam sponge
1cm (½in) circle cutter
Fine paintbrush
A few cocktail sticks
Template (see page 201)
Miniature star cutter
Kitchen paper
Dusting brush

## Cake board

1 Colour 500g (1lb) of sugarpaste (rolled fondant) navy blue, roll out and cover the cake board. Rub the surface with a cake smoother. Trim excess from around the board edge and put aside to dry.

## Pegasus

2 To allow drying time, make Pegasus first (see a). Using 45g (1½oz) of white modelling paste, shape his body flat on the work surface, twisting up a long neck and rounding off the rump. Smooth into the small of his back to create a dip, then gently push down to round off his underside and lift up his rump. As the paste is heavy, the back will flatten so, after a few moments, pick the body up and carefully reshape again.

3 For legs, split 22g (¾oz) of white modelling paste into four pieces. To make a leg, roll one piece into

a

a sausage, fuller at the top for the thigh. Pinch around the bottom of the leg, rounding off the end. Bend the leg half way by pushing gently into the back to indent and pinch out a knee at the front. Stick in place with sugar glue immediately and smooth to blend into the surface of the body. To remove the join completely, rub gently in a circular motion with a little icing (powdered) sugar on your fingertips. Make three more legs in the same way, supporting each in their pose with pieces of foam sponge.

4 Model the head using 7g (¹/₄ oz) of white modelling paste. Roll into an oval shape first and, two-thirds down the length, roll backwards and forwards to indent and lengthen the muzzle, slightly rounding off the end. Stick in place using a dab of royal icing. Push the circle cutter in at an angle to mark the smile. Mark dimples in each corner and two nostrils, using the end of a paintbrush.

5 Stick on two tiny arched eyelids and flattened circles just underneath for eyes. Split a pea-sized amount of white in half and model teardrop shapes for ears. Indent in the centre of each using the end of a paintbrush and stick in place, pointing slightly outward at the top. Smooth the join closed.

6 Model four teardrop shapes for hooves using pea-sized amounts of white modelling paste for each. Stick the hooves onto the bottom of each leg, with the full part at the front. Press the front of each hoof to flatten.

## Cake

7 Trim the crust from each cake and slice the tops flat. Cut a layer in each cake and sandwich back together with buttercream. Spread a thin layer of buttercream over the surface of each cake to help the sugarpaste stick. Place the large cake centrally on the cake board. Roll out 625g (1¹/₄ lb) of

white sugarpaste and cover (see b), trimming excess from around the bottom edge. To obtain a smooth surface, rub gently with a cake smoother in a circular motion over the top and then smooth the sides. To create a smooth top edge, rub gently with the palm of your hand. Cover the remaining cakes on the work surface, using the remaining white sugarpaste. To stack each cake one on top of the other, carefully lift, holding at the bottom, and position centrally. Any finger-marks can then be smoothed away with the cake smoother.

8 Stick Pegasus to the bottom tier of the cake, using a few

b

c

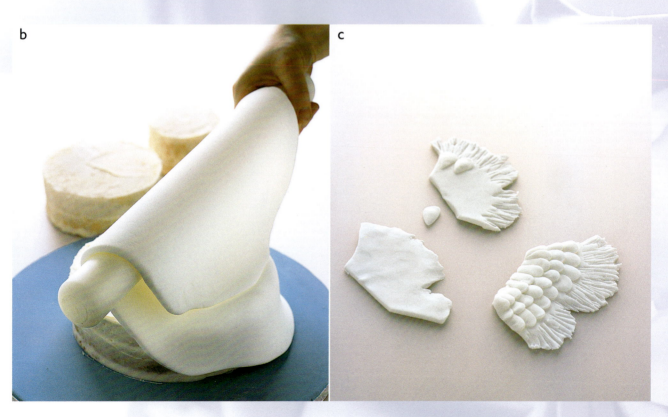

dabs of royal icing, and hold for a few moments until secure. To prevent any slight sinkage that would damage the legs, wedge a piece of foam sponge between him and the cake board to hold in place until completely dry.

9 Build up his mane and tail using different-sized sausages of white modelling paste, each tapering to a point. Keep the shorter lengths on top of his head and curl them up and around (see the main photograph as a guide to the mane and tail).

## Wings

10 To make the wings (see c), thinly roll out 22g ($^3/_4$ oz) of modelling paste and, using the template (see page 201), cut out two wings. Thin and frill around the outside edge by making cuts on both sides, stretching them out and allowing some to break away. Model flattened teardrop-shaped feathers and stick in a line, following the outside shape of the wing. Follow with two more lines, overlapping each on both wings. Carefully turn the wings over and attach more feathers on the reverse side. Stick the wings in place with a little royal icing, using pieces of foam sponge to support them while drying.

## Star and clouds

11 Roll out 7g ($^1/_4$ oz) of white modelling paste and cut out all the stars, using the miniature star cutter, and put aside to dry.

12 To make the clouds (see d), split the remaining white modelling paste into seven different-sized pieces. Each cloud is made from an oval shape first, which is then indented around the edge by pressing in with the paintbrush handle. Press down on the surface of each to flatten and rub around the edge to thin out. Put each cloud upright and bend in the centre slightly, so they will each follow the curved shape of the cake sides.

## Magical touches

13 When the cakes are dry, protect the top of each cake with strips of kitchen paper and then dust a little midnight blue sparkle powder onto the sides of the cake, fading it out around the edge. Stick a cloud in front. Carefully remove the strips of kitchen paper and brush edible gold powder over the cake board in a spiral motion, to give a cloud effect. Stick the stars over the cake and cake board, positioning three stars upright on the centre of the top tier.

14 Brush edible gold powder over all the stars and Pegasus (see e), concentrating more gold on his wings. Sprinkle a tiny amount of edible gold glitter over the cake and Pegasus. Dilute a little navy blue food colouring paste with water, then carefully paint his eyes, using the fine paintbrush. Take care not to have the paintbrush too wet to prevent the colour running.

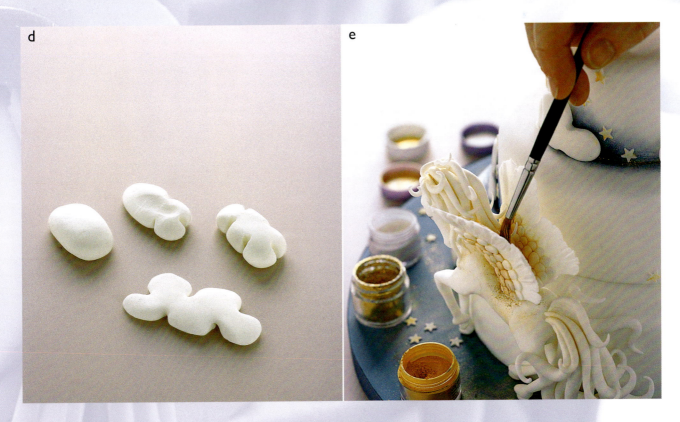

d

e

# Sprite Waterfall

As all children love playing with water, especially when splashing each other, I modelled these little sprites having a fun water fight in a pretty stone effect waterfall.

## Cake & decoration

(See pages 11, 20–1 for recipes and cake chart)

10cm (4in) and 20cm (8in) round cakes

25cm (10in) round cake board

440g (14oz/1¾ cups) buttercream

1.25kg (2½ lb) sugarpaste (rolled fondant)

Black, red, cream, purple, yellow, turquoise, golden brown and yellow food colouring pastes

Icing (powdered) sugar in a shaker

100g (3½ oz) modelling paste

3 sugar sticks

Sugar glue

Apple green and orange edible pollen dusts

Edible gold powder

45–60ml (3–4tbsp) clear piping gel

## Equipment

Plain and serrated kitchen knives

Large rolling pin

Medium paintbrush

Small, medium and large star cutters

1cm (½ in) circle cutter

Small glue brush

A few cocktail sticks

Pieces of foam sponge

Dusting brush

## Cake board and cake

1 Trim the crust from each cake and slice the tops flat. Cut a layer in each and sandwich back together with buttercream. Sandwich the two cakes one on top of the other and position on the cake board, leaving a space at the front (see a). Spread the surface of the cake with buttercream to help the sugarpaste (rolled fondant) stick.

2 Colour the sugarpaste pale grey using black food colouring paste. Roll out 875g (1¾ lb) and cover the cake and cake board completely. Stretch out any pleats and smooth down and around the shape, trimming excess sugarpaste from the edge of the cake board. Mould the trimmings into two angular rocks for the top of the waterfall, one larger than the other, and indent the largest to create a well.

a

**3** Colour 15g (¹/₂ oz) of grey sugarpaste a slightly deeper shade, 7g (¹/₄ oz) mid grey and 7g (¹/₄ oz) dark grey. To give the illusion of deep pools of water, thinly roll out and make the water shadows using the step photograph as a guide *(see b)*, smoothing them to inlay level with the surface of the rock at the top of the waterfall and the cake covering. Using the paintbrush handle, mark lines at the waterfall of both cakes.

**4** Using the remaining grey sugarpaste, edge the waterfall with different-sized angular rocks *(see c)*, marking ridges with the back of a knife. Model flattened pebbles for the cake board. To make white foam, roll tiny white sausages of modelling paste and roll along the length with the paintbrush handle to indent. Stick in position over the rocks at the bottom of each waterfall.

**5** Using 7g (¹/₄ oz) of white modelling paste, shape different-sized teardrop shapes for the base of each toadstool and stick in clusters around the cake. Colour 7g (¹/₄ oz) red and model the teardrop-shaped tops, hollowing out slightly underneath so they each sit neatly on their bases. Model tiny flattened circles of white for the spots.

## Sprites

**6** To make the sprites, first colour 30g (1oz) of modelling paste cream, 7g (¹/₄ oz) each of purple, yellow, turquoise, golden brown, a tiny amount black and another 7g (¹/₄ oz) green using yellow and turquoise food colouring. Make a sprite, one at a time, using the step photograph as a modelling guide *(see d)*, and building up each figure in its pose on the cake.

**7** Just 7g (¹/₄ oz) of cream modelling paste is enough to model the legs, arms and head for one sprite, using half for the head, cheeks and eyebrows, with the other half, split into four pieces, for two arms and two legs. Use another 7g (¹/₄ oz), split into three pieces, for all three bodies. Make the legs first by modelling tapering sausages, bending half way to shape the knee. Model the body, pressing it a little flat, and stick on top of the legs.

**8** To make the costume, thinly roll out modelling paste and cut long tapering strips. From the full end, cut out a 'v' to give a ragged edge, then stick in place, layering around the body. Make the arms next from sausage shapes and pinch around one end to indent a wrist, rounding off the hand. Press down on the hand to flatten, then cut a thumb on one side, and three further cuts along the top to separate fingers. Pinch gently to remove ridges and lengthen slightly.

b

c

Bend the arm half way and pinch out an elbow at the back.

**9** Thinly roll out and cut a star collar, using the medium cutter, and cut repeatedly into the points to make ragged. Stick in place on top of the body, then push a sugar stick down through the body, leaving it half protruding to help support the head.

**10** To make a head, roll a ball and pinch out a pointed nose. Mark the smile, using the circle cutter pressed in at an angle, marking a semi-circle. Smooth the glue brush into the mouth and pull down for the bottom lip. Model teardrop-shaped cheeks, blending the point of each into the surface of the face using the glue brush. Model two eyebrows.

**11** To make wings (see e), thinly roll out the remaining white modelling paste and cut out three large stars. Cut each star in half to make one set of wings. From each

half, cut out triangles, leaving a neat star shape around the edge. Stick to the back of each sprite, using foam pieces for support until completely dry.

**12** For hair, thinly roll out modelling paste and cut a medium and small star. Cut repeatedly into the points, then stick onto the head with the small star on top and flick up a fringe. Colour a tiny piece of modelling paste black and make tiny oval-shaped eyes. Using pea-sized amounts for each boot, first model a long teardrop and pinch up the full end. Hollow this out slightly, using the end of a paintbrush, then stick the boot onto the end of the leg using sugar glue. Use foam pieces for support.

## Grass and flowers

**13** To make the grass, roll the remaining green into different-sized sausages, tapering at one end. Indent down the centre using a cocktail stick (toothpick).

Stick in place in clusters, bending over the tips. For the flowers, thinly roll out yellow trimmings and cut out star shapes with the small cutter. Indent each petal with a cocktail stick and place the flower on a piece of foam. To indent the centre, press the end of the paintbrush down into it, pushing down into the foam sponge to shape the flower.

## Magical touches

**14** Sprinkle green pollen dust around the cake board and put a tiny amount of orange pollen dust into each flower. Brush a small amount of edible gold powder over the rocks.

**15** Add only a tiny touch of turquoise food colouring paste to the piping gel and stir well. Pour the coloured gel into the waterfall and spread out carefully, using the paintbrush. Put a few drips onto the sprites' hands and a few more drips around the cake and board.

d

e

# Sea Witch

Deep under the sea, what would a beautiful Sea Witch live in? I imagined a tall and jagged cave with a treasure of black pearls and a sea serpent to guard it.

## Cake & decoration

(See pages 11, 20–1 for recipes and cake chart)

10cm (4in), 12cm (5in), 18cm (7in) round cakes

30cm (12in) round cake board

1.25kg (2$^1$/$_2$ lb) sugarpaste (rolled fondant)

Jade green, cream, dark green, black, blue and pink food colouring pastes

Icing (powdered) sugar in a shaker

470g (15oz/scant 2 cups) buttercream

Sugar glue

375g (12oz) modelling paste

Dark green powder food colouring

Edible pale blue sparkle powder

Edible green glitter

## Equipment

Large rolling pin

Plain and serrated kitchen knives

Small glue brush

Fine and medium paintbrushes

Pieces of foam sponge

Templates (see page 201)

A few cocktail sticks

No. 4 plain piping tube (tip)

Dusting brush

## Cake board and cake

**1** Colour 375g (12oz) of sugarpaste (rolled fondant) pale jade. Roll out and cover the cake board, marking ridges with the rolling pin. Trim the crust from the cakes and slice flat. Put one on top of the other, graduating in size. Leaving a 2.5cm (1in) circle centrally on the top, cut down at an angle, taking off the top edge of each cake, creating the sloping sides and leaving a ridge around the top of the base cake. Cut out a wedge of cake for the cave opening. Cut a layer in each cake and sandwich back together with buttercream. Colour 875g (1$^3$/$_4$ lb) of sugarpaste jade. Model 15g ($^1$/$_2$ oz) into a teardrop and use to heighten the cake, smoothing the sides level with the cake surface. Roll 60g (2oz) into a tapering sausage, then place the fullest part *(see a)* on the ridge at the back of the cake and bring the two points around to the front. Smooth the sides level with the ridge. Position

a

the cake centrally on the board. Spread buttercream over the surface of the cake.

2 Roll out the remaining jade sugarpaste and sprinkle with icing sugar to prevent sticking. Roll up, place against the cake and unroll around it, pushing gently into the cave opening. Pinch the top into a point. Trim excess at the join, stick together with sugar glue, then rub gently with your fingertips to remove. Trim excess from around the base. Pinch sharp edges around the cave opening and along the ridges to make them angular. Indent more ridges around the cake and mark lines by rolling with the paintbrush handle (see b).

## Sea witch

3 Colour 60g (2oz) of modelling paste deep jade. Put aside 7g (1/4 oz). To make the dress, roll the remainder into a sausage, tapering to a point at one end. Pinch around the full end to shape the waist and round off the chest area,

then cut the top straight (see c). Stick in place and hold until secure.

4 Colour 125g (4oz) of modelling paste jade. To make the cauldron, split 60g (2oz) in half and roll into a ball. Press in the centre to indent and pinch around the edge to create the dish. Using the remaining half, split into three pieces, graduating in size, and model them into angular rocks. Assemble the pieces, sticking with sugar glue.

5 Colour just over 7g (1/4 oz) of modelling paste cream. Put aside two pea-sized amounts and, from the remainder, model the chest and neck area, and separate head and nose. First, shape a sausage with a neck pinched out from the top. Cut the bottom straight and stick in position. For her head, roll into an oval shape and narrow the chin area by stroking downwards either side. Stick in place against the cake, then model her tiny ball nose.

6 Put aside a pea-sized amount of deep jade modelling paste, then split the remainder in half. To make a sleeve, roll a sausage, rounding off one end, and pinch to open up. Twist and roll down the end of the sleeve to a point. Bend the sleeve half way by indenting at the front and pinching out at the back. Make the second sleeve in the same way and stick both in place (see d).

7 Stick on two minute flattened circles of white for eyes and two smaller deep jade circles for the iris. Use the pea-sized amounts of cream to make the hands. Shape one into a teardrop shape. From the pointed end, cut a thumb on one side, then three further cuts at the top to separate fingers. Twist each finger until long and pointed. Pinch gently at the rounded end to make a wrist and stick into a sleeve. If necessary, use a piece of foam sponge for support until dry. Make the second hand, cutting an opposite thumb.

b                                    c

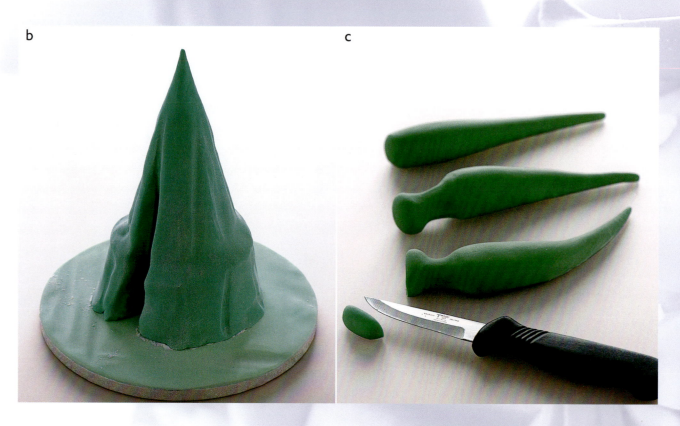

8 Colour 90g (3oz) of modelling paste pale jade. Using the templates, roll out and cut the tail fins and the four dress veils, marking into each by rolling over the surface with the paintbrush handle. Stick the veils in place, with the largest one curling up towards the top of the cave. Colour 7g (¼ oz) of paste dark green for seaweed. Roll into thin sausages of different lengths and press flat. Indent down each side and stroke outwards to round each leaf (see e). Stick in position, following the direction of the dress veils.

9 For hair, colour 45g (1½ oz) of modelling paste black. Shape half into a teardrop and stick onto her head as a frame for her hair, smoothing the point against the cave. Roll the remainder into thin tapering sausage shapes of different lengths. Stick over the frame, twisting them up and securing against the cave. Model some shorter pieces and curl them around her face. Model two tiny pupils for her eyes and roll 10–15 tiny pearls.

## Rocks and sea serpent

10 Using the remaining jade modelling paste, model different-sized spiked rocks by pinching and twisting each upwards, a twisted wand and all the rocks of varying sizes. Stick the wand in the witch's hand and all the rocks around the base of the cake. Colour 15g (½ oz) of modelling paste dusky blue, using blue with a touch of black. Reserve a tiny piece. To make the sea serpent, roll the paste into a tapering sausage and press the full end to flatten the eye area. Cut the mouth open with the knife. With the remaining deep jade, roll two tiny eyes. To make the fin, press a tapering sausage flat and mark lines radiating from the centre using the knife.

## Shells and fish

11 For shells, knead 7g (¼ oz) of white with a little jade until marbled. Shape into teardrops and press in the centre. Turn over and mark radiating lines with a cocktail stick (toothpick). Colour the remaining paste pale dusky blue and make three fish by modelling small sausages and pinching a head at the end. Pinch the opposite end to a point, make a low cut and reshape for the tail fins. Model separate fins, marking each with a cocktail stick; use the tip to indent eyes. Mark the smile by indenting with the piping tube (tip). Stick on tiny dusky blue stripes.

## Magical touches

12 To create shadow, brush dark green powder into the doorway. Brush the cake base and board with sparkle powder. Using sugar glue, paint over the serpent's eyes and the patches, lines over the seaweed and hair, then sprinkle with green glitter. Put glitter into the cauldron. Dilute black food colouring with water and paint the eyeliner and eyebrows. Dilute pink food colouring and paint her lips.

d

e

# Flying Fun

Witches have to learn their craft somewhere. In this school for witches, little apprentices are happily whizzing around the towers, learning to fly broomsticks properly.

## Cake & decoration

(See pages 11, 20–1 for recipes and cake chart)
2 × 15cm (6in) round cakes and 1 × 18cm (7in) round cake
25cm (10in) round cake board
125g (4oz) modelling paste
Brown, green, black, purple, blue, turquoise, yellow, cream and golden brown food colouring pastes
Icing (powdered) sugar in a shaker
45g (1$^1$/$_2$ oz) royal icing
Sugar glue
Edible silver glitter
1.345kg (2lb 11oz) sugarpaste (rolled fondant)
440g (14oz/1$^3$/$_4$ cups) buttercream
3 sugar sticks

## Equipment

Fine paintbrush
Large and small rolling pins
Plain and serrated kitchen knives
Foam sheet
Templates (see page 202)
No.1 plain piping tube (tip)
Miniature, 8cm (3in) and 8.5cm (3$^1$/$_4$ in) circle cutters
1.5cm ($^3$/$_4$ in) and 2.5cm (1in) square cutters
4 paper piping bags
Pieces of foam sponge

## Witches' brooms and door

**1** Make the witches' brooms first to allow plenty of drying time (see a). Colour 45g (1$^1$/$_2$ oz) of modelling paste brown. Split 7g ($^1$/$_4$ oz) into six pieces, with one slightly smaller, and roll the sausage-shaped broom-sticks. Mark the surface, using the paintbrush to indent a wood effect. Roll out 7g ($^1$/$_4$ oz), cut into little strips for twigs and stick around the bottom of five broom-sticks only. Cut strips and wrap around the top of the twigs, crossing over at the front. Colour a quarter of the royal icing light brown and pipe more twigs on each. Brush each broomstick with sugar glue and sprinkle with edible glitter. Place each broomstick on the foam sheet to dry. Roll out the remaining brown and cut out the door, using the template. Mark wood lines with a knife and scratch wood grain with a cocktail stick (toothpick). Using trimmings, make the door handle and then roll out and cut two strips for

a

the door. Stick in place and indent along each strip using the No.1 plain piping tube (tip). Place on the foam sheet to dry.

## Flying school

**2** Colour 315g (10oz) of sugarpaste (rolled fondant) green, roll out and cover the cake board completely, trimming excess from around the edge. Trim the crust from each cake and level the top of each. Cut layers and sandwich the two smaller cakes together, making the base of the school, and position on the cake board. From the larger cake, cut two 8cm (3in) circles and sandwich together for the tower, and an 8.5cm (3¼ in) circle for the roof. Trim the top edge of this roof cake to shape the sloping sides (see b). Spread all cakes with a layer of buttercream to help the sugarpaste stick, including the roof underside.

**3** Colour 15g (½ oz) of sugarpaste dark grey. Thinly roll out and cut the doorway and window, using the templates (see page 202). Stick in place, smoothing the surface with a cake smoother. Colour the remaining sugarpaste pale grey. Using 410g (13oz), roll out a little at a time and cut squares using the square cutters. Cut more squares and oblong shapes from these, making bricks, and build up around the base of the school (see c).

**4** Roll out 100g (3½ oz) of pale grey sugarpaste and cut a circle to cover the top of the base cake. Place the tower cake centrally on top and cover with bricks as before. Roll out 45g (1½ oz) of pale grey, place the base of the roof down onto it and cut around. Roll out 100g (3½ oz) and cover the top, trimming away excess and smoothing into a point (see d). Stick onto the top of the tower with sugar glue.

**5** Knead a touch of purple food colouring paste into 30g (1oz) of pale grey sugarpaste. Roll out and cut a strip the width of the doorway for the path and stick in place, smoothing down each side and trimming excess from the edge of the cake board. Cut out squares for the top edge of the base cake using 75g (2½ oz) of pale grey. With the remaining pale grey, cut out a square, using the larger square cutter, and cut into three strips. Bend each in the centre and use to edge around the underside of the roof. Cut another strip to fit the length of the window ledge. Model three flattened circles to edge the top of the window and doorway, then make the doorbell and roof finial.

## Apprentice witches

**6** To make the witches, first colour just over 7g (¼ oz) of modelling paste blue, then 7g (¼ oz) each of turquoise, purple, yellow and cream, and the remaining piece black. Each figure is built up on a broomstick and allowed to dry before positioning, except for the girl flying out of the

b                                        c

172

tower window, so stick the smaller broomstick into the window, supported by the window ledge.

7 To make trousers, roll 7g (¹/₄ oz) of modelling paste into a fat sausage and press to flatten slightly. Make a cut three-quarters of the way down to separate legs (*see e* for modelled shapes). Smooth to remove the ridges on both sides and pinch half way to bend the knees. Press at the bottom of each leg to flatten and then stick onto the centre of a broomstick. For shoes, roll pea-sized amounts into oval shapes and stick onto each trouser, pinching gently in the centre to arch the foot.

8 To make a top, split just under 7g (¹/₄ oz) of modelling paste in half and, with one half, model a teardrop shape. Indent at the full end to hollow slightly, and stick onto the trousers. Split the remaining piece in half and use to make two sleeves, bending half way and pinching gently to shape the

elbow. Hollow out the end of each sleeve, using the end of the paint-brush, so the hands will slot in easily, and stick in place. Use pea-sized amounts of cream for each hand. Model into teardrop shapes and flatten slightly. Cut a thumb to one side and three cuts along the top of the rounded end to separate fingers. Pinch each finger gently to lengthen and twist at the wrist, bringing up a little point that will slot into the end of each sleeve, and secure with sugar glue.

9 Push a sugar stick down through the top of each figure, leaving half protruding to help hold the head in place. Split the remaining cream into three and model teardrop-shaped heads with tiny ball noses. Make a hole into the base of each using a cocktail stick, then press down onto the sugar stick, securing at the base with sugar glue. Indent smiles using the miniature circle cutter pressed in at an angle, then dimple the corners using the cocktail stick.

10 Split 7g (¹/₄ oz) of black modelling paste into three pieces. Model the three hats from teardrop shapes, hollowing out the full end and pinching a rim, and then twist up a long point. Thinly roll out the remainder and cut the cloaks and collars using the template (see page 202). To mark pleats in each cloak, gently roll over the surface with the paintbrush handle.

11 Split the royal icing into three and colour dark brown, light brown and golden brown. Stick the remaining two figures and broomsticks against the school, using royal icing, and hold for a few moments until secure. Using the piping bags, with a small hole cut into the tip, pipe the hair, flicking up at the ends. When the cake is dry, dilute black colouring paste with a little water and paint their eyes using the fine paintbrush. Randomly paint a little sugar glue over the cake and figures, and sprinkle with a little edible glitter.

d

e

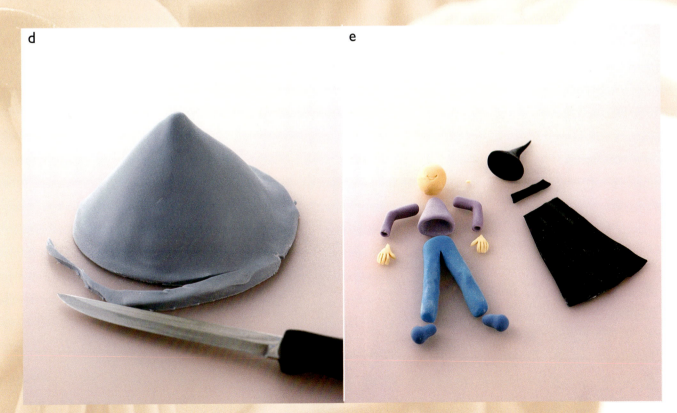

# Fairy Godmother

A book filled with magical cakes wouldn't be complete without a friendly Fairy Godmother waving her wand, sprinkling magic star dust everywhere and granting birthday wishes.

## Cake & decoration

(See pages 11, 20–1 for recipes and cake chart)

2 litre (4 pint/10 cup) bowl-shaped cake

35cm (14in) round cake board

1kg (2lb) sugarpaste (rolled fondant)

Pink, blue, cream and black food colouring pastes

Icing (powdered) sugar in a shaker

315g (10oz) modelling paste

Sugar glue

410g (13oz/1$^1$/$_2$ cups) buttercream

8–10cm (3–4in) sugar stick or food safe dowelling

30g (1oz) royal icing

Edible pink sparkle powder

Edible silver glitter

## Equipment

Large rolling pin

Plain and serrated kitchen knives

Small glue brush

Paintbrush

Templates (see page 202)

A few cocktail sticks

Nos. 1, 4 and 17 plain piping tubes (tips)

Piping bag

Dusting brush

Pieces of foam sponge

## Cake board and wand

1 Colour 250g (8oz) of sugarpaste (rolled fondant) pink and 750g (1$^1$/$_2$lb) blue. Knead the pink and 250g (8oz) of blue together until streaky. Roll out and cover the cake board completely, trimming excess from around the edge, then put aside to dry.

2 To allow drying time for the wand, roll just under 7g ($^1$/$_4$oz) of white modelling paste into a sausage, then put aside to dry.

## Fairy godmother's head

3 Make her head first to allow it time to set (see a). Colour 75g (2$^1$/$_2$oz) of modelling paste flesh, using cream food colouring paste with a touch of pink. Put aside 7g ($^1$/$_4$oz), roll the remainder into a ball and pinch out a rounded nose. Cut a curved line for her smile underneath, and smooth along the line with the

a

damp glue brush to open it up. Put a little more pressure at the centre of the bottom lip to pull it down slightly. Smooth along the bottom lip to round it off. Dimple each corner, using the end of the paintbrush. Roll two large pea-sized amounts and press onto her cheeks. Moisten either side of her nose with sugar glue, then blend the cheeks into her face to smooth and remove the joins completely.

## Cake

4 Trim the crust from the cake and slice the top flat, keeping a rounded edge. Cut a layer in the cake and sandwich back together with buttercream. Trim around the shape to create the pleats and folds. Use trimmings to make them deeper, sticking them in place with buttercream (see b). Spread a layer over the surface of the cake to help the sugarpaste stick.

5 Roll out the remaining blue sugarpaste and cover the cake completely, smoothing around the

shape and tucking any excess sugarpaste underneath. Position the cake on the cake board. Gently pinch the pleats for the gown to define them.

## Gown and cloak

6 Colour 75g (2¹/₂ oz) of modelling paste blue. For her bodice, roll 45g (1¹/₂ oz) into an oval shape, then roll in the centre to indent. Stick on top of the cake towards the front, so the skirt is fuller at the back (see c). Split 30g (1oz) in half and use for sleeves. First, roll into a sausage, fuller at one end. Pinch into the full end to open up the sleeve and smooth around the edge to round off. Mark the elbow by bending half way, then pinch out at the back. Stick each sleeve in place level with the top of the bodice, bringing them together at the front with one sleeve slightly higher than the other. Secure against the gown.

7 To make the cloak, first colour 140g (4¹/₂ oz) of modelling

paste mauve, using pink and blue food colouring pastes. Roll out 75g (2¹/₂ oz) and cut the cloak, using the template (see page 202). Moisten around her shoulders with sugar glue, then stick the cloak in position, pulling it around until joined at the neck. There will be a little excess around the top: just smooth it down, then press a little dip into it so that it will cradle the head. Push a sugar stick down into the body, leaving half protruding. Push the head down onto the sugar stick, securing with sugar glue at the base and tilt slightly.

8 Shape 30g (1oz) of mauve modelling paste into a teardrop shape and press into the full end, pinching up a rim. Stick in place on top of her head as a support for the hood. Roll out the remaining mauve and cut out the oblong-shaped hood, using the template (see page 202). Lay it against the front of the support (see d) and smooth the two far corners down, joining at the back

and tucking the two front corners under her chin. Glue the join at the back, then rub in a circular motion with the palm of your hand to remove completely.

9 Thinly roll out the mauve trimmings and cut the bow, using the template (see page 202). Mark the surface to create pleats, fold each over and stick together under her chin. Finish the bow with a little square tie.

### Glasses and eyes

10 Colour 7g (¼ oz) of modelling paste pale grey, using a touch of black food colouring paste. To make the glasses, roll out a pea-sized amount and cut out three circles using the No. 17 plain piping tube (tip). From the centre of each, cut out another circle, using the No. 4 plain piping tube. Cut a little piece from one circle, making a bridge for the glasses, and assemble the glasses using sugar glue, and then set aside to dry. Split the remaining

grey in half and make her hair, tucking the ends around her face. Mark lines on the surface using the handle of the paintbrush.

11 Stick on two tiny flattened oval-shaped eyes using white modelling paste, with two smaller oval-shaped iris using blue trimmings. Colour a minute amount of modelling paste black and make two pupils. Roll a tiny amount into two very thin sausages and use for eyelashes. Stick the glasses onto the end of her nose.

### Hands

12 Split the remaining flesh-coloured modelling paste in half and use to make the hands, using the step photograph as a modelling guide (see e). Model two pea-sized amounts into teardrops and press slightly flat. Make a cut on one side for the thumb, then three cuts along the top to separate fingers. Pinch each finger to remove ridges and then pinch around the wrist to lengthen and

create an anchor that will slot easily into the end of each sleeve. Stick the hands to the wand, turning out each wrist, and then stick each wrist into the end of each sleeve. Secure the end of the wand to the dress.

### Magical touches

13 Pipe small lines in a circle for the sparkles over her dress and the cake board, using royal icing and the piping bag fitted with the No. 1 plain piping tube. When dry, dust her cheeks and some of the sparkles with pink sparkle powder. Finally, dust a little edible silver glitter over the sparkles on the cake board.

d
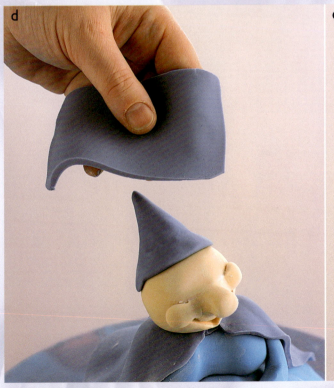

e

# Gold Mine

Little dwarfs, working busily in their gold mine, make an enchanting cake for any child. The pools of candlelight radiating from lamps, and sparkling nuggets of gold, complete the magic.

## Cake & decoration
(See pages 11, 20–1 for recipes and cake chart)
20cm (8in) square cake
30cm (12in) round cake board
500g (1lb) modelling paste
Brown, black, cream, red and mauve food colouring pastes
Icing (powdered) sugar in a shaker
Sugar glue
410g (13oz/1$^1$/$_2$ cups) buttercream
1.22kg (2lb 7oz) sugarpaste (rolled fondant)
Edible gold powder
Yellow powder food colouring

## Equipment
Large rolling pin
1.5cm ($^3$/$_4$ in) square cutter
Plain and serrated kitchen knives
Small glue brush
A few cocktail sticks
Ruler
Medium paintbrush
Dusting brush
No. 4 plain piping tube (tip)
Pieces of foam sponge

## Pickaxes and ladder

1 To allow drying time, make three pickaxes and the ladder first. Colour 170g (5$^1$/$_2$ oz) of modelling paste brown and 60g (2oz) grey. For the ladder, roll out 30g (1oz) of brown and cut out four squares in a line, with a step between each, using the square cutter. Cut around, creating a ladder with three steps. Mark the surface with a cocktail stick (toothpick) for a wood effect. For a pickaxe handle, roll a pea-sized amount of brown into a sausage and mark the surface as before. For the axe, roll a pea-sized amount of grey into a tapering sausage and stick to the handle. Bend the tip down. Make two more, then a brown ball for the tops.

## Cake and cake board

2 Trim the cake crust and slice the top flat. Cut as the cutting diagram (see page 203 and below). Trim the large and small rock cakes to round off, cut a

a

layer in each and sandwich back together with buttercream. Place the large rock cake towards the back of the cake board and sandwich the smaller rock on top. Trim at either end of the two carriage cakes, so they slope inwards towards the base. Arrange trimmings to create some steps around the large rock and pile a little at the front of the board. Spread the cakes with buttercream.

3 Colour 1kg (2lb) of sugarpaste (rolled fondant) grey using black food colouring paste. Roll out and cover the cake and cake board completely, smoothing around the shape and trimming excess from around the edge. Pinch around all rocks to make them angular and, using your fingers, stroke lines in the direction of the track. Model different-sized rocks with trim-mings and pile up around the board, putting one on top of the small rock cake. Using 75g (2½oz) of brown paste to make the track, thinly roll out and cut strips

measuring 8cm (3in). Mark the surface of each by scratching wood lines using a cocktail stick, then stick in place. Roll out and cut two long strips for either side, stick in place and trim any excess (see b).

## Carriages and bucket

4 Colour 45g (1½oz) of sugarpaste black. Thinly roll out and place the top of a carriage down onto it and cut around. Cover the base and then cover the second carriage in the same way. Colour the remaining sugarpaste brown. To cover the carriage sides (see c), roll out a little at a time and indent evenly spaced lines by pressing in with a ruler. Scratch wood lines with a cocktail stick. Measure and cut out pieces to fit the sides, keeping them slightly higher than the cake. Cover the two longest sides first, then the ends. Stick both carriages onto the board, securing with sugar glue.

5 To make the bucket, roll 7g (¼oz) of brown modelling

paste into a ball and indent into the top to open. Press both ends down onto the work surface to flatten and roll the sides straight. Mark lines for wood, then stick onto the carriage. Roll out and cut a tiny strip for the handle, loop around and stick in position. For the wheels, split 15g (½oz) of brown modelling paste into eight pieces and shape into flattened circles. Stick in place with a tiny ball on the centre of each.

## Gnomes

6 To make the gnomes (see d), colour 45g (1½oz) of modelling paste dark cream, 60g (2oz) cream, 45g (1½oz) pale cream, 7g (¼oz) red, 15g (½oz) pale mauve and 22g (¾oz) orange, using red colouring with a little cream. Make one gnome at a time and build up each on the cake.

7 Use 7g (¼oz) of brown modelling paste, split in half, to make boots. To model, roll into a sausage and bend up one end,

b

c

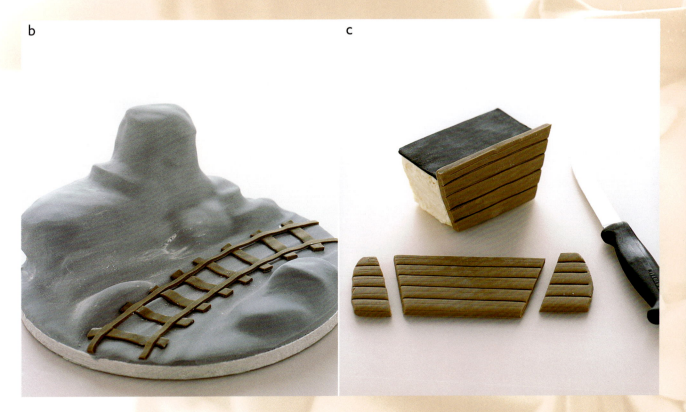

pinching up a rim and hollowing it out slightly. Mark the pleats by pressing in and rolling a cocktail stick over the surface. The trousers are modelled from a 7g ($^1/4$ oz) slightly flattened square. Cut down the centre to separate legs and smooth the ridges to remove. Mark pleats as before. Stick these directly onto the boots.

8  Each top is made from just under 15g ($^1/2$ oz) of pale cream. Split in half and shape into a slightly flattened circle. Press one side down on the work surface to flatten the bottom. Split the remaining half in half again for two sausage-shaped sleeves, marking pleats as before. Indent into the end of each sleeve to open up so the hands will slot in easily. Bend each arm half way, press in at the front and pinch out at the back for elbows. Thinly roll out 7g ($^1/4$ oz) for the tunic, then cut an oblong measuring 8 × 4cm (3 × $1^1/2$ in) and place over the top and shoulders. Squeeze the sides together and

wrap a thinly cut strip of brown paste around the waist, crossing over at the front for a belt.

9  To make a head, roll just under 15g ($^1/2$ oz) of cream modelling paste into a ball and pinch out a nose. Stick on two tiny flattened circles of white modelling paste for eyes and two pupils, made from black sugarpaste. Shape two small pea-sized teardrops for cheeks and edge each eye with tiny tapering sausages. The hands are made from slightly larger pea-sized amounts. Model into a teardrop and press slightly flat. Make a cut on one side for the thumb, then two cuts along the top to separate fingers. Pinch each finger to remove ridges and then pinch around the wrist to lengthen and create an anchor that will slot easily into the end of each of the sleeves.

10  For the hat, roll a tapering sausage using just under 15g ($^1/2$ oz) of paste. Pinch deeply into the full end to open up, so it

fits neatly on top of the head. Bend and stick the end of the hat against the tunic. Using white modelling paste, model different lengths of tapering sausage shapes for hair, eyebrows, beard and moustache.

## Magical touches

11  With the remaining grey paste, model little handles for the end of the carriages and all the small nuggets. Stick nuggets around the cake in clusters, put some spilling out of the bucket, and fill the second carriage. Paint the surface of the nuggets with sugar glue and leave until tacky. Brush over edible gold powder.

12  For lamps (see e), colour the remaining modelling paste bright yellow and roll into balls. Using brown paste, make the lantern cases, cutting a hole into the handle at the top, using the No. 4 tube. Mix yellow powder with icing sugar and brush the cake near the lanterns for candlelight. Brush gold powder over the cake.

d

e

# Giant Troll

Children love stories about giants, and it doesn't matter whether they're scary or kind. I decided to make a friendly giant troll, about to squash everything in sight with his great boots.

## Cake & decoration

(See pages 11, 20–1 for recipes
and cake chart)
18cm (7in) and 20cm (8in) round
cakes
30cm (12in) round cake board
2kg (4lb) sugarpaste
(rolled fondant)
Flesh, mauve, cream, brown, black,
golden brown and green food
colouring pastes
500g (1lb/2 cups) buttercream
Icing (powdered) sugar in
a shaker
Sugar glue
8cm (3in) sugar stick or length
of food-safe dowelling
Mauve and green powder food
colourings

## Equipment

Plain and serrated kitchen
knives
Large sable paintbrush
Large rolling pin
Small glue brush
Pieces of foam sponge
Ball or bone tool
Templates (see page 203)
Small, pointed scissors

## Troll's head

**1** Make the head first to give time to set before being positioned. Colour 235g (7½ oz) of sugarpaste (rolled fondant) flesh and roll 140g (4½ oz) into a ball-shaped head. For the smile, press in the tip of a knife on either side, then stroke along the bottom edge to create the bottom lip. Push the end of a paintbrush into the mouth corners and push up slightly (see a). For the chin area, press in on both sides, using your thumbs. Push the paintbrush into the base of the head to make a hole for when the head is positioned later. If the back has flattened, reshape by gently rolling.

## Cake and cake board

**2** Trim the crust from each cake and slice the tops flat. Put the smaller cake centrally on top of the larger cake. Leaving a 5cm (2in) circle centrally on the top, cut down at an angle to the base to create the

a

sloping sides of the mountain shape. For the rounded top, place a large piece of cake trimming on top of the cake and trim again.

3 Position the shaped cake on the cake board. Sandwich all the layers together with butter-cream. Spread the surface of the cake with buttercream to help the sugarpaste stick. Cut some more cake trimmings into strips and position these strips around the base of the cake (see b), then spread with buttercream.

4 Colour 875g (1 3/4 lb) of sugarpaste pale mauve. Roll out and cover the cake and cake board, smoothing into the ridges around the cake, and then trim excess from around the board edge. To make the snow, model several teardrops in different lengths, using 125g (4oz) of white sugarpaste. Stick around the top of the mountain, smoothing the joins closed at the top to resemble a snow-capped mountain (see c).

## Troll's clothes

5 Colour 265g (8 1/2 oz) of sugarpaste cream. Using 140g (4 1/2 oz), roll a teardrop shape for the troll's shirt and pinch into the full end to hollow out. Press deeply into the surface, using the paint-brush handle to mark pleats, and press to flatten the neck area. Stick in place with the neck area level with the top of the mountain. (See back view photograph on page 182.) Split 60g (2oz) in half and roll sausage-shaped sleeves, marking pleats as before using the paintbrush handle. Bend the sleeves at the elbow and then secure with sugar glue.

6 Colour 220g (7oz) of sugarpaste mid brown. Roll 200g (6 1/2 oz) into a fat sausage. Cut down the centre to separate legs and pinch around the bottom of each to widen and hollow out. Mark deep pleats as before, then stick against the mountain in a wide-legged pose. Smooth gently to round off and shape his bottom.

7 With the remaining mid brown, thinly roll out and cut a trouser patch, then roll out and cut two slightly thicker strips for braces. Stick the braces over the shoulders, tucking into all the pleats, and cross over at the back. Stick the patch onto the trousers and mark different-sized stitches around the edge using a knife. Shape a flattened circle for a collar, using 15g (1/2 oz) of cream, then cut out a 'v' from the edge to the circle centre.

## Troll's face

8 Push the sugar stick or dowelling into the top of the mountain, leaving half protruding. Push the head down onto the sugar stick and secure at the base with sugar glue. Using 15g (1/2 oz) of flesh, model two flattened circles for cheeks, shape his nose and make his toe, marking the toenail with a knife, then put aside. Split just under 7g (1/4 oz) of flesh in half and make two ears, indenting in the centre of each

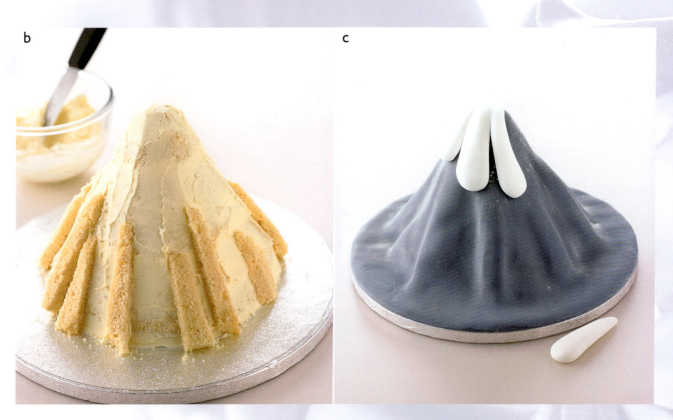

b

c

with your finger. Stick the two ears in place either side of his head, level with his nose.

9 With pea-sized amounts of white for each eye, make two flattened oval-shaped eyes, then roll out and cut a small tooth. For the iris, model two flattened oval shapes using mid brown trimmings. Colour a pea-sized amount of black sugarpaste and model two pupils, and two tiny sausage-shaped eyebrows.

## Boots, hands and hair

10 To make the troll's boots, first colour 185g (6oz) of sugarpaste pale brown. Split in half and shape into ovals. Pinch to narrow the heel and round off the toe area. Mark pleats in the boots using the paintbrush handle (see d). Cut a line at the front to mark the sole on one boot only, and then push into the toe area to open up. Stick the troll's boots in place, then position the toe made earlier. Use foam pieces for

support until the boots are completely dry.

11 Split the remaining flesh in half to make the hands. Shape one piece into a teardrop shape and press to flatten slightly. Cut on one side for the thumb and cut twice into the top to separate fingers. Smooth to remove ridges and press down at the fingertips to widen. Stick in place, and then make the second hand, cutting the opposite thumb. Mark nails using a knife. Split the remaining cream sugarpaste in half and model the two cuffs, marking pleats with the paintbrush handle. Stick in place, hiding the join between the sleeves and hands.

12 Colour 75g (2¹/₂ oz) of sugarpaste golden brown. Using the templates (see page 203), roll out and cut the hair pieces, one at a time, starting with the largest piece first. Stick these in place on top of the troll's head and flick up some of the points.

Finish the hair by sticking on a small pointed trimming and smooth the join closed.

## Trees

13 Colour the remaining sugarpaste green and split into several different-sized pieces. To make a tree (see e), model into a teardrop shape and then snip into the tree at an angle using scissors. Start at the top and make small cuts, gradually cutting in deeper as you spiral down, and then cut away the excess paste at the base. Bend one of the trees at the tip.

## Magical touches

14 Mix mauve and green powder colourings separately with a little icing (powdered) sugar and then dust mauve into the ridge recesses around the mountain and dust green around the base, using the large paintbrush. Stick the trees in place, positioning the bent tree directly under the troll's boot.

d

e

# Crystal Ball

Here is a wizard with his giant crystal ball, large enough to play around with all the stars in the universe and turn the whole world in a spin.

## Cake & decoration

(See pages 11, 20–1 for recipes and cake chart)

2 x 1 litre (2 pint/5 cup) bowl-shaped cakes

30cm (12in) round cake board

1.25kg (2$^1$/$_2$ lb) sugarpaste (rolled fondant)

Blue, purple and cream food colouring pastes

Icing (powdered) sugar in a shaker

315g (10oz) modelling paste

Sugar glue

280g (9oz/1 generous cup) buttercream

Sugar stick

Edible silver glitter

## Equipment

Large rolling pin

Serrated and small/medium plain kitchen knives

Various star cutters

Small glue brush

Cake smoother

Template (see page 203)

Paintbrush

Pieces of foam sponge

A few cocktail sticks

Dusting brush

1 Colour 750g (1$^1$/$_2$ lb) of sugarpaste (rolled fondant) pale blue and 500g (1lb) purple. Knead together 200g (6$^1$/$_2$ oz) of pale blue and 170g (5$^1$/$_2$ oz) of purple until streaky and colours are just starting to blend. Roll out and cover the cake board, trimming excess, then put aside to dry. Trim the crust from both cakes and level the tops. Put the cakes together and check they make a ball shape. Sandwich the two cakes together. Spread the surface with buttercream and leave to set.

### Stars and crystal ball

2 Colour 45g (1$^1$/$_2$ oz) of modelling paste lilac using blue colouring paste with a touch of purple. Save just over 7g (1/4 oz) for the hat and belt, then roll out the remainder and cut the different-sized stars (see a). Stick a group together for the wizard's hand. Leave to dry. Add a little more buttercream to the cake. Knead the remaining sugarpaste until streaky as before, roll out and cover the cake. Pull up a pleat and cut away

a

excess, without cutting away too much (see b). Pinch the join together and rub with icing sugar to remove. Smooth around the shape and trim. Position on the board.

## Wizard

3 Colour 220g (7oz) of modelling paste deep mauve using blue and purple food colouring pastes. To make the wizard, model a long teardrop-shaped body 12cm (5in) in height, using 140g (4½oz), and press down on the full end to flatten. Thinly roll out 60g (2oz) of deep mauve and cut the cloak using the template (see page 203). Roll the paintbrush handle over the surface to create pleats. Stick in place, pulling out at the back for fullness and letting excess drape onto the cake board. For the staff, roll the trimmings into a sausage, tapering to a point. Flatten the top and pinch the surface to indent.

4 Reserve a tiny amount for eyes, then split the remaining deep mauve paste in half for the sleeves. Model long teardrop shapes first, then pinch into the full end to open up. Twist down the end of each sleeve to a tapering point. Bend the arm half way and pinch out an elbow. Stick in position with the shoulders, level with the top of the body, one arm against the cloak and the other resting against the cake. Stick the staff in place using foam for support (see c). Push the sugar stick down through the top of his body, leaving a little protruding.

5 Colour 7g (¼oz) of modelling paste cream and put aside two pea-sized amounts. Using the remainder, model an oval-shaped nose and roll a ball-shaped head. Mark the smile using the end of a paintbrush. Push the head down onto the sugar stick and secure at the base. Stick on his nose. For the rope belt, roll a thin sausage, using a little lilac modelling paste. Indent along the length at an angle, using the side of a cocktail stick. Cut into three strips and assemble his belt. For his hat, roll the remaining lilac paste into a teardrop with a long point. Indent at the full end to hollow and pinch out a wide rim. Stick onto his head slightly towards the back and hold until secure.

6 Using the remaining white paste, make his hair and beard. Stick two long pieces under his nose for a moustache. For hands, see page 173, step 8. Stick into the sleeve ends, with one hand holding stars and the other the staff. Model tiny oval eyes, using deep mauve paste, and stick on tiny white sausages for eyebrows, marking hairs by pressing along the length at an angle with a cocktail stick. Moisten a line, spiralling around the cake and board, with sugar glue. Stick on all the stars, some flat, with others upright, and sprinkle along the line with a tiny amount of glitter. Brush glue over his hat, staff, eyes, around the cloak edges, and randomly over the stars, then brush with glitter.

b

c

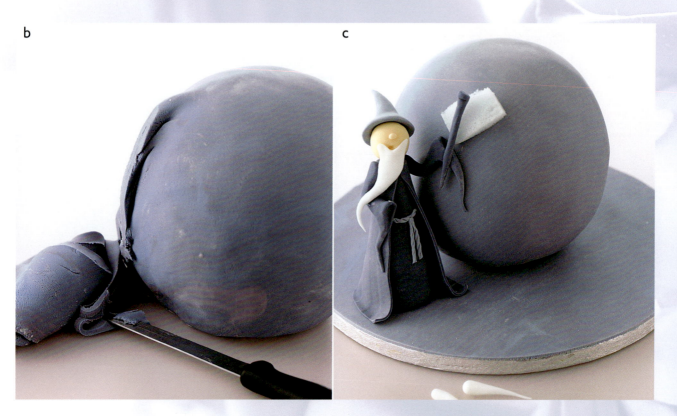

# Templates

**Pixie Teapot House:**
teapot decoration
(pages 92–96)

**Pixie Teapot House:**
door curtain
(pages 92–96)

**Peter Pan:**
roof edge
(pages 72–75)

**Busy Elves:**
window and frame
(pages 80–83)

**Pixie Teapot House:**
woodstore roof
(pages 92–96)

**Enchanted Castle:**
door
(pages 64–67)

**Busy Elves:** door
(pages 80–83)

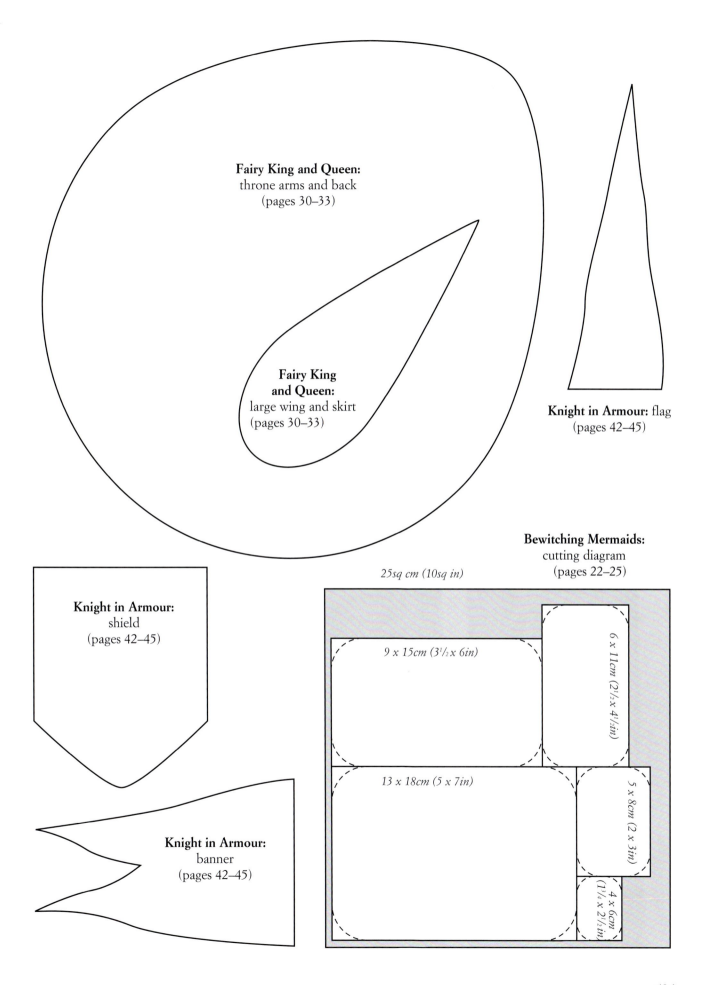

**Fairy King and Queen:**
throne arms and back
(pages 30–33)

**Fairy King
and Queen:**
large wing and skirt
(pages 30–33)

**Knight in Armour:** flag
(pages 42–45)

**Knight in Armour:**
shield
(pages 42–45)

**Bewitching Mermaids:**
cutting diagram
(pages 22–25)

*25sq cm (10sq in)*

*9 x 15cm (3¹/₂ x 6in)*

*6 x 11cm (2¹/₂ x 4¹/₂in)*

*13 x 18cm (5 x 7in)*

*5 x 8cm (2 x 3in)*

*4 x 6cm
(1³/₄ x 2¹/₂in)*

**Knight in Armour:**
banner
(pages 42–45)

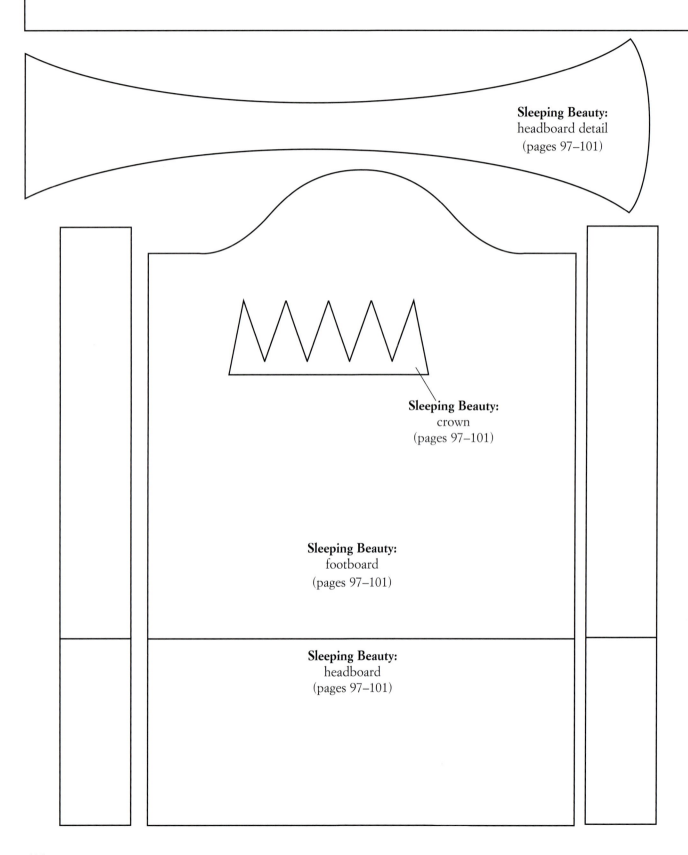

**Sleeping Beauty:**
side pieces x 2
(pages 97–101)

**Sleeping Beauty:**
headboard detail
(pages 97–101)

**Sleeping Beauty:**
crown
(pages 97–101)

**Sleeping Beauty:**
footboard
(pages 97–101)

**Sleeping Beauty:**
headboard
(pages 97–101)

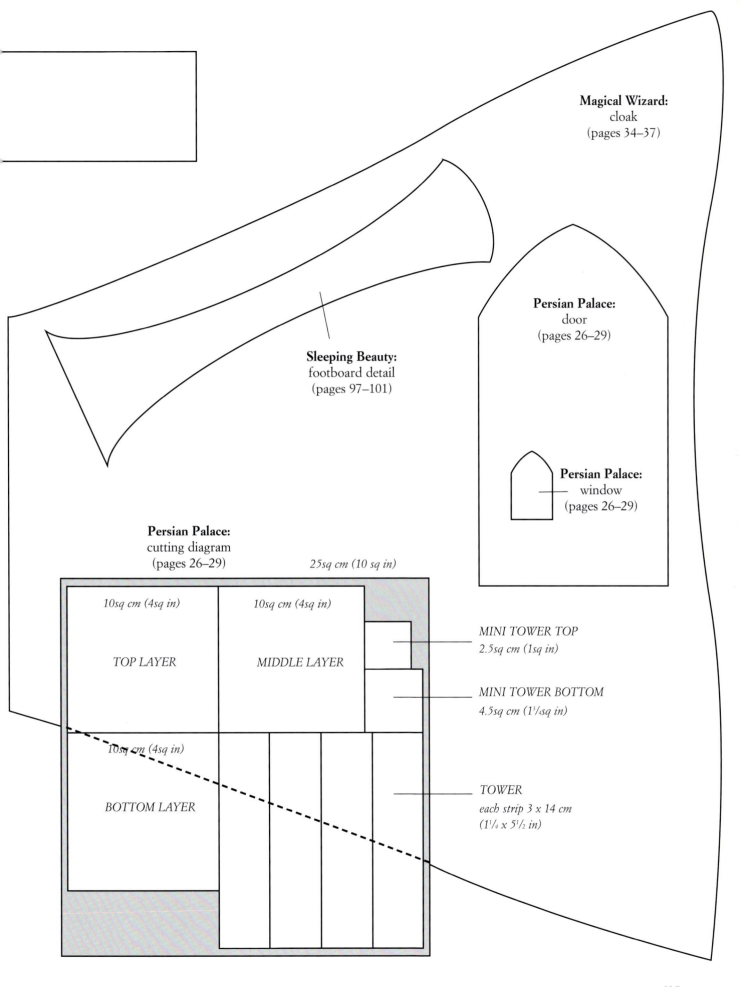

**Magical Wizard:**
cloak
(pages 34–37)

**Sleeping Beauty:**
footboard detail
(pages 97–101)

**Persian Palace:**
door
(pages 26–29)

**Persian Palace:**
window
(pages 26–29)

**Persian Palace:**
cutting diagram
(pages 26–29)

*25sq cm (10 sq in)*

*10sq cm (4sq in)*

*TOP LAYER*

*10sq cm (4sq in)*

*MIDDLE LAYER*

*MINI TOWER TOP*
*2.5sq cm (1sq in)*

*MINI TOWER BOTTOM*
*4.5sq cm (1³⁄₄sq in)*

*10sq cm (4sq in)*

*BOTTOM LAYER*

*TOWER*
*each strip 3 x 14 cm*
*(1¹⁄₄ x 5¹⁄₂ in)*

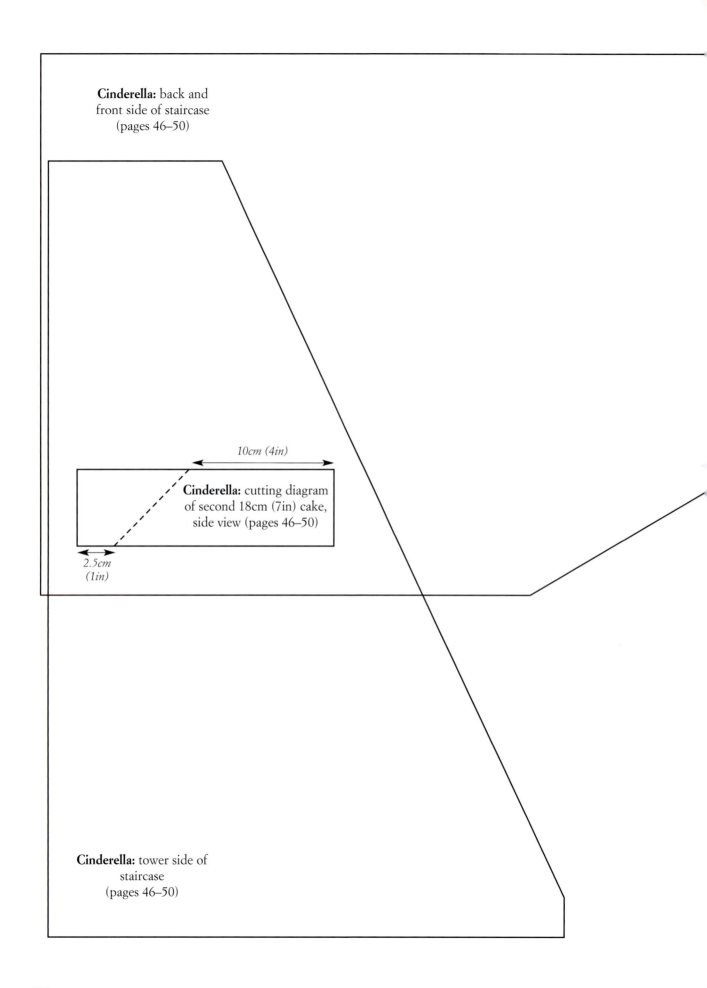

**Cinderella:** back and
front side of staircase
(pages 46–50)

*10cm (4in)*

**Cinderella:** cutting diagram
of second 18cm (7in) cake,
side view (pages 46–50)

*2.5cm
(1in)*

**Cinderella:** tower side of
staircase
(pages 46–50)

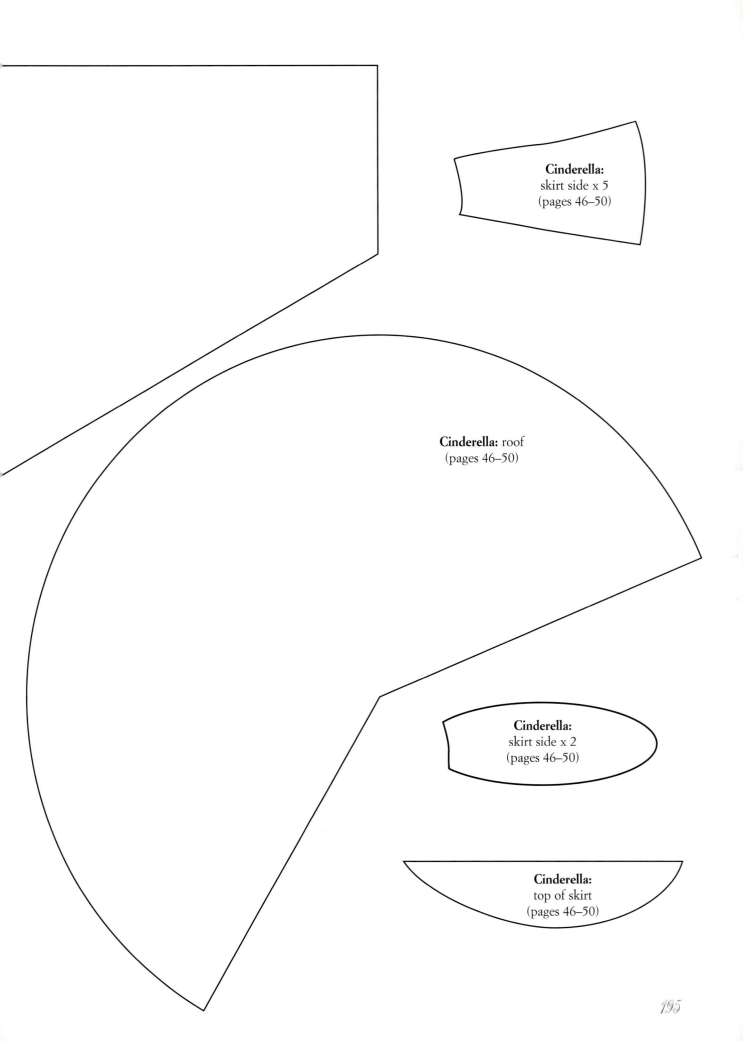

**Cinderella:**
skirt side x 5
(pages 46–50)

**Cinderella:** roof
(pages 46–50)

**Cinderella:**
skirt side x 2
(pages 46–50)

**Cinderella:**
top of skirt
(pages 46–50)

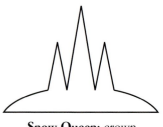

**Snow Queen:** crown
(pages 68–71)

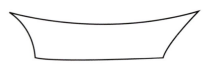

**Snow Queen:** collar
(pages 68–71)

**Snow Queen:** wings
(pages 68–71)

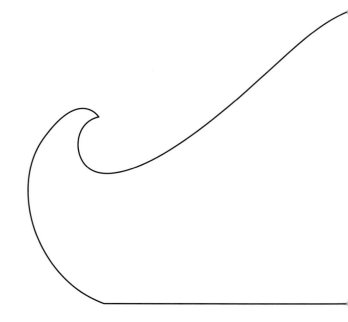

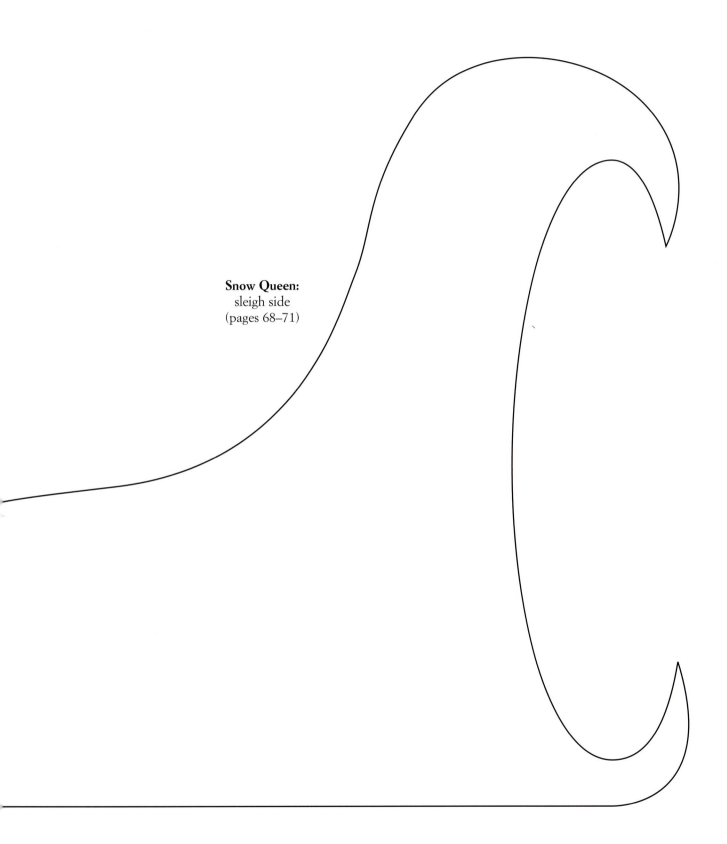

**Snow Queen:**
sleigh side
(pages 68–71)

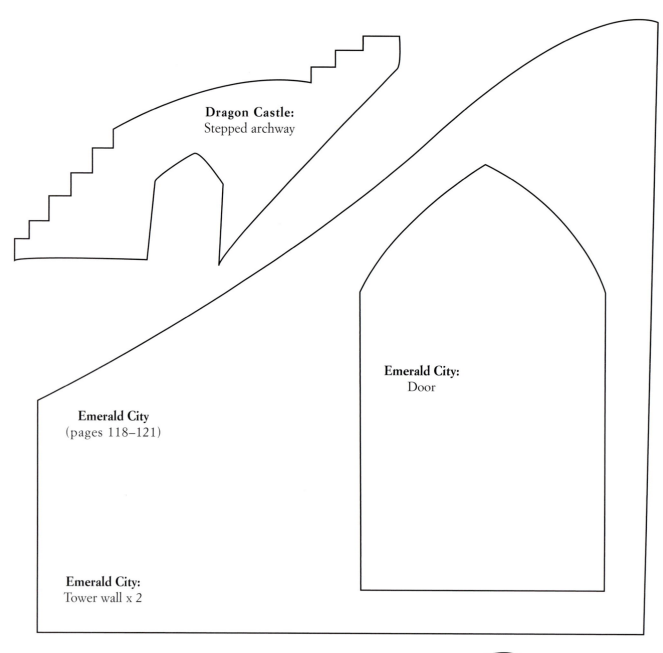

**Dragon Castle:**
Stepped archway

**Emerald City:**
Door

**Emerald City**
(pages 118–121)

**Emerald City:**
Tower wall x 2

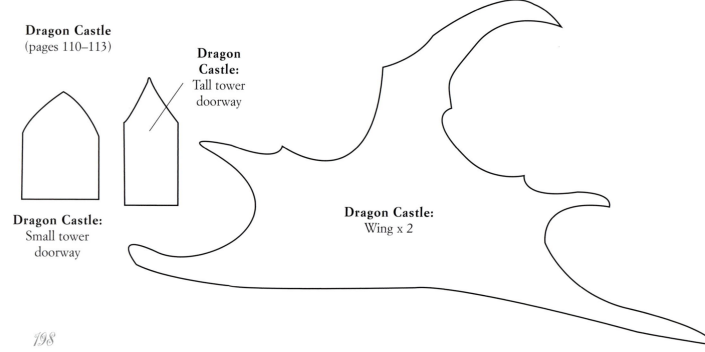

**Dragon Castle**
(pages 110–113)

**Dragon Castle:**
Tall tower doorway

**Dragon Castle:**
Small tower doorway

**Dragon Castle:**
Wing x 2

**Ramshackle Village**
(pages 122–125)

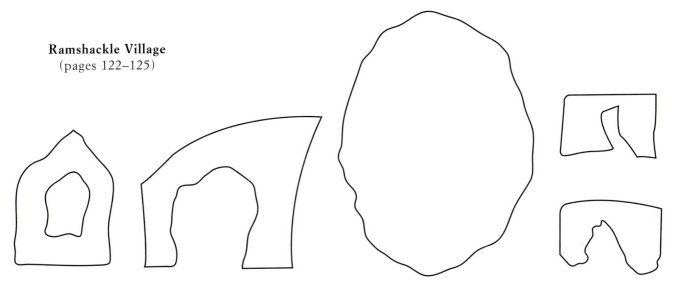

**Ramshackle Village:**
Dormer
large house

**Ramshackle Village:**
Roof dormer
large house

**Ramshackle Village:**
Troll tunic x 2
(Score paste, then tear)

**Ramshackle Village:**
Small dormers either
side of small house

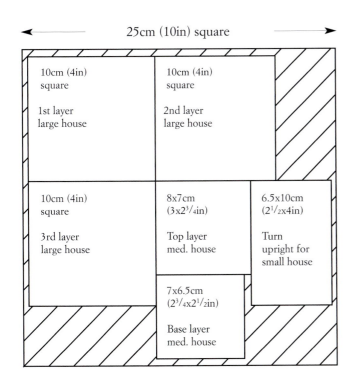

25cm (10in) square

| 10cm (4in) square 1st layer large house | 10cm (4in) square 2nd layer large house |
| 10cm (4in) square 3rd layer large house | 8x7cm (3x2³/₄in) Top layer med. house | 6.5x10cm (2¹/₂x4in) Turn upright for small house |
| | 7x6.5cm (2³/₄x2¹/₂in) Base layer med. house | |

**Ramshackle Village** (pages 122–125)
Cutting diagram

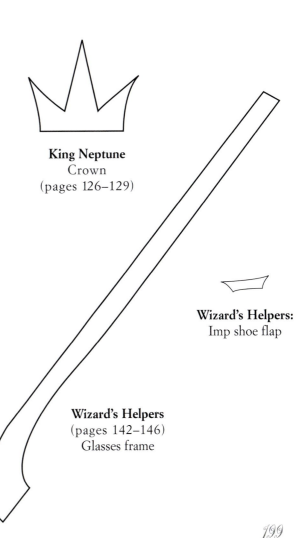

**King Neptune**
Crown
(pages 126–129)

**Wizard's Helpers:**
Imp shoe flap

**Wizard's Helpers**
(pages 142–146)
Glasses frame

**Wizard Owl** (pages 130–133)
Cutting diagram

25cm (10in) square

11x12.5cm
(4³/₄ x 5in)

Chair seat

11x12.5cm
(4³/₄ x 5in)

Chair back

8x10cm
(3¹/₄ x 4in)

Arm

8x10cm
(3¹/₄ x 4in)

Arm

8x6cm
(3x2¹/₄ in)
Owl

8x6cm
(3x2¹/₄ in)
Owl

**Wizard Owl:**
Cloak

**Pirate Dreams**
(pages 138–141)

**Pirate Dreams:**
Headboard

**Pirate Dreams:**
Footboard

**Pirate Dreams:**
Crossbones on boy's hat

**Pirate Dreams:**
Crossbones on pyjamas

**Pirate Dreams:**
Flag

**Pirate Dreams**
Teddy's
waist-coat x 2

**Pirate Dreams:**
Crossbones on teddy's hat

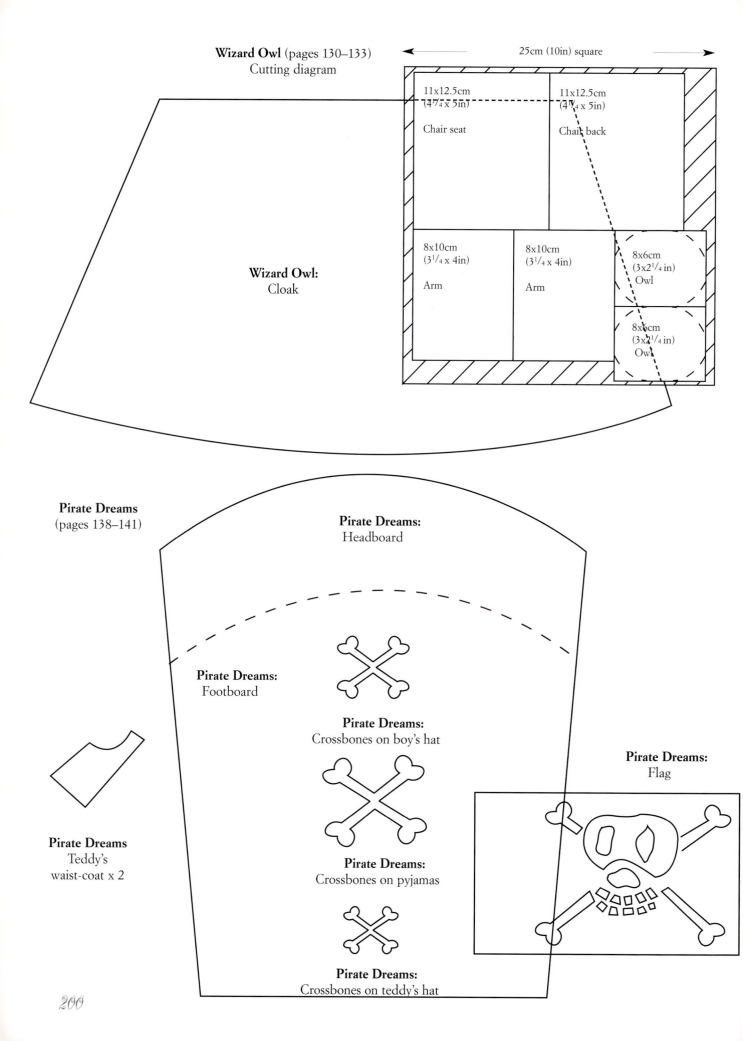

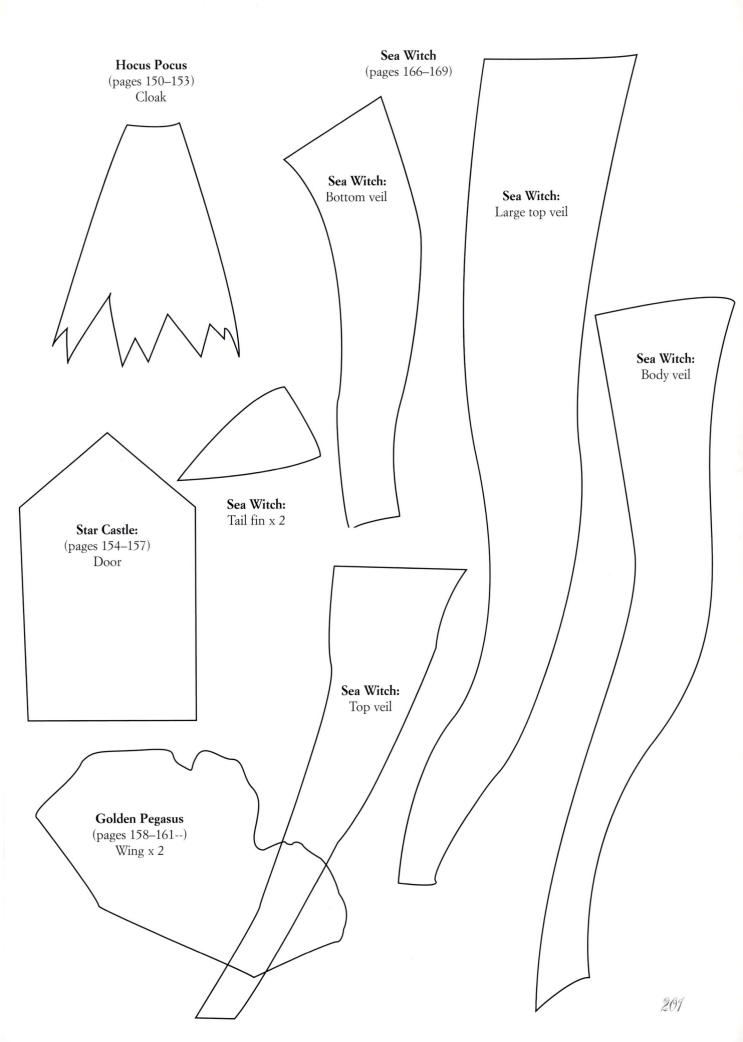

**Hocus Pocus**
(pages 150–153)
Cloak

**Sea Witch**
(pages 166–169)

**Sea Witch:**
Bottom veil

**Sea Witch:**
Large top veil

**Sea Witch:**
Body veil

**Sea Witch:**
Tail fin x 2

**Star Castle:**
(pages 154–157)
Door

**Sea Witch:**
Top veil

**Golden Pegasus**
(pages 158–161--)
Wing x 2

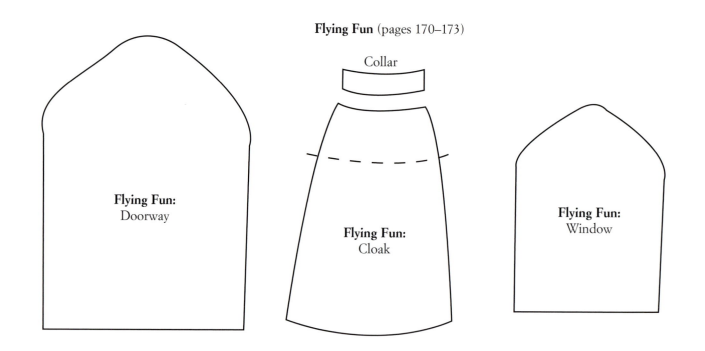

**Flying Fun** (pages 170–173)

Collar

**Flying Fun:**
Doorway

**Flying Fun:**
Cloak

**Flying Fun:**
Window

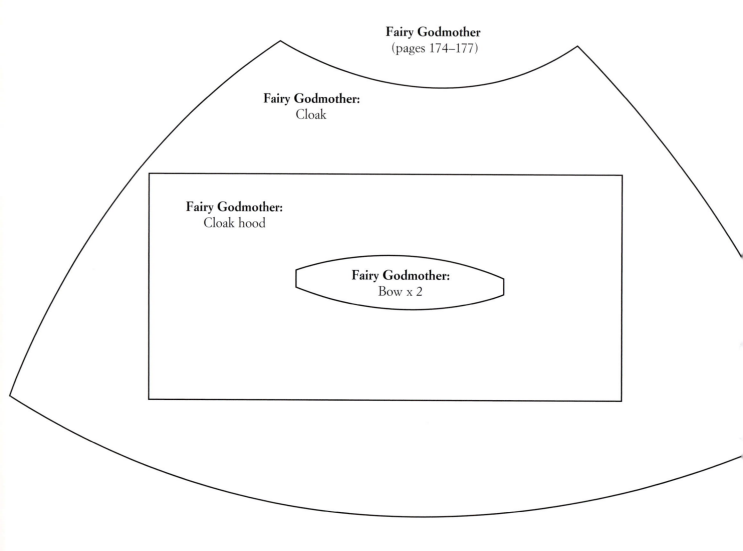

**Fairy Godmother**
(pages 174–177)

**Fairy Godmother:**
Cloak

**Fairy Godmother:**
Cloak hood

**Fairy Godmother:**
Bow x 2

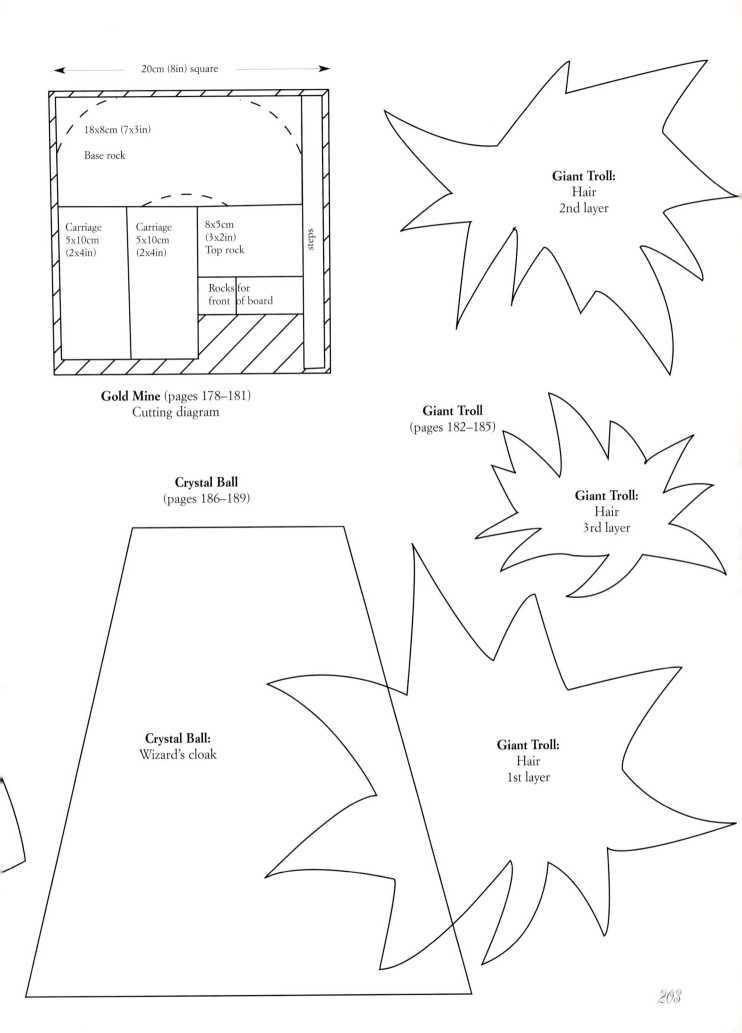

20cm (8in) square

18x8cm (7x3in)

Base rock

Carriage
5x10cm
(2x4in)

Carriage
5x10cm
(2x4in)

8x5cm
(3x2in)
Top rock

Rocks for
front of board

steps

**Gold Mine** (pages 178–181)
Cutting diagram

**Giant Troll:**
Hair
2nd layer

**Giant Troll**
(pages 182–185)

**Giant Troll:**
Hair
3rd layer

**Crystal Ball**
(pages 186–189)

**Crystal Ball:**
Wizard's cloak

**Giant Troll:**
Hair
1st layer

# Index

# Acknowledgements

Firstly, I would like to say thank you to my husband, Paul, for his unstinting support. The many hours sitting in traffic and transporting box after box containing fragile cakes to the centre of London, and getting them all there in one piece, is a feat in itself; and for his patience and understanding throughout the duration of producing the book, when the house is taken over by them.

Thank you to my best friends, Elaine and Aysa, and my mother Pam, who were all a little neglected during the intensity of producing this book, and warned not to call and chat for hours when the deadline loomed. We have a lot of catching up to do now!

To Pam and Ray Herbert, my dear mother and father, for their love and support always.
To my grandmother, Winnie Herbert for being so proud.
To my grandmother, Eliza Lewis, always by my side.
To Aysa for being such a good friend.
To Barbara Croxford, for always being at the end of the telephone during a panic.
To Clive Streeter, for his magical photographs.
To my husband Paul for being the greatest help of all.
To Doris and George Brown, the nicest mother and father-in-law anyone could wish for.

As I can be very indecisive when it comes to anything creative, thank you to my daughter Laura for her impeccable taste in colour and design – she helped me clear my thoughts and go with first instincts. Thank you to my sons, Lewis and Shaun, for helping with all the research: they enlightened me on all the differences that there could be between these mythical creatures.

Many thanks to Barbara Croxford, a brilliant editor and very good friend, whose talent and professionalism shines through every time. Along with Barbara, thanks also to Catie Ziller and Shahid Mahmood, whose vision and creative minds helped form this beautiful book.

Thank you to Clive Streeter for the magical photographs and for his wit, charm and easygoing nature. He took the worry out of frantic days with hundreds of pieces needing to be arranged and photographed.

Thank you to Renshaw's for providing all the Regalice sugarpaste used throughout the book. A high quality sugarpaste that works as you want it to is invaluable. Thanks also to Edable Art, Squires Kitchen, Sugarflair and European Cake Gallery for their rainbow of wonderful edible powders, glitters and sparkles.

Last, but not least, a big thank you to all the people I have met through sugarcraft, especially my students, some of whom have become good friends. They keep me on my toes with anything new they would like to see and give me inspiration to keep producing books.

This edition published in 2012 by Murdoch Books Pty Limited
Reprinted 2012

This edition is a compilation of:
*Enchanted Cakes* first published in 2000 by Merehurst Limited, an imprint of Murdoch Book UK Ltd
*Magical Cakes* first published in 2002 by Murdoch Books UK Ltd


Murdoch Books Australia
Pier 8/9
23 Hickson Road
Millers Point NSW 2000
Phone: +61 (0) 2 8220 2000
Fax: +61 (0) 2 8220 2558
www.murdochbooks.com.au

Murdoch Books UK Limited
Erico House, 6th Floor
93–99 Upper Richmond Road
Putney, London SW15 2TG
Phone: +44 (0) 20 8785 5995
Fax: +44 (0) 20 8785 5985
www.murdochbooks.co.uk


Chief Executive: Juliet Rogers
Publishing Director: Kay Scarlett
Production: Nikla Martin
Photography: Clive Streeter

ISBN 978-1743361948

A catalogue record for this book is available from the British Library.

Colour separation by Spitting Image
PRINTED IN CHINA.

IMPORTANT: Those who might be at risk from the effects of salmonella poisoning (the elderly, pregnant women, young children and those suffering from immune deficiency diseases) should consult their doctor with any concerns about eating raw eggs.

OVEN GUIDE: You may find cooking times vary depending on the oven you are using. For fan-forced ovens, as a general rule, set the oven temperature to 20°C (35°F) lower than indicated in the recipe.